New researches
on the religion and mythology
of the Pagan Slavs

Collection
« Histoire -mythes - folklore »

2014
Mikhaïl Dragomanov et Lydia Dragomanova
Travaux sur le folklore slave, suivi de Légendes chrétiennes de l'Ukraine
Viktoriya et Patrice Lajoye
Sadko et autres chants mythologiques des Slaves de l'Est

2017
Patrice Lajoye
Fils de l'orage
Patrice Lajoye
Charmes et incantations. Biélorussie, Russie, Ukraine
Georges Dumézil
Contes et légendes des peuples du Caucase, 1

À paraître
Mitrofan Dikarev
Contes grivois et chansons paillardes de l'Ukraine

New Researches on the religion and mythology of the Pagan Slavs

edited by
Patrice Lajoye

LINGVA

© 2019, Lingva, Patrice Lajoye and the authors
Éditions Lingva
22 A rue de la Gare
14100 Lisieux (France)
lingva.france@gmail.com
www.lingva.fr

Foreword

Patrice Lajoye

Nothing serious, for decades, has appeared in English concerning the mythology of pagan Slavs. The most recent book[1], published in 2019, could give hope that, finally, academics would seize this subject. Alas, it is entirely based on a false premise: there is no common pantheon to all Slavs. This is a surprising position that shows that the two authors are not aware of the most recent work in this area. So we wanted to bring together some of the best researchers in this field, to enable them to publish in English their most recent, most innovative work. Thus, Jiří Dynda translates and comments all the ancient texts pertaining to the myths of the creation of Man. Alexander V. Ivanenko returns to the etymology of the name of the god Stribog. Oleg V. Kutarev is interested in the god Rod and the Rožanicy, criticizing the old Soviet studies. Kamil Kajkowski makes an inventory of known pagan idols in Pomerania (northern Poland). Stamatis Zochios tries to identify who were the Slav gods linked to death. Marina M. Valentsova studies the names of Slovak mythological creatures. Aleksandr Koptev is interested in the mythical mode of accession to royalty involving three brothers. I have studied the concepts of sovereign and sovereignty among pagan Slavs. Finally, Roman Zaroff, with a large synthetic article, offers us a view of the Baltic religion, neighbours of the Slavs. This book is not a synthetic monograph, but a collection of various works. However, they cover the whole field of current research on pagan Slavs, and by the sources that they quote, or by the abundant bibliography which accompanies them, they offer a way of access to a mythology still largely unknown in the West.

---

1. Judith Kalik and Alexander Uchitel, *Slavic Gods and Heroes*, 2019, London and New York, Routledge, 186 p.

Slavic Anthropogony Myths

Body and Corporeality in the Slavic Narratives about the Creation of Man

Jiří Dynda

Institute of Slavonic Studies of the Czech Academy of Sciences, Prague

dynda@slu.cas.cz

Abstract. The paper analyzes four narratives attested in chronicles, religious treatises and folk legends that it considers to be possible remnants of Slavic anthropogony myth that has partially survived after the Christianization of Slavs. The conclusion is that even though these narratives were considerably influenced by and syncretized with Christian (apocryphal) tradition, the archaic narrative and motivic core with many common traits with the other Indo-European anthropogony traditions can be positively identified in them. The special focus is laid on the role of human body and corporeality and its connection to the material of earth and the body of deities.

Keywords. anthropogony; body; corporeality; myth; syncretism; apocrypha

ANTHROPOGONY MYTHS, or the myths about the origins of humanity, are attested in many Indo-European mythologies. From the Pre-Christian Slavic symbolic system no such myth has survived *as a myth*. Of the Slavic tradition that speaks directly of the creation of man or the origin of his soul, only Christian apocryphal and/or folklore narratives have survived. The ratio of the Christian (i.e. non-canonic) apocryphal traditions and the original pagan influences in them is difficult to estimate. In this paper, we attempt to analyze these narratives and try to uncover their most significant motives, leading to a reconstruction of basic outlines of a Slavic anthropogony tradition.

Jan Vyšatič, *volchvy*, and God's bath

The first non-traditional (i.e., non-Biblical) narrative about the creation of man comes from the so-called *Primary Chronicle* (in OCS *Pověstь vremennychъ lětъ*, hereinafter referred to as *PVL*). In the record *sub anno* 1071, it mentions that two *volchvy*, i.e. East Slavic wandering sorcerers, appeared in the neighborhood of Běloozero.[1] They allegedly killed many people, claiming them to be witches holding crops. The *Volchvy* cut their bodies apart and pulled out of them grain and fish they had allegedly stolen from the Běloozero people, thus causing a famine.[2]

When Jan Vyšatič, prince Svjatoslav's tax collector, became aware of such unauthorized exercise of executive power, he had both *volchvy* arrested and interrogated them. The *volchvy* stated that they pulled the crops out of the people who had stolen it and had been holding it, and that they were willing to show it to the interrogators on demand. Jan said that their statements are nonsense, because he knows very well that God created man out of earth (ѿ землѣ *Lavr*)[3] and that man is made up of flesh and bone (сставленъ костьми • и жылами ѿ крове • нѣ в немь ничтоже • и не въсть ничтоже *Lavr*), so it is not possible to pull crops out of people. But the *volchvy* objected that it was not so and they said they knew how a man was *actually* made – and they explained it to Jan:[4]

бъ мывъса въ мовници и вспотивъса ѿтерса[5] вѣхтемъ[6] • и верже с нбсе на землю • и распръса сотона с бмь • кому в немь створити члвка • и створи

---

1. For *volchvy* see Gazo 1898; Zguta 1974; Téra 2005 and others.
2. For South-European analogies of this phenomenon *cf.* Ginzburg 1966.
3. Of course, it is an allusion to Gn 2:7.
4. *PVL* 1999, 76; collation Ostrowski 2003/3: 1418–1421.
5. Thus *Radz, Acad*; ѿтерьса *Hypa*; ѿ са *Laur*.
6. Thus *Acad*; ветъхомъ *Laur*; ветхй *Radz*; въхтемь *Hypa*; вѣтѣ *Chle*. Similarly (ве/ѣхтемъ nebo ве/ѣхътьмь) also every other redaction. The lexeme ветъхъ is in this semantics documented in the Old Russian literature only once, and that is at this place in two copies of the *PVL* (*Laur* fol. 59d3, *Radz* fol. 103v10), *cf.* Tvorogov 1984: 33 (every other, younger manuscript copy of *PVL* uses въхтемь). *SDRJa* I (1988, 400) denotes semantics of ветъхъ as *тряпка*, 'rag, cloth, piece of cloth' (nevertheless, this semantics is derived only from this one occurrence in the *PVL*). The lexeme въхъть is then interpreted by *SDRJa* I as *пучок*, 'tuft of straw, budle of brushwood'; it is etymologically related to Czech *vích* or *věchet* with the same meaning (*SSJČ* IV, 38 a 84). The only other occurrence of this lexeme is in the manuscript *Hypa* fol. 301v [*sub anno* 1288], where it is explicitly interpreted as a "tuft of straw": и вземь [tj. володимѣръ] соломы в роукоу • ѿ постела своее • рекъ хота быхъ ти рци • братъ мои • тот въхотъ соломы далъ • того не даваи по моемь животъ никомоу же (*SDRJa* II, 1989, 308).

ДЬІАВОЛЪ ЧΛ̅ВКА • БЪ Д̅ШЮ В НЬ[7] ВЛОЖИ • ТѢМ ЖЕ АЩЕ ОУМРЕТЬ ЧΛ̅ВКЪ В ЗЕМЛЮ ИДЕТЬ ТѢЛО • А Д̅ША К Б̅У

> While God was bathing in the bathhouse, he sweated and wiped himself with a tuft of straw and dropped [it] from the sky on the Earth. And there was a dispute between Satan and God, who will create a man from it. The devil created a man, and God put a soul in him. Therefore, when a man dies, the body goes into the earth, but the soul goes to God.

In the end of the story, the *volchvy* stated under interrogation that they believed in the Antichrist, who dwelt in the bottomless abyss. Consequently, Jan had them tortured and executed.

The testimony of the *volchvy* is particularly valuable because in it we have a unique opportunity to glimpse another narrative manifestation of the dualistic principle so popular in many alternative Slavic cosmologies known to us: whether it is apocryphal (e.g. the so-called *Legend of the Tiberias Sea*),[8] or oral-folklore narratives.[9] In those stories, two antithetic beings – one active and the other passive – always create the world in synergy. As well as with these much younger alternative cosmogonies, also in the *PVL* the character interpreted as a "Devil" is an active element, whereas "God" always plays only the role of a passive observer who, as a matter of fact, participates only indirectly in the creation of the world. In the *PVL*, his creative role is condensed into the act of throwing out the tuft of straw (вѣхъть) after a bath. Over this bundle of straw a dispute arises whether God or Devil should create man from it; the dispute is surprisingly won by Devil. Only in the end, God is involved in finalizing the creation of man by breathing in his soul.

A similar anthropogony narrative is also known from the abovementioned stories of dualistic cosmogony. After the creation of the world itself, man is also created by two antagonistic figures, but their roles are the opposite: God creates man (with everything), but Devil spits on him in order to make him prone to illness, to become mortal, etc. This is completely in compliance with the overall ethos of these narratives: everything negative in the world (such as swamps, mountains, diseases, etc.) arises from the activity of Devil during the first days of the creation.

---

7. Thus *Radz, Acad*; в не *Laur*.
8. Text has survived in at least twenty manuscript copies ranging from 17th to 19th cent.; yet the subject matter is with the highest probability much older than that; text of the apocrypha has been published by Barsov 1866.
9. *Cf.* Tomicki 1976; Kuznecova 1998; Mil'kov 1999; Johns 2005.

Let us emphasize, however, one remarkable motif in the narrative of the Běloozero *volkhvy*: that strange tuft or wisp of straw (вѣхъть), that is, the bundle of straw mixed with sweat of God from which man is created.[10] This вѣхъть appears to be a purely utilitarian thing – cleaning, wiping and drying with bundles of straw was quite common (but also, straw could be used as a thermal insulation or fire starter). In Slavic folklore, however, the meaning of вѣхъть was often apotropaic or forbidding: вѣхъть on a tree symbolized that it was not allowed to collect fruit from it (or it was supposed to drive off birds), вѣхъть on a pin on a footpath symbolized that it was not allowed to trespass. Also, вѣхъть could have a bit more positive signaling character: a tuft of straw at the gate of a tavern showed that the tavern had the right to sell beer or wine.[11] That is all we know of the symbolic function of вѣхъть and it does not help much in our understanding of the scene in the narrative; everything else is hidden behind unknown semantic horizons.

Regardless of this, the use of such motif in the *PVL* in the story about creation of man is very remarkable and we will return to it later with an attempt to interpret it. The most important aspect here is probably not the thing itself, but rather the fact that God wipes his sweat with it, as we will see.

Rod and lumps of soil

The second interesting narrative also comes from the Old Russian literary milieu. It is a short text that was found in a 15th century compilation manuscript, which contains various spiritual and legal writings of church fathers and comments on them. After the text deals with the creation of man, there is a very brief passage, in essence only half a sheet, which is entitled: *On breathing the Spirit into a man* (о вдѹновении дѹха в человѣка). Here, among other things, it is said:[12]

> единъ вдымаеть вседръжитель • иже единъ безсмѹртенъ и непогибающихъ творецъ • дѹнѹ бо емѹ [человѣкѹ] на лице дхъ жизни • и бысть чкъ в дшю живѹ • то ти не родъ • сѣда на вздѹсѣ мечеть на землю грѹды и в том ражаютса дѣти • и паки аггли вдымаеть дѹшю • или паки иномѹ ѿ чкъ или ѿ аггла сѹдъ бгъ предасть • сице бо нѣции еретици глаголють ѿ книгъ срачиньскихъ и отъ проклатыхъ волхаръ • о такихъ блѹдословцехъ пррокъ рече • попелъ срдце ихъ и персти хѹже надежа ихъ и безчестнѣе кала житие

---

10. *SSJČ* IV, 38: s.v. *věchet*; *SSJČ* IV, 84: s.v. *vích* (*věch*).
11. For all meanings cf. *SSJČ* IV, 38 a 84.
12. It was discovered and made famous by Gal'kovskij 2013 (1913[1]): 360–362; it is from his edition I publish this text, I only supplement it with the biblical citations.

ихъ • ако не раꙁꙋмѣша творца своего • съꙁдавшаго их и вдохнꙋвшаго въ нихъ дꙋхъ жиꙁни и вложившаго дꙋшꙋ дѣиствену • всѣмъ бо есть творецъ богъ а не родъ

The only one who breathes the soul in is All-ruler [i.e. God], who alone is the immortal and non-transient Creator. For he *breathed into his nostrils the breath of life, and the man became a living being* [Gn2:7].[13] **And not that Rod, sitting in the air, throws lumps [of soil?] on the earth and thus the children are born**, or that angels are those who breathe in the souls, or even that God passes the right [to breathe in the soul] to somebody of men or angels, as some heretics say, inspired by Saracen books and by forsaken Bulgarians. About such heresy-talkers the prophet says: *their heart is made of ashes, their hope is cheaper than dirt and their life is not worth as much as his clay, because he never came to know the God who shaped him, who breathed into him a breath of life and a real soul.*[14] The Creator of all men is God, not Rod.

The basic point of the text, the warning that the supreme Creator is only God and not a figure called Rod, is thus repeated in the text once more (всѣмъ бо есть творецъ богъ а не родъ). Immediately after this passage, there follows a treatise on the physicality and how it goes with the seed and the mother's womb, or how the wisdom of God has arranged it that even the small seed can create a large body (ѿколе мала сѣмене • велика бывають величествїа телеса).

In that castigating depiction of a mythological being called Rod, sitting in the heavens and throwing on the ground the lumps [of earth] (сѣдѧ на вꙁдꙋсѣ мечеть на ꙁемлю грꙋды) from which children are born (и в том ражаютсѧ дѣти), we find an interesting revelation of one of the functions of this enigmatic figure called Rod. This figure otherwise appears only sporadically in medieval Russian homiletics. The homiletic texts usually prohibit praying to and preparing the sacrifices on the altars or tables (трапеꙁы) for *Rod* (M.sg.) and *Rožanice* (F.pl.) – in the Old Russian homiletics the prohibition of sacrifices and prayers for

---

13. *Cf.* for example the reading of Gn2:7 in one of the oldest Old Church Slavonic *prophetologion* (Lat. *paroemiarion*, Rus. *паремийник*), that is in the *Paroemiarion Grigorovičianum* (ed. Ribarova & Xauptova 1998: 77): и съꙁда бъ чл҃вка прьстиѧ ѿ ꙁема ∴ и доунѫ на лице его дъхновение животное ∴ и бъ | чл҃вкъ въ дш҃ѫ живѫ ∴ (Grig fol. 19v-20r). Similar reading are in *Paroemiarion Zacharianum*: пьрстью ѿ ꙁемлѧ (Zach fol. 41аβ) and *Paroemiarion e collectione Lobkoviana*: прьстиѫ ѿ ꙁема Lobk (fol. 27v).

14. Paraphrasing Sap15:10–11: „His heart is ashes, his hope is cheaper than dirt, and his life is of less worth than clay, because he failed to know the one who formed him and inspired him with an active soul and breathed into him a living spirit."

these beings is a frequent literary trope.[15] Rožanice are usually interpreted as *genii familiares*, beings closely related to the household, family succession and child-birth.[16] From other texts we also know that the term *rožanice* was used in Old Church Slavonic translations of Greek texts as the equivalent of the Greek concepts of *tuchē* and horoscopic genealogies.[17] They were closely related to the progression and predestination of human life. About Rod, who always appears in these texts as a masculine singular, we know much less.

The treatise *On breathing the spirit into a man* is thus the only text in which we can see Rod's competences and it also gives us some hints that he could once have been conceived as a supreme mythological being – at least in the imagination and beliefs of some non-traditional religious schools (as a matter of fact, Boris Rybakov used this treatise in his absolutely uncritical attempt to create from Rod the key deity of his fictitious reconstruction of the Slavic pantheon).[18] Interestingly, this text does not refer to any mythical *illud tempus* when man was originally created, but it rather attempts to convey the idea of how the world is routinely working in this day – that is, how new children's souls are actually coming into being.

What is also important is that here we are again confronted with the idea that the existence of a person depends on the fact that a divine agent **throws something out of the sky** (wisp of straw or lumps of earth), from which then a new human life is created in contact with the earth as such. This is a remarkable moment. We can compare this tradition with, for example, the Greek story of Deucalion, who, after the flood of the world, together with his wife Pyrrha threw "the bones of the mother of the earth", that is stones, on the ground. From these stones falling on the earth a new generation was born (Apollodorus, *Bibl.* I,7.2);[19] Pindar called this new people "progeny of stone" (λίθινον γόνον, Pindar, *Olymp.* 9.45).[20] So the

---

15. Sreznęskij 1855.
16. *Slovo někojego Christoljubca, Slovo sv. Grigorja Bogoslovcja, Slovo Isaja Proroka, Vъprosto čto estъ trebokladenъe idolъskoe eže reče sv. Vasilij* etc. (*cf.* manuscript variants of these sermons in editions of Buslaev 1861; Tixonravov 1862; Gal'kovskij 1913; Barankova, Savel'eva & Sapožnikova 2013; commentaries: Sreznęskij 1855; Aničkov 1914; Petruxin 2000; Mansikka 2005).
17. *Cf.* Gal'kovskij 2013: 104-130.
18. Rybakov 1981: 438-470. For methodological criticism of Rybakov's work, his attitude to mythology and sources, see Petruxin 2000: 236-243; Klejn 2004: 68-104.
19. Ed. Frazer 1921 (*LCL*), vol. 1, 52-55. *Cf.* Kerényi 1996: 173.
20. Ed. Race 1997 (*LCL* 56), vol. 1, 152-153.

motive is not unique. Some variants of this trope can be also found elsewhere among the Slavs; they suggest that the common structure of these traditional stories, namely that an element or particle of God falls from heaven to earth and creates man, has been developed in many ways. Let us look closer at these Slavic traditions.

Particle of God falls down to the Earth

One Hutsul oral story tells about the creation of the world and explains the origin of man again as arising from the conflict between the passive God and his active adversary, who in this narrative bears the name Aridnyk. The result of the dispute is that a piece of skin from the hand of God falls from heaven to earth, and from this skin Adam is created, "pure as God Himself."[21] One Slovene/Croatian folk etiological legend (recorded by Janez Trdina in the village of Menge š in Kranjska, near Ljubljana) also speaks of the origin of man in a very similar manner: God, after a long journey, has become sweated (similarly to the God of *volchvy* who sweated in the bath) and the sweat from his forehead fell from heaven to earth – when the drop came to life, Man was created:[22]

> Bog [... p]utuje te putuje, nu nigde konca ni kraja. Putujuć dodje i do naše zemlje, nu već se biaše umorio: pot mu se čela hvataše. Na zemlju padne kap znoja – kap se oživi, i eto ti prvoga čovjeka. Božja mu rodbina, nu stvoren ne bi za razblude, iz znoja se rodio, već početkom mu sudjeno bilo, da se muči i znoji.
>
> God travels and wanders, but there is no end or edge anywhere. Wandering, he comes to our country, but he gets tired: the sweat drips from his forehead. A drop of sweat falls on the ground - the drop comes alive and, behold, here is the first man. He has a God-like origin, but he was not made of sin, he was born of sweat; he was destined from the beginning to be troubled and sweated.

In another Trdina's version of this story its moral lesson is even more literal: man is made of God's sweat in order to remember forever that he has to work in the sweat of his face to survive.[23] In addition, folk tradition aids folk etymology: man

---

21. Koenig 1936: 370; in fact, he cites Szuchiewicz 1908.
22. Trdina 1858: 60; *cf.* Kropej 2012: 17.
23. See Trdina 1881: 164: „[...] Bog se je naveličal popotovati in se je vrnil nazaj na našo zemljo. Z obličja mu pade na zemljo kaplja potu in iz te kaplje rodil se je prvi človek. **Ustvarjen je bil iz božjega potu v večni spomin, da si mora s potom svojega obličja svoj kruh služiti.**"

is called *človĕk*, since he originated from the forehead (*čelo*) of God – he is only a drop of sweat from the forehead of God.

The moral lesson and folk etymology are probably only secondary. For us, it is very important that in this story we find already a fourth instance of a motif that something from God – and, again, that something had a contact with God's "body" – falls to the ground: (1) the tuft of straw in which the sweated God has wiped himself (in *Primary Chronicle*); (2) a piece of skin from his hand (in Hutsul narrative); (3) the sweat that came from his forehead (in Slovenian narrative); (4) and finally the lumps of soil he held in his hand and threw on the ground (in the Old Russian treatise *On breathing the Spirit into a man*).

The texts themselves perceive these items positively – even though it is the sweat from the forehead, the skin from the hand, the sweat on the towel or the lumps of soil, the most important thing is that these objects have had contact with the deity and are therefore considered to be good *par excellence*. However, we should keep in mind the ambiguous symbolic meaning of these "marginal objects" and parts of the human body (such as fallen off skin, cut off hair, dripped sweat or other body fluids) that they have in many cultures of the world.[24] This ambivalence gives symbolic power and peculiarity to these marginal corporeal objects and is crucial for our understanding of those stories.

In the first three instances of the motif (tuft, skin, and sweat), the contact with God's body is quite straightforward and obvious. In the fourth example, Rod's "lumps [of soil]" (гроуды), the situation is a bit more complicated. Rybakov, for one, interpreted Rod's lumps as a metaphor of droplets of fertile rain falling from the clouds,[25] even despite the fact that the whole context of the treatise *On breathing the Spirit into a man* refers exclusively to the mystery of the origin of human body, or to the mystery of the inspiration of soul. There is not even the smallest mention of any agricultural practices in the treatise.[26] It is therefore

---

24. *Cf.* particularly a classic social-anthropological work on this issue: Douglas 1966: 122.
25. *Cf.* Rybakov 1981: 450.
26. Rybakov based his interpretation on lexical data that had been published by Sreznevskij 1893/I: 600. Rybakov, however, didn't choose the lexeme гроуда („lump of soil, heap, pile'), but he used meanings of a lexeme грѹдиѥ/гряждиѥ, which is attested denoting only 'drops of dew' (βώλους δρόσου, glebas roris; particularly in a translations of Jb38:28), undoubtedly based on their roundness and lumpiness. And yet, Rybakov's грѹдиѥ (when we consider Sreznevskij's dictionary thoroughly) is not once attested with the meaning "raindrops"! So even when we reconsider Rybakov's lexical sources, his conclusion makes no sense.

more fruitful to consider the lumps in the context of symbolic meaning of various bodily elements, which is a prism brought to us by the three other presented anthropogony narratives. The question is, then, whether the semantic horizons of the lexeme гроүды, as it appears in the Old Russian literature, allow this way of interpretation?

The context of the whole treatise, that is, a thorough discussion of the origins of soul in relation to seed and impregnation, can bring us to the question of whether these „lumps of something" (гроүды) cannot also be a metaphor for some kind of Rod's genetic material or for a part of his body? Not just the immediate context of our source, but also the comparative data can lead us to this conclusion. A comparative mythology can be very illustrative in this case: just as the motif of the creation from the soil can be compared to the widespread tradition of the Old Testament (Gn 2:7, where man is "dust of the ground"), and the birth from thrown stones can be compared with the Greek story of Deucalion and Pyrrha, for the remarkable motif of the creation of man from the divine genetic material we have an analogy in Indo-European mythological tradition. In the Greek mythology we know the story about the origins of Athenians, who were allegedly born from earth: one version of this myth states how Hephaestus passionately desired the goddess Athena and he tried to rape her, but he ejaculated on her thigh. Athena then wiped his semen away from her skin with a tuft of wool she then flung to the earth (εἰς γῆν ἔρριψε). The contact of the divine semen on the wool (*erion*, ἔριον) with the earth (*chthōn*, χθῶν) gave birth to a creature called Erichthonius, the ancestor and the first human king of all the Athenians, the descendant of still virgin goddess Athena (*cf.* Apollodorus, *Bibl.* III, 14.6).[27] The story was supposed to prove the fact of Athenian autochthony: the fact that the Athenians were born directly from the soil they lived on, and thus they have the greatest claim to it.[28]

---

27. Ed. Frazer 1921 (*LCL*), vol. 2, 88–95. *Cf.* other version of this myth in *Iliad* II.546–551; Herodotus VIII.55; Pausanias I.2.6; Augustin, *De civitate* 18.9, ad. Etymology of Erichthonios, derived from the words *erion* and *chthōn* is much later, though. Apollodorus uses along with *eris* the word *gē* (γῆ, ‚Earth'), Herodotus calls Erichthonius *gēgeneos* (γηγενέος, ‚born from earth'; Herodotus VIII.55, ed. Godley 1925, vol. 4, 50–51). Other versions in which the folk etymology is derived from the word *eris*, ‚discord', meaning discord between the two deities (i.e. Athena and Hephaestus), are summarized by Kerényi 1996: 97.
28. *Cf.* Bonnefoy & Doniger 1991: 341; Kerényi 1996: 97–98; Kerényi 1998: 158–159; Redfield 2003: 121–122; Munn 2006: 33.

I do not mean to suggest that Rod's гроуды refer to his semen as such; for such a claim we completely lack arguments in the source material itself. I only want to claim that this lexeme does not have to necessarily refer to "lumps *of earth*", but that it can have a broader meaning, in which the genetic material interpretation can give more sense. There is definitely no doubt that the word as such was perceived as denoting something rather unclean, as the lexical evidence of the term гроуда in the Old-Russian literature attests. We know of three occurrences in the literary works written between 11th and 14th century:[29]

1. In the so-called *Lobkovskij Prolog*, i.e. in the Novgorod manuscript dated to year 1262 or 1282, which contains a number of biblical and hagiographic texts meant for liturgical readings from September to January, the Old Testament story *Bel and Dragon* is paraphrased (Βῆλ καὶ δράκων in the Septuagint;[30] in the Vulgate it is also referred to as Chapter 14 of the Book of Daniel). In the story, the Prophet Daniel pulls out his hair, he wraps it with a cloth, "he rolls it up into a гроуда" (сверте въ гроудоу) and smears it with pitch and oil. When the dragon approaches him and wants to devour him, Daniel throws this weapon into his mouth (врьже гроудоу въ оуста кго) and the dragon falls dead to the ground.[31]

2. In one of the sermons of Gregory the Theologian in a 14th century manuscript, there is an allusion to the abovementioned story. It is paraphrased similarly: Daniel "boiled together" pitch and his hair, thus creating a гроуда (и створи груду), which he threw into the dragon's mouth and killed him with it.[32]

3. The last known occurrence of the lexeme is perhaps the most interesting one for us. It can be found in the homiletic anthology called the *Golden Chain* (*Златая цепь*) and dated to the 14th century. In the sermon on the topic of Gn

---

29. Cf. SDRJa II, 396.
30. Cf. Rahlfs 1952/II: 936–941.
31. Dn14:27: и оурвавъ своихъ власъ и скоутъ арона ризы • сверте въ гроудоу и помаза смолою и масломъ • иде къ змию • змии же оучютивъ кго • идаше к немоу съ гнѣвомь • и ѩко зиноу хота пожрети данила • дани|лъ же врьже гроудоу въ оуста кго • бѣ змии мьртвъ (Пролог „Лобковский" сентябрьской половины, MS ГИМ, Хлуд. № 187, fol. 95a–95b). In the Greek original of Septuagint, from which the OCS version was translated, Daniel also takes "pitch, fat, and hair" (πίσσαν καὶ στῆρ καὶ τρίχας; variants in Rahlfs 1952/II: 940) and he makes small balls or lumps out of them (μάζας; figuratively also ,cakes'); he throws these balls into the dragon's mouth.
32. възвари вкоупь смолу и власы • и створи груду и вверже въ оуста змикви (Григория Богослова 16 слов с толкованиями Никиты Ираклийского, MS ГИМ, Син. № 954, fol. 140a).

2:7 about the creation of man, it is explicitly stated that God created man from the clay (пеȓьсть) and *not from the lumps* (а не гру̂), not from "rough soil" (не дєбєлю зємлю), but from good soil (но добру пєрсть).³³

In the first two examples, гроуда is an impure mass of something, formless and artificially put together: in this case a tuft of hair wrapped in cloth and pitch (nota bene: quite an unexpected analogy to Athena's tuft of wool with Hephaestus' sperm on it, or God's sweat wiped away with a tuft of straw, albeit in a narrative with a completely different plot).

In the case of the third occurrence, the sermon explicitly mentions the word гроуда as something unclean, as a bad or rough (дєбєлıа) soil, and puts this object in direct contradiction to the "good soil", called here as clay or soil (пєрьсть).³⁴ This word – in the standardized OCS form: пръсть – is in the oldest extant Slavonic translations of *Prophetologion* the most common translation of the Greek χοῦς, 'dust' (in a common collocation: "the dust of the ground", χοῦς ἀπὸ τῆς γῆς, пръсть ѿтъ зємѧ).³⁵

When the treatise *On breathing the Spirit* quotes Gn 2:7 about the creation of man from the earth and then it talks about Rod's грȣды, it builds the same rhetorical opposition as the sermon from the *Golden Chain*, which draws its topic also from Gn 2:7. The conclusion of both literary works is, undoubtedly, that *the soil* of earth (пръсть) is good, but *the lump* of earth (гроуда) is bad. There is perhaps an analogy to the manner in which the Hutsul oral story considers it necessary to emphasize that Adam, originating from God's skin, is "pure as God himself", and in which the Slovenian legend points out that the creation of man from God's sweat is a proof of his original creation "without sin", that is non-bodily creation – even though it is in both cases in a direct contradiction with the *ultimate physical and bodily nature* of creation of man in these stories.

At the moment of Rod's throwing of "lumps", the reader automatically makes in his mind an association of lumps with *lumps of earth*, mainly because of the immediately preceding quotation of Gn 2:7 about the creature of man from the

---

33. и взѧ̂ бъ пєрсть ѿ зємли рукою • нарчєть творѧщюю ѥго силу и створи ѹ̂лвка и взѧ̂ пєрьсть а не гру̂ не дєбєлю зємлю • но добру пєрсть (Златая цепь, MS РНБ, Тр.-Серг. № 11, fol. 49d). Similar reading of this passage (и созда ѹ̂лка не взат реч груду пєрсти ни велику зємлю но дробну пєрсть и созда ѹ̂лка) can be found, according to СРЯ (4: 144), also in *Paleja tolkovaja* dated to 1477 (Палея толковая, MS РНБ, Син. № 210, fol. 31b).
34. Cf. *ESSJa* 7, 146–148, where there are interesting parallels for *gruda* in various Slavic languages: sand, grain, frozen land, stones... See also *ESRJa* I, 181.
35. See evidence in *SJS* 3, 403; *Cf.* also above, footnote N°. 13.

earth. And yet, wouldn't it be a bit strange if Rod threw from the heavens *down to the earth lumps of earth*? Of which, when they came in contact *with earth again*, the children would be born? A rhetorical question: is it really productive to sow *soil into the soil*?

Thus, all the evidence gradually suggests that Rod's lumps do not necessarily have to be lumps of earth, but that the word гроудa denotes some kind of unspecified material that probably has to do with Rod's body and corporeality – as the structural parallels with other Slavic narratives and also the comparative Greek parallel suggest. These lumps were perceived both as something unclean, but also as something non-ordered and formless – as the semantic horizons of the Old-Russian texts suggest. Гроудa can be a formless lump of hair, straw or wool, which is in any case mixed with some bodily liquid.[36] In the context of anthropogony, it is also extremely interesting that it is only from the initial formlessness that something as complicated as man can arise; whether it is the formlessness of the Biblical dust of the ground, the Rod's mysterious lumps, the sweat of God, or the human seed as such.

Human body and body of Earth

The above-mentioned parallel of Rod's "lumps" with the sperm can, of course, be completely rejected. It cannot be read literally, but rather metaphorically. Just as in the joke about Freud's cigar,[37] here too sweat is sometimes only sweat and a lump is only a lump. However, the striking parallel with the Greek myth of autochthony, the creation from the earth, remains important. It is not only the analogy of creation from earth as in the Old Testament, but in particular the motif common to the creation story about the God of the Běloozero *volkhvy*, the God of the Slovene and Hutsul oral tradition, and the goddess Athena: some object that is corporeal or that has been in contact with the body of the deity is by his/her agency thrown to the ground and then man is created from it...

We have some hints that there could have been some archaic notion of the autochthonous birth of the people from the earth among the Slavs before the

---

36. In case of the prophet Daniel's pitch on hair it is not a bodily liquid *per se*, but this resin from tree, turned into a flammable pitch, which can be perceived as a bodily liquid *sui generis* (a liquid from the body of a tree).

37. It is an apocryphal story making fun of Freud's fallic symbolism theory: Asked by one of his students, whether also his iconic cigar, tubular, with hot, red end and emitting fragrant smoke can also be perceived as a symbol of penis, Freud allegedly replied: "A cigar is sometimes just a cigar."

adoption of Christianity (which only later mediated the Old Testament tradition of creation to the Slavs). First, among various Slavs there was quite a widespread tradition about the underground people: e.g. Lusatian *ludki*, Polish *krasnoludki*, Slovakian *lútci*, etc.[38] They were said to have been born from the earth similarly to the Old Norse *dvergar*,[39] and the Lusatian Serbs believed that *ludki* were the first inhabitants of the land; their extinction began, as the folk tradition says, with Christianization and the practice of bell ringing. We can also associate this idea with a fairly widespread narratives that the giants, born from the rocks, were the first generation of beings on earth. In both of these examples, we find a motive of the creation of some pre-human beings from natural elements (i.e. earth or stone), from which they must later "emancipate" and become regular people.

A supporting argument to the interesting and intricate relationship of man and his body to the earth can be also shown in the North-Russian folklore apocrypha, appertaining to the genre of so-called spiritual songs (*духовные стихи*): an epic poem *Golubinnaja kniga* (*GK*). This story can, in my opinion, illuminate both the intricate relation of humans to the earth, and also to the deities.

In many variants of the text of the *GK*, we find the story of the creation of the world from some pan-cosmic, gigantic Proto-Being, which at the beginning of the ages was killed (or sacrificed), and from its body parts rocks, trees, the sky, the sun, the moon, etc. were then created.[40] Interestingly, side by side with the description of emergence of the world from the body of the Proto-Being, we can find in the *GK* also the depiction of how the human body, i.e. bodies of the individual people, comes from the material of the world as such. It is nicely described by one variant of *GK*:[41]

> У нас ум-разум самого Христа,
> наши помыслы от облац небесныих,
> у нас мир-народ от Адамия,
> кости крепкие от камени,
> телеса наши от сырой земли,
> кровь-руда наша от черна моря.

---

38. Máchal 1995: 79–86.
39. See Snorri Sturluson, *Gylfaginning* 14 (*dvergar* born from the ground as maggots; ed. Faulkes 2005: 15), cf. *Völuspá* 9 (born *ór Brimis blóði ok ór Bláins leggjum*; ed. Kristjánsson & Ólason 2014: 293), or *Alvíssmál* 35 (Alvís turns to stone at daylight; ed. Kristjánsson & Ólason 2014: 443).
40. Lincoln 1986; West 2007: 343–345.
41. Oksenov 1908: 304–311, verses 81–86.

> We have the mind of Christ himself,
> our thoughts from heavenly clouds,
> we have the world-people from Adam,
> strong bones from stone,
> *our bodies from the damp land,*
> our red blood is from the Black Sea.

A similar description of the elements of the human body created from the natural elements appears also in other variants of *GK*,[42] but also in other spiritual songs (e.g. in the song *Svitok Jerusalimskij*) or apocrypha (*Povestvovanije o tom, kak sotvoril Bog Adama* from the 17th century,[43] or fragments of a 15th century treatise called „On body", *O tele*[44]). This motif is clearly much more than just an allusion to Gn 2:7, which would work with the analogy "human body = dust of the earth". Perhaps it is a reflection of more archaic and much more variegated ideas, known from other Indo-European traditions in which the world is made up from a cosmic Proto-Being.[45]

In all of these narratives, the human body is depicted as a microcosm, which is the mirror image of the whole macrocosm. Moreover, there is a third, ultimate meta-level, that is the body of a cosmic Proto-Being, from which the macrocosm has been created in the first place. Therefore, the world as such can be, in light of these traditions, understood as a transition stage between the divine and the human existence. Earth and its "body" is a kind of cosmic transducer, a mediator between body material coming from God (or other mythological being) and between the human body coming from the Earth itself. This is precisely what, in my opinion, we can see in the background of all four of the abovementioned Slavic narratives of the creation of man from a particle of God. From this particle man is born when it comes into the contact with the earth as the mediator of creation.

The presented reading and interpretation of those four structurally similar narratives may, among other things already mentioned, indicate that the concept of man as an "earthling" or "terrestrial being" may not only be a reflection of

---

42. *Cf.* Bahna 2007.
43. MS RGB, Rumjac. sobr. № 370, fol. 147a–174a (ed. Mil'kov 1999: 422–429); fol. 147a–148a: Со‹з›дати в земли мадїа‹м›стеи ҃чка взе‹м› земли горсть ото осми ҃ча‹о›те‹и› | •а҃• ѿ земли тѣло •в҃• ѿ камени ко‹с›ти •г҃• ѿ мора кровь •д҃• ѿ с҃нца очи •е҃• ѿ облака мысли •ѕ҃• ѿ свѣта свѣ‹т› •з҃• ѿ | вѣтра дыханїе •и҃• ѿ огна теплота • и поиде г҃ь б҃гъ очи има‹ти› ѿ со‹л›нца и остави адама едино‹г› лежаща на зе‹м›ли •
44. MS RNB, Kir.-Bel. sobr. № 11/1088, fol. 279b–280b (ed. Mil'kov 1999: 442–443).
45. *Cf.* Lincoln 1975 and 1986; West 2007, 343-345; Lajoye 2013.

the Old Testament tradition based on Gn 2:7, but that it is grounded in a very archaic notion, already expressed not only in the abovementioned Proto-Indo-European cosmogony-anthropogony myth, but also in the semantic relation of the words "man" and "earth" in some Indo-European languages (such as e.g. Latin *humanus–humus*, Lithuanian *žmogus–žeme*, all from PIE *$(d^h)g^homon$*.[46] Thus, on the assumption that a person is connected in a metonymic and inseparable way to the earth from which he was born, on which he walks, and to which he is going to eventually return. Or, as one Moravian folk song summarizes aptly:

> Ze země jsem na zem přišel,
> po ní chodím jako pán.
> Na zemi jsem rozum našel,
> do ní budu zakopán.

> From earth I came to be on earth,
> on it I walk like a lord.
> I've found my wisdom on earth,
> in it I will be buried.

Literature

Primary sources

Apollodorus, *Bibl.*: Apollodorus, *The Library*, with an English translation by Sir James George Frazer. Cambridge, Harvard University Press, Loeb Classical Library, 2 vols., 1921 (reprint 1954).

Pindar, *Olymp.*: Pindar, *Olympian Odes; Pythian Odes*, edited and translated by William H. Race. Cambridge, Harvard University Press, Loeb Classical Library vol. 56, 1997.

Snorri Sturlusson, *Snorra Edda*: Snorri Sturluson, *Edda: Prologue and Gylfaginning*, edited by Anthony Faulkes. London, Viking Society for Northern Research, 2005.

Kristjánsson & Ólason 2014: Jónas Kristjánsson & Vésteinn Ólason (eds.), *Eddukvæði I: Goðakvæði*. Reykjavík, Hið Íslenzka Fornritafélag, 2014.

Manuscripts and edition of *PVL*
Edition:

PVL 1999: *Povet'vremennyx let*, podgotovka teksta, perevod, stati i kommentarii D. S. Lixačeva; pod redakcej V. P. Adrianovoj-Peretc, izdanie vtoroe ispravlennoe i dopolennoe. Saint-Petersburg, Nauka.

---

[46] *Cf.* West 2007, 180. *Cf.* also Greek folk etymology that lies at the basis of the story about Deucalion: the word for 'people' (λαοί) is in Pindar associated with the plural of ‚stones' (λᾶες). Cf. Pindar, *Olymp.* 9.46, ed. Race 1997 (LCL 56), vol. 1, 152–153.

Collation:

Ostrowski, Donald, 2003: *The Povĕst' vremennykh lĕt: An Interlinear Collation and Paradosis*, vol. 1–3. Harvard, Harvard University Press.

Manuscripts:

Laur = Laurentian Codex. PSRL. T. 1. *Lavrent'evskaja letopis'*. Leningrad, 1926–28. http://expositions.nlr.ru/LaurentianCodex/_Project/page_Show.php
Radz = Radziwiłł Codex. http://chronologia.org/rare/radzivil/index.html
Acad = Academic Codex. http://old.stsl.ru/manuscripts/medium.php?col=5&manuscript=236&pagefile=236-0001
Hypa = Hypatian Codex. PSRL. T. 2. *Ipat'evskaja letopis'*. Saint-Petersburg, 1908.

Bibliography of literature, dictionaries and editions of OCS sources:

Aničkov, E. V., 1914: *Jazyčestvo i drevnjaja Rus'*. Saint-Petersburg, Tipografija M. M. Stasjuleviča.

Barankova, G. S., Savel'eva, N. V., Sapožnikova, O. S., 2013: *Antologija pamjatnikov literatury domongol'skogo perioda v rukopisi XIV v.: Sofijskij sbornik*. Saint-Petersburg, Al'jans-Arxeo.

Barsov, E., 1866: „O Tiveriadskom more: Po spisku XVI v. ", *Čtenija v Imperatorskom obščestve istorii i drevnostei possijskix pri Moskovskom universitete* 2/2, *Materialy istoriko-literaturnye*: 1–8.

Bonnefoy, Yves, Doniger, Wendy 1991: *Mythologies: A restructed translation of "Dictionnaire des mythologies et des religions des sociétés traditionnelles et du monde antique"*, Vol. 1, compiled by Bonnefoy; prepared under the direction of Wendy Doniger; translation by Gerald Honigsblum. Chicago – London, University of Chicago Press.

Buslaev, F. I., 1861: *Istoričeskaja xristomatija: cerkovno-slavjanskogo i drevnerusskago jazykov*. Moscow, Univerzitetskaja tipografija.

Douglas, Mary, 1966: *Purity and Danger*. London, Routledge.

ESRJa: *Etimologičeskij slovar' russkogo jazyka, tom. I, G*. Moscow, Izdatel'stvo Moskovskogo universiteta, 1972.

ESSJa: *Etimologičeskij slovar' slavjanskix jazykov, tom. 1-37*. Moscow, Nauka, 1975–2011.

Gal'kovskij, M., 1913: *Bor'ba xristijanstva s ostatkami jazyčestva v drevnej Rusi, tom. II, Drevne-russkija slova i poučenija, napravlenyja protiv ostatkov jazyčestva v naroda*. Moscow, A. I. Snegirev.

Gazo, A. (Gazeau, A.) 1898: *Šuty i skomoroxi vsex vremen i narodov*, perevod i dopolnenija N. Fedorovoj. Saint-Petersburg, tipografija A. L. Trunova.

Ginzburg, Carlo, 1966: *The Night Battles: Witchcraft and Agrarian Cults in the Sixteenth and Seventeenth Centuries*, translated by J. and A. Tedeschi. Baltimore: John Hopkins Press.
Johns, Andreas 2005: „Slavic Creation Narratives: The Sacred and the Comic", *Fabula* 46 (2005): 257–290.
Kerényi, Karl 1996: *Mytologie Řeků I: Příběhy bohů a lidí*, z německého originálu přeložil Jan Binder. Prague, Oikoymenh.
Kerényi, Karl, 1998: *Mytologie Řeků II: Příběhy héróů*, z německého originálu přeložil Jan Binder. Prague, Oikoymenh.
Klejn, L. S., 2004: Voskrešenie Peruna: k rekonstrukcii vostočnoslavjanskogo jazyčestva. Saint-Petersburg, Evrazija.
Koenig, Samuel 1936: „Cosmogonic Beliefs of the Hutsuls", *Folklore* 47: 368–373.
Kropej, Monika, 2012: *Supernatural Beings from Slovenian Myth and Folktales*. Ljubljana, Založba ZRC.
Kuznecova, V. S., 1998: Dualističeskie legendy o sotvorenii mira v vostočnoslavjanskoj fol'klornoj tradicii. Novosibirsk, Izdatel'stvo SO RAN OIGGM.
Lajoye, Patrice, 2013: „Puruṣa", *Nouvelle Mythologie Comparée / New Comparative Mythology* 1: 23–58.
Lincoln, Bruce, 1975: „The Indo-European Myth of Creation", *History of Religions* 15/2 (1975): 121–145.
Lincoln, Bruce, 1986: *Myth, Cosmos, and Society: Indo-European Themes of Creation and Destruction*. Cambridge, Harvard University Press.
Máchal, Jan, 1995 ([1]1907): *Bájesloví slovanské*. Olomouc, Votobia.
Mansikka, V. J., 2005 ([1]1922): Religija vostočnyx slavjan. Moscow, IMLI RAN.
Munn, Mark Henderson, 2006: *The Mother of the Gods, Athens, and the tyranny of Asia a study of sovereignty in ancient religion*. Berkeley – Los Angeles, University of California Press.
Oksenov, A. V., 1908: *Narodnaja poesija: Byliny, pesni, skazki, poslovicy, duxovnye stixi, povesti*. Saint-Petersburg, Sinodal'naja tipografija.
Petruxin, V. Ja., 2000: *Iz istorii russkoj kul'tury, t. I, Drevnjaja Rus'*. Moscow, Jazyki russkoj kul'tury.
Redfield, James M., 2003: *The Locrian maidens: Love and death in greek Italy*. Princeton – Oxford, Princeton University Press.
Ribarova, Z., Xauptova, Z. (eds.), 1998: *Grigorovičev parimejnik, 1, Tekst so kritički aparat*. Skopje, Makedonska akademija na naukite i umetnostite.
Rybakov, B. A., 1981: *Jazyčestvo drevnej Rusi*. Moscow, Nauka.
SDRJa: Slovar' drevnerusskogo jazyka (XI-XIV vv.), tom. I-II. Moscow, Russkij jazyk & Azbukovnik, 1988–1989.
Sreznevskij, I. I., 1855: *Roženicy u slavjan i drugix jazyčeskix narodov*. Moscow, tipografija A. Semena.

Sreznevskij, I. I., 1893: *Materialy dlja slovarja drevnerusskogo jazyka, tom. I, a-k*. Moscow, tipografija Imperatorskoj Akademii Nauk [reprint 1958].

SRJa: *Slovar' russkogo jazyka XI-XVII vv., tom 1-30*. Moscow, Nauka, 1975–2004.

SSJČ IV: *Slovník spisovného jazyka českého IV (V-Ž; Doplňky a opravy)*. Prague, Academia, 1971.

Szuchiewicz, Włodzimierz, 1908: *Huculszczyzna*. Lwów, Muzeum im. Dzieduszyckich, tom 4.

Téra, Michal, 2005: „Staroruští volchvové a jejich souvislosti s indoevropskými a eurasijskými duchovními tradicemi", *in* M. Příhoda (ed.), *Kulturní, duchovní a etnické kořeny Ruska: Tradice a alternativy*. Červený Kostelec, Pavel Mervart: 13–47.

Tixonravov, N., 1862: *Letopisi russkoj literatury i drevnosti, tom IV, otd. III*. Saint-Petersburg, tipografija V. Gračeva.

Tomicki, Ryszard, 1976: „Slowiański mit kosmogoniczny", *Etnografia polska* 20/1: 47–97.

Trdina, Janez, 1858: „Narodne poveisti iz staroslovinskoga bajeslovja", *Neven: Zabavan, poučan i znansten list* 7/4: 60–62.

Trdina, Janez, 1881: „Verske bajke na Dolenjskem", *Ljubljanski zvon* 1/3: 164–170.

Tvorogov, O. V., 1984: *Leksičeskij sostav Povesti vremennyx let: Slovoukazateli i častotnyj slovnik*. Kiev, Naukova Dumka.

Zguta, Russell, 1974: „The Pagan Priests of Early Russia: Some New Insights", *Slavic Review* 33/2: 259–266.

Towards the PSl. *Stribogъ origin

Alexander V. Ivanenko

National Academy of Sciences of Ukraine, Institute of the Ukrainian language
skifetym@gmail.com

Abstract. The article deals with the origin of the PSl. *Stribogъ theonym. Grounding the literary monuments and the new Iranian lexicographic sources, the author substantiates the old «windy» etymology of the PSl. *Stribogъ ‹ East-Iranian *S(t)rī-baya "the wind, storm or thunder god".

Keywords. theonymy, Slavonic theonymy, semantical reconstruction, Iranian studies, Slavonic studies, The Lay of Igor's Warfare

THE NAME OF STRIBOGЪ mentioned for the first time in 980 AD: "И нача княжити Володимеръ въ Киевѣ единъ, и постави кумиры на холму внѣ двора теремнаго: Перуна ... и Хърса, Дажьбога, и Стрибога ... - I nača knjažyti Volodiměr vŭ Kijevě jedinŭ, i postavi kumiry na xolmu vně dvora teremnago: Peruna ... i Xŭrsa, Dažĭboga, i Striboga[1] (And began to rule Volodimer in Kiev solely, and erected the idols on the hill, out the palace garden: Perun ... and Hors, Dazhbog and Stribog ...)».[2]

In the *The Lay of Igor's Warfare* the theonym *Stribog* fixed in the possessive adjective: "Се вѣтри, Стрибожи внуци, вѣютъ съ моря стрѣлами на храбрыя плъки Игоревы! - Se větri, Striboži vnutsi, vějutŭ sŭ morja strělami na xrabryja plŭki Igorevy (There winds, *Stribog's* grandsons, blow by the arrows on the Igor regiments the brave)».[3]

The theonym *Stribog* is fixed in a raw of the East- and West Slavonic place names: *Stribozhe ozero*, *Stribozhya* – a river in Kiev region, *Stribozh* – villages (in the

---

1. There ŭ = ъ, ĭ = ь and ě = ѣ.
2. PVL 1996: 37.
3. Vinogradova 1965: 17.

Zhytomir and Nodgorod regions), *Strzyboga* – a Polish town[4] as well.

Nowadays, there are many hypotheses concerning the personality of the god, his functions and the etymology of his name.

Thus, some scholars, such as M. Kastorsky, P. Stroyev, F.I. Buslayev, A.N. Afanas'yev, S. Gedeonov, V.I. Petr saw in *Stribog* a god of the air, wind or storm.

At the same time, grounding on the assumption of the evil entity *Stribog*, which grandsons blows by the arrows on the Igor's regiments, some authors (Y.G. Butkov, S.V. Russov, E.V. Barsov, E.G. Katarov) have considered him the formidable and severe god of the element, god of cold winds, storm, wirlwind, bizzard and a swift wind.[5]

I.V. Serebryansky saw in the *Stribog* image a gloomy power, fighting against the good power. Following this thought, D.K. Zelenin points out the PSl. *striti (*sъtьri))* "to destroy", characterising the *Stribog* as the destroying, extirpating god. This attitude is supported by A.S. Orlov and Y.E. Borovsky. M.P Pogodin considered *Stribog* as the god of the war (in connection with the OUD *střít* "argument = discussion".[6]

M.R. Fasmer explained the Slavonic *Stribog* theonym from the OIr. *Srībaya* "sublime god": cf. Hephthalit. *Śribaya-* with the typologically relative Sanskr. *Çrīsōmadēvas* "sublime S.".[7] M. Vey saw Stribog as the transformed PIE. **pater dyeus* "father" with the PIE. **dyeus* – **bhagos* substitution, cf. Av. *baya*, OPers. *baga*, Slav. *богъ*.[8] K. Moshynsky tied the *Stribog* with Sanskr. *sá-sr-i-* "to run, to hurry".[9]

V.N. Toporov and Vyach. Vs. Ivanov examined *Stribog* along with *Dažbog*. Both gods complements each other: the first vest the goods and the second (as the winds god) spread them.[10]

Of all the comparatively new versions, we should to make mention of V.V. Martynov etymology. According to this etymology, the theonym *Stribog* (~ Iran. **sri-baya* "good god", cf. Sanskr. *śrī* "good, good-looking, kind") opposites to *Dažbog* (~ Iran. **duš-(duž)-baya* "evil god").[11]

---

4. ESPI 1995: 5, 68.
5. ESPI 1995: 5, 69.
6. Fasmer 1987: 3, 777; ESPI 5, 69.
7. Fasmer 1987: 3, 777 with the versions review.
8. Vej 1958: 96.
9. Mozsyński 123.
10. Toporov, Ivanov 1965: 23-24. For the history of the problem, see: Fasmer 1987: 3, 777; ESPI 1995: 5, 69.
11. Martynov 1989: 72-73.

Reminder the *Stribog* theonym etymologies are: *Stribog* ~ PSl. **ster-* (to reach out): "sowing god" – A.G. Preobrazhensky; *Stribog* ~ **sterti,*stъrǫ* – R. Jakobson; *Stribog* ~ *стрибать* (*stribat'*) – A. Brückner; *Stribog* ~ **strojiti, striti*: "the good organizer" – E. Berneker.[12]

However, the Iranian material allows explaining the *Stribog* theonym as the 'Lord of wind'.

In addition, to reveal the theonym **Sri-baya* origin and to define the times and ways of this one appearance in the Slavonic territories allows the limited data about the Iranian-spiking tribe of the Hephthalites. Taking into the attention the fact that Hephthalitan kingdom unites the highland tribes of the Pamir and Hindu Kush[13] we can to suppose that in the **Sri-baya* (god and theonym) genesis took part not only Iranian, but and the Indian lingual material.

The theonym *Śri-baya* – Stribog origin, as testifies a brief versions review, is controversial. In etymology that proposed, we based upon the Iranian material from the H. Junker article on the Hephthalites. The significance of this material for the Slavonic etymology has been for a long time depreciated.

The factors, defining our etymological positions, are:

> 1. The context of the «Lay...» allows attesting the god *Stribog* unambiguously as the god, having the atmospheric functions.

> 2. The *Śri-baya* theonym is marked on the Iranian-speaking Hephthalites tribe coins: ΣΡΙ ΒΑΓΟ ΟΖΡΟΒΑΔΙ ΣΟΓΟΝΔΑΝΟ ΒΑΓΟ ΧΟΔΑΥΟ and ΣΡΙ ΒΑΓΟ ΟΖΟΡΟΒΑΔΙ ΣΟΓΟΝΑΝΟ ÞΑ ΒΑΓΟ ΧΟΔΑΥΟ.[14] These inscriptions are written in Parthian script and belong to the Northern-East Iranian branch.[15] The attempts to interpret these inscriptions see in cited Junker's article.

In reference to the component **ΣΡΙ ΒΑΓΟ**, we can say the following. After the manner of M.R. Fasmer[16], we assume that it is the Iranian composite. However, at the same time the *Śri* name had been used in conjunction with other lexemes[17], allowing to suppose that the *Śri* name could be used as the self-sufficient proper name.

---

12. Fasmer 1987: 3, 777.
13. Gumilev 1959: 140.
14. Junker 1930: 650.
15. Junker 1930: 646.
16. Fasmer 1987: 3, 777.
17. See examples *in* Junker 1930: 646-648.

The origin of the component ΣPI was considered in conjunction with *Candâra ~ Čand(r)ōr-bay-* = Čandror-Prince or with the *Śri vad(r)o-ra*, but in this case the *bay*-element semantics must be "a prince, supreme governor, sovereign".[18]

The word **ОZРОВАΔI**, which is treated by H. Junker as the *vožroβaδi*[19], as we consider, can be interpreted in junction with the CSogd. *w'zt* (pl.) "wings", *zwz-* "to fly up" (+ **uz-*), Parth. *wz-* "blow [of wind]; to move, go, fly"; (+ **fra-*) *frwz-* "to fly", BMP *wc-* / *waz-* "to move"; "blow [of wind]", MMP (+ **para-*) *prwz-* "to fly", Chor. *wz-* "to swim, fly"?, *w'zy-*² (caus.) "to lead to, cause to run; to chase (away)". All this material traced to the Iran. **u̯az-* "to carry, drive (chariot, vel sim.)".[20]

In connection with **the atmospheric functions** of the ORuss. *Стрибогъ-Stribog* (borrowed, finally, from the East-Iranian continuum), we can to reconstruct the common sense of the Hephthalitan inscriptions first part as: "Śri, the prince = god of wind ...".

Following the Iranian and the Indo-Arian material we can to explain the origin of the «Hindo-Scythian» theonym **Sri-baya* quite adequately as the "Lord of winds". Moreover, this name and it's treatment thoroughly conforms to above-mentioned "atmospheric" lexica with the meaning such as: "to shoot, break" etc. With the atmospheric nature of **Śribaya-* = *Стрибог* (as the Winds lord) perfectly correlates to the Sanskr. *sr̥ij* (= *sarj*) "wind", *sr̥ika* "wind", "fire", *sr̥iká* "wind", *sr̥idāku* "the wind"[21] – noun derivating from *sr̥i* "to run, flow, speed, glide, move", "to blow (as wind)", "to run away, escape", "to go against, attack, assail", "to blow violently (as the wind)".[22] The atmospheric semantics reflected in certain way in the Sanskr. *sr̥ita* "going, moving", "flight"[23] as well. All these words could be fetching to the Ar. **sar-* "to run quickly, flow" ~ IE. **ser-* "to flow, to move quickly; to go (along with)" ‹ **sr-eu-* "flow", cf. Russ. *струя*. With the Ar. **sar-* correlates the Sanskr. *sar-* : *sr̥-*.[24]

As the structural and typological parallels to the «Hindo-Scythian» **Śribaya-* "The winds prince" we see the Sogd. *dšny w't βy y* "Wind god"; *w'trt'w* – Pers. *wāt-artāw* "righteous wind". In the text: *w't βy yy* "Wind-god".[25]

---

18. Junker 1930: 646, 648.
19. Junker 1930: 647.
20. Cheung 2007: 429-431.
21. MW 1899: 1245.
22. MW 1899: 1244.
23. MW 1899: 1245.
24. ESLJa 2000-2015: 3, 369.
25. Gharib 1995: 145, 399.

As to *Stribog's* grandsons' **abilities to push the arrows**, it is essential to adduce some derivatives, which could be useful to these abilities clarifying: *cf.* Shougn. *xivāzn* "staff", Yagnob. *xəvežn* "spear (-length)" – **sri-wājina*?[26] To this group is ranked and the Sanskr. *śṛi* "to crush, rend, break".[27] In addition, there similar things names fixed in Sanskr.: *cf. sṛídāku* "a thunderbolt"; *sṛikāyín* "having an arrow or spear", *sṛika* "a thunderbolt"; *sṛikṁvat* "having an arrow or spear".[28] As concern to winds flair to hit by the arrows to (smb. or smth.), the most indicative in this sense is Sanskr. *sṛik* "to be pointed".[29]

Both above-mentioned lexica and the YAv. *sari-* "piece, fragment", Sanskr. *śari* "to shatter, break" may be tied with the Iran. **sarH³* "to break".[30] However, this material can be estimated as the result of the semantic evolution of the Arian. **sar-* "to run, flow" cluster: **"to shoot" ← "to beat, destroy, break" ← "to run".

***

Thus, we take the quite acceptable interpretation of the god **Śri-baya-* name: probably, this god originally *was in charge of streams* (watery or airy) in general, but it was not a personified *wind* or *storm*. In addition, only with time **Śri-baya-* became the god of the wind, storm and thunder. Further, according to our god *Stribog* origin version, we have to admit the opinion of V.N. Toporov: there winds gods could be functioning as the thunderers embodiments very often.[31]

The reliability of etymology that proposed confirms the fact, that the *Lay ...* first publishers named *Stribog* as the Slavonic *Aeolos*. This figurative comparison confirmed both these gods functional parallelism and the similarity of the Greek and Sanskrit lexical material: *cf.* AGr. Αἴολος – *Aeolos*, the Hyppotos son[32], lord of winds. Properly – Rapid or Changeable: *cf.* αἰόλος "quick-moving, nimble"[33], αἰόλος "changeable, diversified"[34].

In connection with the fact of the *Stribog's* grandsons blowing by the arrows in the Igor's regiments, we can see an interesting parallel in the AGr. αἰολο-βρόντης

---

26. Morgenstierne 1974: 104.
27. MW 1899: 1088.
28. MW 1899: 1245.
29. MW 1899: 1245.
30. Cheung 2007: 338.
31. SD 1995-2012: 1, 209.
32. Dvoreckij 1958: I, 53.
33. Liddell, Scott 1996: 41, 40.
34. Dvoreckij 1958: I, 53.

"thunderer (of Zeus)".[35] Therefore, the B.A. Rybakov treatment of *Stribog* as the "sky, air, wind god" and the comparison of the Slavonic *Stribog* with the Scythian *Papay*[36] is grounded: it is well established in literature the Herod's correlation between the *Papay* and *Zeos*.[37] As well, Greek *Zeos* had traditionally named the *Thunderer* and the *Clouds Persecutor*. Thus, the Slavo-Iranian *Stribog* had the same functions. Therefore, the Scythian *Papay-Zeos* must have had the same functions.

Further, knowing the place (Pamir Upland) and the time (IV-VIth cc. AD) Hephthalites inhabitation, we can say that with the god *Śri-baya-* the Slavonic tribes have to know in the first half – middle part of the Ith m. AD. in the result of the ethno-lingual contacts Slavs with the Iranian or the Iranian-spiking tribes living in the Northern Sea Coast. Let alone the fact that the Vladimir prince established *Stribog's* idol in 980 AD in Kiev.

Finally, in purely linguistic facet the theonym *Śri-baya-* (and the god properly) ought to examine as the Iranian-Sanskrit (Ancient Indian) hybrid. Formally, the theonym *Śri-baya-* might become yet on the East-Iranian ground analogically to the Iranian*stri-* ‹ *sri-* "woman".[38] Moreover, most probably, in such form it was borrow by the Slavonic culture, where it was adapted (resp. reconsidered) under the influence of such lexemes as the PSl. *striti* or something else. Nevertheless, the functions those were inherent to the East-Iranian (Hephthalitan?) theonym *Ś(t)ri-baya-*, were conserved.

Abbreviations

AGr. – Ancient Greek
Ar. – Arian
Av. – Avestan
BMP – Book Pahlavi / Zoroastrian Middle Persian
Chor. – Choresmian = Khwarezmian
CSogd. – Sogdian in Christian texts
Hephth. – Hephthalitan
IE. – Indo-European
Iran. – Iranian
MMP – Manichaean Middle Persian

---

35. Dvoreckij 1958: I, 53.
36. Rybakov 1994: 433.
37. Abaev 1990: 89.
38. Abaev 1979: 194.

OIr. – Old Iranian
OPers. – Old Persian
ORuss. – Old Russian
OUD – Old Upper Deutsch
Parth. – Parthian
PSl. – Pre-Slavonic
Russ. – Russian
Sanskr. – Sanskrit
Scyth. – Scythian
Slav. – Slavonic
Shougn. – Shoughni
Sogd. – Sogdian
YAv. – Young Avestan

References

Abaev, V. I., 1979: *Istoriko-etimologičeskij slovar' osetinskogo jazyka*. Moscow, Nauka, III.
Abaev, V. I., 1990: "Kul't semi bogov u skifov", *in* Abaev, V. I., *Izbrannye trudy. Religija, fol'klor, literatura*: V 4-x t. / Otv. red. V. M. Gusalov. Vladikavkaz, Ir., I, 388-395.
Černyx, P. Ja., 1999: *Istoriko-etimologičeskij slovar' russkogo jazyka*. Moscow, Russkij jazyk, T. I-II.
Cheung, J., 2007: *Etymological Dictionary of the Iranian Verb*. Leiden, Boston, Brill.
Dvoreckij I. X., 1958: *Drevnegrečesko-russkij slovar'*. Moscow, GIINS, I-II.
ESLJa – Rastorgueva, V. S., Edel'man, D. I., 2000-2015: *Etimologičeskij slovar' iranskix jazykov*. Moscow, Vostočnaja literatura, T. 1-5.
ESPI – *Enciklopedija «Slova o polku Igoreve»: v 5 tomax*. Saint-Petersburg, Dmitrij Bulanin, 1995. – T. 5: *Slovo Daniila Zatočnika – Ja. Dopolnenija. Karty. Ukazateli.*.
Fasmer, M., 1987: *Etimologičeskij slovar' russkogo jazyka*. Moscow, Progress, T. 1-4.
Gharib, B., 1995: *Sogdian Dictionary. Sogdian-Persian-English*. Tehran, Farhangan Publications.
Gumilev, L. N., 1959: "Eftality i ix sosedi v IV v.", *Vestnik drevnej istorii*, 1, 129-140.
Junker, H. F. J., 1930: "Die hephtalitischen Munzinshriften", *Sitzungberichte der Preussischen Akademie der Wissenschaften, Philos.-hist. Klasse*, XXVII., 641-664.
Liddell, H. D., Scott, R., 1996: *A Greek-English Lexicon compiled by Henry George Liddel and Robert Scott, revised and augmented throughout by Sir*

Henry Stuart Jones with the assistance of Roderick McKenzie and with the cooperation of many scholars. With a revised Supplement. Oxford, Oxford University Press.

Martynov, V. V., 1989: "Sakral'nyj mir ⱪ lova o polku Igoreve⟩⟩ , *Slavjanskij i balkanskij fol'klor. Rekonstrukcija drevnej slavjanskoj duxovnoj kul'tury.* Moscow, Nauka, 61-78.

Morgenstierne, G., 1974: *Etymological Vocabulary of the Shougni Group.* Weisbaden, Dr. Ludwig Reichert Verlag.

Mozsyński, K., 1957: *Pierwotny zasięg języka prasłowiańskiego.* Wrocław, Zakład narodowy inmenia Ossolińskich, Wydawnictwo PAN, 1957.

MW – Monier-Williams, Sir, 1899: *A Sanscrit-English dictionary etymologically and philologically arranged. With special reference to cognate Indo-European languages.* Delphy.

PVL – Povest'vremennyx let. [Ros. akad. nauk]; Podgot. teksta, per., st. i komment. D. S. Lixačeva; Pod red. V. I. Adrianovoj-Peretc; [Dop. M. B. Sverdlova]. – 2-e izd., ispr. i dop. Saint-Petersburg, Nauka, 1996.

Rybakov, B. A., 1994: *Jazyčestvo drevnix slavjan.* Moscow, Nauka.

SD – Slavjanskie drevnosti. Etnolingvističeskij slovar' pod redakciej N. I. Tolstogo. Moscow, 1995-2012, 1-5.

Toporov, V. N., Ivanov, V. V., 1965: *Slavjanskie semiotičeskie modelirujuščie sistemy.* Moscow, Nauka.

Vej, M., 1958: "K etimologii drevnerusskogo 'Stribog'» *Voprosy jazykoznanja,* 3, 96-99.

Vinogradova, V. L., 1965: *Slovar'-spravočnik «Slova o polku Igoreve».* Moscow, Leningrad, Nauka, 1.

Description of Rod and Rožanicy in Slavic mythology

B. A. Rybakov and his predecessor's interpretations

Oleg V. Kutarev

Russian Christian Humanitarian Academy
(191011, St Petersburg, Fontanka embankment, 15)
etnogenez@mail.ru

Abstract. Such characters of Slavic mythology as Rod and Rozhanicy have been scientifically studied for more than 150 years. It seems that quite a true notion of them should have been formed and spread for such a long period. However, is the most commonly encountered approach introduced in 1980s by academician B. A. Rybakov, which was popular among the considerable circles of neopagans, true? Analyzing Old Russian sources, folklore and studies of scholars preceding Rybakov, the author tries to answer this question, considering findings of this famous academician with regard to Rod and Rozhanicy.

Keywords. Rod and Rožanicy, Slavic mythology, Russian neopaganism, B.A. Rybakov, "The paganism of early Slavs", Rodnoverie

The largest Slavic neopagan trend in Russia is Rodnoverie[1] (Rus. "native faith"; connection with god Rod is also possible). Despite the highly considerable differences in communities of rodnoverie now and then, which may be expressed both regarding the text sources and pantheon, rites and religious practices, there are principles common almost to all representatives of rodnoverie. First of all, it is their basis in attracting the scientific sources of Boris Aleksandrovich Rybakov's (1908–2001) works, academician and great researcher of paganism of early Slavs and Old Russia.

---

1. Kutarev 2014.

Meanwhile, in scientific Slavonic studies, as early as publication of B. A. Rybakov's main works[2], they were perceived quite carefully. In the course of time, there were a lot of pointed remarks; only familiarization and systematization of considerable archaeological, ethnographical and other material[3] and his critical studies of such late forgeries as *Velesova kniga* (*Book of Veles*)[4] were acknowledged as his undoubted service for study. However, it is findings of Rybakov's main works that had crucial importance for the representatives of rodnoverie; to some extent B. A. Rybakov became "an apostle of Rodnoverie". Coincidence of propagation time and achieving fame of his works and collapse of the Soviet Union created a situation, in which academician Rybakov's main works became the main source of many first neopagan trends appeared just at that period[5]. To the present day, influence of Rybakov's ideas on neopagan, popular and even (to a lesser extent) academic literature should be acknowledged as an excessive one. At the same time, it is necessary to note that even the first Soviet editions of two main Boris Aleksandrovich's books numbered 25,000 copies for *The Paganism of early Slavs* (1981) and 95,000 copies for *The Paganism of Old Russia* (1988): after the breakup of the USSR and decline in Russian science and economics, perhaps, ALL scientific publications on the Slavic paganism of 1990s taken together had comparable scale. Thus, from the date of issue, B. A. Rybakov's "voice" has overridden the whole fair criticism against him for two decades, crucial for forming rodnoverie.

One of the most important issues, in which Boris Aleksandrovich's findings have not been met with support in scientific world, is reconstruction of Slavic pantheon. At the same time his highly disputable and sometimes quite contradictory findings to those of preceding and subsequent studies underlie the beliefs of rodnoverie. This article considers this fact by the example of Rybakov's approach to Rod and Rožanicy[6], the characters of Slavic mythology that have been studied since the

---

2. Rybakov 1981, 1987. These works had a great circulation and have new editions.
3. See, for example, Egorov 2012, Klejn 2011, Novosel'cev 1993 and others; on request it is possible to list a lot of articles and books, criticizing one or another Boris Aleksandrovich's findings.
4. Buganov, Žukovskaja, Rybakov, 2004. *Vleskniga* or *Book of Veles* (Veles is one of ancient main Slavic gods, who is a shaman and patron of poetry and cattle) was made by Yuri P. Mirolubov (Юрий Петрович Миролюбов) in 1950s, but was presented as text of pagan Russian author of IX century.
5. Gajdukov 2004.
6. Russian and Old Russian word "Рожаница" [Rožanica] (literally translation "[feminine who giving] birth") is singular form; "Рожаницы" [Rožanicy] is plural form.

middle of XIX century. We will try to consider Rybakov's views against a background of studies preceding his ones (without touching upon the subsequent ones), seeking for revealing their grounds. Note that if considering the subsequent works, a series of critical opinions on academician's findings will be revealed; but we are interested in differences between Rybakov's ideas and findings of his predecessors (and many scholars after him) and what are the grounds for such his views rather than review of critique. Having distinguished various views of an issue and revealed differences between them, we will try to determine which view is more valid as far as possible.

* * *

For the first time Rod and Rožanicy are mentioned in Old Russian texts (although many scholars note possible borrowing of these text fragments from South Slavs)[7]. *The Tale of Some Who Loves Christ* and *The Tale of Idols*[8], representing sermons against paganism and attributed by different researchers[9] to XI–XIII centuries, are generally (including Rybakov) acknowledged to be the oldest. They similarly mention Rod and Rožanicy, for example, in *The Tale of Idols*: "… *the Slavs create and make treba* (a sacrifice) *to Samodivas, Mokoš, Diva, Perun, Xors, Rod and Rožanica*"[10] (these names basically are the names of Slavic gods, known from other sources). In the following centuries in Old Russia several other texts appear mentioning these characters of Slavic mythology. However, such sermons add almost no new data on the essence of Rod and Rožanicy; in essence, they just repeat what is already known[11] according to these two *Tales*:

So, if we write "Rožanicy" it means plural. In Old Russian sources it's possible to find this word in singular, plural and even dual form (doesn't exist in modern Russian).

7. Sreznevskij 1855, Mansikka 2005: 142 and others.

8. *The Tale of Idols* is a conventional shortening (for example, in E. V. Aničkov); its full Old Russian name is *Слово святого Григорья, ізобрѣтено въ толцѣхъ о томъ, како первое погани суще языци кланялися ідоломъ і требы им клали; то і нынѣ творятъ* (Гальковский 2013: 281–299). The same relates to *The Tale of Some Who Loves Christ* – *Слово нѣкоѥго Христолюбца, и ревнителя по правой вѣрѣ* (Ibid.: 300–312).

9. See, for example, Aničkov 2009: 190, 199; Mansikka 2005: 142; *Pis'mennye pamjatniki istorii Drevnej Rusi* 2003: 153–157.

10. Translation from Old Russian is ours. In the original: «требоу кладоуть и творять, и словеньскыи языкъ, Виламъ, и Мокошьи, Дивѣ, Пероуноу, Хърсоу, Родоу и Рожаници» (Gal'kovskij 2013: 287).

11. See, for example, *Слово Ісаія пророка истолковано святымъ Иоаномъ Златаоустомъ о поставляющихъ вторую трапезу Роду и Рожаницамъ* (Gal'kovskij 2013: 348–355); *Слово нѣкоего Христолюбца и наказаніи отца духовного* (Sreznevskij 1863:

food was sacrificed to Rod and Rožanicy and they were worshipped along with other pagan characters: deities, Samodivas (fairies), etc., only occasionally allowing themselves highly unskillfully comparing them to the deities of other mythologies (Semitic, Egyptian, Greek). Only one source, communicating original information, is distinguished among the ancient ones mentioning Rod. It is a comment to the Gospel of XV century under the name *О вдуновеніи духа в человѣка* (*On blowing in the spirit to a human* in Old Russian), reporting: "The Almighty, the only one who is immortal and the Creator of nondyings, blows in immortally and agelessly <…>; it is not Rod, sitting in the air, throws heaps to the earth, and children are born in him <…>. It is God who is Creator rather than Rod"[12] (Slavic word "*груды*" (heaps?) has a lot of possible meanings). Thus, this text points out fallacy (from Christian point of view) of the idea that Rod gives birth to souls, which he sends down from the "air" with the "heaps", i.e., according to Rybakov, who was supported by many researchers, with the raindrops[13].

Another domain of data of our interest in medieval texts concerns the relations between these characters and astrology[14] (which were translated as "rozhestvoslovie"[15]) and fate. In *The Tale of Idols* "*халдѣйскаіа астрономіа и родопочитаніе*" ("Chaldea astronomy and ancestor worhip" in Old Russian) rank with one another[16]; and in general, as V. J. Mansikka convincingly shows, "a number of cases is known, when Greek words τύχη and εἱμαρμένη (literally "fate" and "destiny, doom" – O.K.) were translated as "Rod" and "Rožanicy"; moreover, the word "Rožanicy" often conveyed the words γένεσις and γενεαλογία (literally from Greek "origin, origination" and "genealogy" – O.K.) equal to it"; "perhaps, sometimes it is more correct to consider it as merely philological phenomenon, an attempt to convey τύχη, fortune, idea of fate in

---

699–700); Aničkov 2009: 125–152 and others.

12. Translation from Old Russian is ours. In the original: «Вдуновение бесмртное нестарѣюще единъ вдымаетъ вседръжитель, иже единъ безсмртенъ и непогибающихъ творецъ <…>; то ти не Родъ, сѣдя на вздусѣ мечеть на землю груды и в том ражаются дѣти <…>. Всѣмъ бо есть Творецъ Богъ, а не Родъ» (Gal'kovskij 2013: 360-362).

13. Rybakov 1981: 450. It is worth noting that other authors (e.g. V.Y. Petrukhin and others) have another point of view as for definition of "heaps" in this text (heaps of earth etc.).

14. Sreznevskij 1855: 9.

15. Mansikka 2005: 145.

16. Gal'kovskij 2013: 288.

Slavic rather than really existing Slavic "idols" in Rod and Rožanicy"[17]; at any rate, sometimes we can claim it for sure. Rod and Rožanicy were worshipped the next day after Christmas[18] and the Nativity of the Blessed Virgin Mary[19], and the sermons had been issued for several centuries, which condemned offering gruel and any pastries that day, devoted to Rožanicy; later child's first hair trimmed sacrificed to Rožanicy[20]. In essence, it is all direct data, which may be obtained from Old Russian texts. It is worth noting that Rod and Rožanicy are known only through the texts, condemning *dvoeverie* ("dual faith", period in first centuries after Russia's baptism in 988 AD with strong paganism's influence), and there are no references to their idols, oaths, etc. (in contrast to other main gods), what is noted by Rybakov as well[21]. At any rate, Rod and Rožanicy are not mentioned under these names in the texts, describing pre-Christian epoch in Russia, and unknown to other early Slavs' sources on pre-Christian epoch, e.g. Polabian and Baltic Slavs, about whose paganism is known quite a lot.

Extra data are reported by folklore, not only of the East and South Slavs, but even that of the West Slavs, although to a lesser extent. Jan Máchal writes on Rožanicy in the Slavic world: "they were also called Sudice ('Givers of Fate'), Sudjenice, Sujenice (Croatian), Sojenice, Sujenice (Slovenian), Sudženici (Bulgarian), or Sudičky (Bohemian). The Bulgarians have their own name for them, viz. Naručnici (narok, 'destiny') or they call them Orisnici, Urisnici, Uresici"[22], Russian Dolya and Udelnica and Serbian Srecha[23] are similar to them as well as Živica, Deklica, etc.; thus, worship of them appears to be "one of Common Slavic ancient remains"[24]. According to folklore sources, it is known that women, often wearing something white, sometimes holding candles and wearing wreaths on the head, and "the Bohemians believe that after sending deep sleep upon a woman lying in childbed, the Destinies put the infant upon the table and decide his or her fate. Usually three Destinies appear, the third and oldest being the most powerful; but mention is also made of one, four, five, seven or nine, with a queen at their head[25].

---

17. Mansikka 2005: 134-135.
18. Gal'kovskij 2013: 114-115.
19. Zubov 1995: 46-48.
20. Mansikka 2005: 140–141, 225; Gal'kovskij 2013: 358.
21. Rybakov 1981: 442.
22. Máchal 1918: 250.
23. *Ibid.*: 251-252.
24. Sreznevskij 1863: 10-21.
25. It also happens that there are two of them or even one for each person. See: *Ibid.*

Their decisions often thwart one another, but what the last says is decisive and will be fulfilled. The chief matters which they determine are how long the child will live, whether it will be rich or poor, and what will be the manner of its death. According to a wide-spread belief, the first spins, the second measures, and the third cuts off the thread whose length signifies the duration of life of the new-born mortal"[26]. Similar ideas, known to the Slavic folk art (*cf.* poet Alexander Pushkin: "Three fair maidens, late one night / Sat and spun by candlelight"[27]), have obviously parallels to Indo-European mythologies. Germanic deities of fate are three "Norns, those, who come to every baby born and endow with the fate"[28]. The same archetype is revealed by the Roman Parcae and their analogies – Greek Moirai, on whom Hesiod writes that there were three of them, that "they assign misfortune and fortune to people at birth"[29], and who are also conceived as spinners. At the same time the role of Rožanicy is related not only to the fate: they are also ancestors, embodying progenitresses and particularly protecting women. This idea also has analogies: "Similarly the Roman Junones (protectors of women) were originally souls of the dead, while the Dísirs of Scandinavian mythology are spirits of deceased mothers that have become dispensers of fate"[30]. It is also possible to find other analogies: in legends of European folklore on three fairies, or in Hittite (tracing back to Hurrians) *The Song of Ulikummi* (XIV century B.C.), in which "goddesses of fate and protecting goddesses" are repeatedly mentioned. Thus, "in the course of time in exposers' consciousness an idea of deceased ancestors, whose cult had extremely great propagation among the Slavs" joined to the "astrological meaning of Rod and Rožanicy <…>: Rod and Rožanicy seemed to the exposer to be identical with the deceased relatives"[31]. In this connection it is worth noting considerable similarity of worshipping such characters as Rod, Domovoj and, for example, Bulgarian Stopan: meals were sacrificed to all of them, all of them were considered to be masters of the fate of their descendants, and it is possible to easily find (and in Rod's case fairly suppose) in worship of them the image of the deceased ancestor[32].

---

26. Máchal 1918: 250-251.
27. In Russian original: "Три девицы под окном / Пряли поздно вечерком..". Puškin 1982: 339. Every Russian knows this fairy-tale.
28. *Prose Edda*, *Gylfaginning*, 15.
29. Hesiod, *Theogony*, Lines 218-219.
30. Máchal 1918: 249.
31. Mansikka 2005: 135.
32. Máchal 1918: 238-240.

Let us make the first conclusions. First of all, Rod and Rožanicy appear to be the embodiment of the fate, at the same time in paganism Rod probably gave people souls, and Rožanicy – the fate. Moreover, meal is set for them and respect is properly shown; thus, Rod is a set of ancestors, deified kind of man and soul creator. Perhaps, they are gods, but not main in pagan time: their value increased just after baptism (when real main gods disappeared). Ancestors, not gods, were the basis of this cult: and that's why cult of Rod and Rožanicy exceeded meaning of other pagan gods in some late period, after all Christianity favored ancestor respect too.

Now, having briefly considered the data, which old texts and folklore provide us, we will examine Rybakov's idea of Rod and Rožanicy. He writes quite a lot about them and devote at least almost two chapters (out of ten) to them in *The paganism of early Slavs*[33]. His quoting of Galkovsky is fair as Galkovsky stated that the issue of Rod and Rožanicy was one of the most complex and complicated, however, it is strange that distinguishing general trends of its examination, he only notes the approach to Rod as Domovoj (absolute identity of whom he fairly denies[34]), without trying to analyze for some reason, say, V. L. Komarovich's view that "Rod is a set of ancestors of a particular family"[35], Rybakov criticizes his entirely different theses[36]. Subjecting the remark that Rozhanicy were brought together with astrology to criticism and pointing to the fact that in this case we deal with homonym, Rybakov, however, does not even have a thought that similar property could be one of Rozhanicy's attributes, which is just confirmed by this homonymy[37].

One of Rybakov's main arguments in favour of interpretation of "Rod as significant Slavic deity"[38] is notorious "periodization" of the author of "The Tale of Idols", which reports that *"the Slavs began setting the meal to Rod and Rožanicy before Perun* (one of main Slavic gods, warrior and thunder god)*, their*

---

33. Rybakov 1981: 438-470, chapter 8. "Род и Рожаницы" ("Rod and Rožanicy").
34. Ibid.: 438-441.
35. Ibid.: 439.
36. It is worth noting that the form of article does not allow considering in detail all aspects of views on Rod and Rozhanicy in the studies. E.g., following Komarovich, Rybakov considers that this cult was public and national (see ibid.: 439-440), while N. M. Galkovsky notes: "worship of Rod and Rožanicy was a family thing, the private one" (Gal'kovskij 2013: 120); it is possible to distinguish a lot of similar views.
37. Rybakov 1981: 441.
38. Ibid.: 443.

deity. And before treba (a sacrifice) was made to Upirs (vampires) and Berehinyas (water spirits, sometimes emerged from drowned people, close to Samodivas)"[39]. Out of this actually unremarkable phrase, which does not develop in *The Tale of Idols*, Rybakov makes quite significant conclusions. Thus, he draws up a picture, according to which he clearly identifies historical periods, social formations and technological innovations. Relying upon only one phrase, Rybakov starts examining material only in those limits which he has just outlined, forgetting about the fact that there are other sources and that it is firstly necessary to approach to this very "periodization" critically. Meanwhile, in several decades prior to that, E. V. Anichkov has almost undoubtedly proved that acknowledged diversity and mosaicism of the text by Rybakov[40] is explained by the plenty of insertions and later additions[41]. L. R. Prozorov's remarkable short article convincingly shows that information on the Slavs' order of worship of Upirs and Berehinyas, later – of Rod and Rozhanicy, and finally of Perun in the stated quotation of ancient *The Tale of Idols* should be perceived as description of the ritual stages rather than the evolution stages of religion, which, undoubtedly, was unknown to the Old Russian scribe. L.R. Prozorov confirms his theory not only with extra Slavic medieval and ethnographical materials, but with surprisingly eloquent analogies from Indian culture[42]. However, Rybakov continues seeing intrinsic logic through "incompleteness, as it were the draft of *The Tale*"[43]. Out of these lines he at once understands that it is Metholithic period and the late Stone Age when Upirs and Berehinyas were worshipped, that they were origins embodying evil and good, respectively, although he at once admits that we do not have even close data on these creatures in terms of time. As for Metholithic period, it is early to apply even Proto-Indo-European religion[44] to this period, and we know little about its very grounds. However, Rybakov continues developing his idea in I and VIII chapters of *The Paganism of early Slavs*, without particularly attracting at least any sources on this topic. The same relates to Rod that is, according to Rybakov, a dominating deity at the period of transfer "from appropriating economy to

---

39. Translation from Old Russian is ours. In the original: «словенѣ начали тряпезу ставити, родоу и рожаницямъ, переже пероуна бога ихъ. А преже того клали требы оупиремь и берегынямъ» (Gal'kovskij 2013: 288-289).
40. Rybakov 1981: 11-12.
41. Aničkov 2009: 101-120.
42. Prozorov 2017: 55-57.
43. Rybakov 1981: 12.
44. Eliade 2002: 174-178.

producing one"[45], i.e. from the beginning of the late Stone Age to nearly historical time, when, according to Rybakov, Perun strengthened himself as the main deity. Meanwhile, in the middle of VI century Procopius of Caesarea noted: the Slavs *"consider that it is only the God, creator of lightning, that is the lord over people, bulls are sacrificed to him and people perform other solemn rites"*[46]. However, Rybakov considers Rod rather than Perun a creator of lightning; he puts forward many other original (whether defensible?) assumptions instead of arguments, just adding that it "could be". As a result, Rybakov concludes that Rod is a deity of "the universe, the whole nature and fertility", and Rožanicy take the same place which was taken by humble to Zeus Moirai in Greek mythology. At the same time, there are only two Rožanicy, for the author could be able to find only such an example in well-known to him archaeological materials[47]. In order to verify the fact of Rod significance, Rybakov notes that monotheistic Christianity contrasted the only God with Rod. But what could the Christianity contrast with any pagan deity instead of the only God?

It is worthy of respect that in contrast to many other authors, Rybakov pays particular attention to Rod rather than Rožanicy, despite the fact that Rod, in essence, is unknown from folklore and ethnographic materials, what makes this material more complicated for any conclusions. However, Rybakov's conclusions are quite controversial. The academician says that "manifold complex of Old Russian words contains 'rod' root"[48] may play a significant role in explanation of Rod's properties and functions, at the same time associating him with water (e.g. Russian *родник [rodnik]* – 'spring'), nature (e.g. Russian *природа [priroda]* – 'nature', etc. from root *родить* – 'to spawn, birth'), red colour and even with ball lightning, without ever coming to the most evident conclusion that Rod could be a deity of... family (Russian *род [rod]*). Thus, it would be more logical for Rybakov to come to a justified conclusion that Rod is a Parent (Slavic *родитель [roditel']*) as well. His conclusion regarding relations between the symbolism of the 6-wire wheel and Rod is highly questionable, in essence, he does not advance any argument in favour of that aside from the fact that this symbol related to the light and the main deity that suddenly became Rod in the course of another Rybakov's speculation. There are also no grounds for the comparison between "main" East Slavic deity, Rod, and the main deity of West Slavic Rani tribe, Sventovit,

---

45. Rybakov 1981: 20.
46. Procopius of Caesarea, *Gothic War*, III.14.
47. Rybakov 1981: 24.
48. *Ibid.*: 451.

that is considered by the academician, focusing on his own interpretations of well-known Zbruč idol rather than the texts of Helmold and Saxo Grammaticus, having reliably described worship of him[49].

Idol from Fischerinsel
XI-XII century, oaken statue of West Slavic Veleti tribe, found in 1969 at Fischerinsel island in Tollensee lake, Germany. Neubrandenburg Regional Museum.

As for Zbruč idol, even the correlation between him and Sventovit is in no way proven, what is also admitted by Rybakov[50], let alone bringing together Rod and Sventovit. However, Rybakov devotes several pages to the examination of this idol as Rod (perhaps allegedly uniting several cults, because on Zbruč idol there are several characters). To this day, Rybakov's interpretation of the Zbruč idol's images, completely unreliable, is the most widely known.

Addressing to other idols, Rybakov talks about Rožanicy, insisting that there were two of them, although folklore shows different numbers of them, and the dominated one is three. As a result, the academician refers to Rožanicys as

---

49. Main sources (XII–XIIIth centuries) about West Slavic god Sventovit: Helmold of Bosau, *Chronica Slavorum*, I. 52, II. 12; Saxo Grammaticus, *Gesta Danorum*, XIV.39.
50. Rybakov 1981: 462. Zbruč idol (X–XI centuries, limestone statue of some East (or West?) Slavs, found in 1848 at Zbruč river, now Ukraine). Kept in Archaeological Museum of Kraków. Criticism of its non-Slavic or late origin is not sufficiently thorough.

famous dual idol from Fischerinsel (XI–XII century, oaken statue of West Slavic Veleti tribe, found in 1969 at island in Tollense lake, Germany), without paying attention to the fact that these "Rožanicy" have moustache[51].

The academician refers only to Siberian and Greek myths, unlikely containing any data on Rod and Rožanicy, as an argument in favour of their duality. The only assumption, which, however, also requires further studies, is an idea that among other things the cult of Rod and Rožanicy could have an agrarian essence as well[52]. Boris Aleksandrovich's view regarding the identification of Rožanicy as Lada, Lelya and other goddesses[53] is also highly questionable.

A valid question arises: if Rod was the main Slavic deity, why, even if it is possible to explain absence of idols to him by the exclusiveness of his properties, he was nowhere mentioned as the main one? Why was he mentioned only in Russian sources? Why do chronicles keep silent about him, why does not he exist in any folklore (opposed to Rožanicy), why is he mentioned in no external sources as Perun, for example, why are there no manifestations of him in the cult of Christian saints or, on the contrary, in the late demonology as other main gods?

As we see, Rybakov overemphasizes Rod and raises Rožanicy to him; if his views of Rožanicy are not so far away from the generally accepted ones, rise of Rod is at the least groundless. Rybakov disagrees with the scientific majority and quite obvious sources data. The significant number of authors, starting with the earliest research, for example, that by I. I. Sreznevsky in 1855[54] (while study of them started in 1850s)[55], points to the interpretation of Rod and Rožanicy as the masters of fate and embodiment of ancestors and the whole family as well. Before Rybakov, as to this issue, the similar view was shared, for example, by A. N. Veselovsky[56], A. N. Sobolev[57], Jan Máchal[58], E. V. Anichkov[59], V. L. Komarovich[60], M. Gimbutas[61] and others. Among the researchers, who

---

51. *Ibid.*: 465.
52. *Ibid.*: 469.
53. *Ibid.*: 465-470.
54. Sreznevskij 1855.
55. Klejn 2004: 182-183.
56. Veselovskij 1890: 192-261.
57. Sobolev 1999: 79-88.
58. Máchal 1918.
59. Aničkov 2009: 215-218.
60. Komarovič 1960: 84-104.
61. Gimbutas 2008: 207.

have written on that later, we may point out V. V. Ivanov and V. N. Toporov[62], V. Y. Petrukhin[63], L. S. Klejn[64] etc. Finally, it is worth making a reservation that, although Procopius of Caesarea has written that the Slavs *"do not know the fate and do not acknowledge it"*, he then points out that they *"make fortune-telling as well"*[65]. And as we see now, "surely, Procopius has noted not without the sense that the Slavs did not acknowledge the fate, but they acknowledged goodness and power of the divine intent"[66], that the fate is not blind and automatic for them, but it is embodied by some deities, namely Rod and Rožanicy, what Rybakov has never admitted, having drawn up original but generally groundless theory on Rod as an absolute and supreme deity of the Slavic paganism.

This article was first published in Russian: Kutarev O. V., « Xarakteristika Roda i Rožanic v Slavjanskoj mifologii : interpretacii B. A. Rybakova i ego predšestvennikov », *Religiovedenie*, 2013, 4, 170-177. It is amended a little for this edition.

References

Aničkov, E. V., 2009: *Jazyčestvo i Drevnjaja Rus'*. Moscow, Akademičeskij proekt.
Buganov, V. I., Žukovskaja, L. P., Rybakov B. A., 2004: "Mnimaja «drevnejšaja letopis' »", in O. V. Tvorogov, A. A. Alekseev (eds.), *Čto dumajut učenye o «Velesovoj knige»*. Saint-Petersburg, Nauka, 38-46.
Egorov, V. B., 2012: "Kogda voznikla Kievskaja Rus'?", *Istorija v podrobnostjax*, 2012, 3, 32-43.
Eliade, M., 2002: *Istorija very i religioznyx idej*, T. 1. Moscow, Kriterion.
Gajdukov, A. V., 2004: "Legitimnost' slavjanskogo neojazyčstva: osobennosti vzaimootnošenija s gosudarstvennoj vlast'ju", *Gercenovskie čtenija: Aktual'nye problemy social'nyx nauk*. Saint-Petersburg, ElekSis, 274-278.
Gal'kovskij, N. M., 2013: *Bor'ba xristianstva s ostatkami jazyčestva v Drevnej Rusi*. Moscow, Akademičeskij proekt.
Gimbutas, M., 2008: *Slavjane. Syny Peruna*. Moscow, Centrpoligraf.
Ivanov, V. V., Toporov, V. N., 1995: "Rod", *Slavjanskaja mifologija. Enciklopedičeskij slovar'*. Moscow, Ellis Lak, 335.
Klejn, L. S., 2004: *Voskrešenie Peruna. K rekonstrukcii vostočnoslavjanskogo jazyčestva*. Saint-Petersburg, Evrazija.
Klejn, L. S., 2011: "Akademik Rybakov i partijnaja linija", *Troickij variant*, 2011, 73, 14.

---

62. Ivanov, Toporov 1995.
63. Petruxin 2000: 236-243.
64. Klejn 2004: 182-196.
65. Procopius of Caesarea, *Gothic War*, III.14.
66. Sreznevskij 1863: 14.

Komarovič, V. L., 1960: "Kuľt Roda i zemli v knjažeskoj srede XI–XIII vv.", *Trudy otdela drevnerusskoj literatury*, XVI, 84-104.

Kutarev, O. V., 2014: "Neojazyčestvo Evropy", *Filosofija i kuľtura*, 2014, 12, 1801-1810.

Máchal, J., 1918: "Slavic Mythology", *Mythology of all races*, Vol. III. *Celtic and Slavic Mythology*. Boston, Marshall Jones Company, 215-330, 351-361 (Notes), 389-398 (Bibliography).

Mansikka, V. J., 2005: *Religija vostočnyx slavjan*. Moscow, IMLI RAN.

Novoseľcev, A. P., 1993: "«Mir istorii» ili mif istorii?", *Voprosy istorii*, 1993, 1, 23-32.

Petruxin, V. Ja., 2000: *Drevnjaja Rus'. Narod. Knjaz'ja. Religija*, in *Iz istorii russkoj kuľtury*. Moscow, Jazyki russkoj kuľtury, 11-410.

Pis'mennye pamjatniki istorii Drevnej Rusi, 2003: *Pis'mennye pamjatniki istorii Drevnej Rusi*. Saint-Petersburg, Blic.

Prozorov, L. R., 2017: "'Preže Peruna, boga ix': k voprosu o mnimoj 'perdiodizacii slavjanskogo jazyčestva'", *Vostočno-Evropejskij naučnyj vestnik*, 2017, 3, 55-57.

Puškin, A. S., 1982: "Skazka o care Saltane", in Puškin, A. S., *Sočinenija v 2 t.*, T. 1. Moscow, Xudožestvennaja literatura, 339-348.

Rybakov, B. A., 1981: *Jazyčestvo drevnix slavjan*. Moscow, Nauka.

Rybakov, B. A., 1987: *Jazyčestvo Drevnej Rusi*. Moscow, Nauka.

Sobolev, A. N., 1999: *Zagrobnyj mir po drevnerusskim predstavlenijam*. Saint-Petersburg, Lan'.

Sreznevskij, I. I., 1855: *Roženicy u slavjan i drygix jazyčeskix narodov*. Moscow, Tipografija A. Semena.

Sreznevskij, I. I., 1863: *Drevnie pamjatniki. Izvestija Imperatorskoj Akademii nauk po Otdeleniju russkogo jazyka i slovesnosti*, T. 10, vyp. 7. Saint-Peterburg, Imperatorskaja Akademija Nauk.

Veselovskij, A. N., 1890: "Razyskanija v oblasti russkogo duxovnogo stixa", Gl. XIII, "Suď'ba-Dolja v narodnyx predstavleniax slavjan", *Otdelenie russkogo jazyka i slovesnosti*, 1890, 46, 6, 172-261.

Zubov, N. I., 1995: "Naučnye fantomy slavjanskogo Olimpa", *Živaja starina*, 1995, 3 (7), 46-48.

Idols of the Western Slavs in the Early Medieval period

The example of Pomerania (northern Poland)

Kamil Kajkowski

West-Cassubian Museum in Bytow
kamilkajkowski@wp.pl

Abstract. Research on the religions of pagan Slavs is extremely difficul topic. This is mainly due to the limited (but contrary to appearances, not so limited as well) and the one-sided character of written sources as also the significance of archeological data. Amongst the latter, sculptures identified as idols deserve our special attention. Unfortunately, just a small number of these objects have a clear archaeological context. Most of them is known from accidental discoveries, including the 19th century. In the case of Poland the 19th century was a period of state and national identity crisis. All of this was the reason for searching for the so-called Slavic Antiquities. Programmatically, they were to legitimize the rights to Polish lands and to testify its cultural autonomy. Therefore, it needs especially cautious to approach the findings from this period because not all of them could be authentic, not all came from the early Middle Ages and finally not all could be regard as pagan idols. The aim of the author's considerations is to analise available information about the findings of sculptures considered as idols that have been found so far in the area of Pomerania (Northern Poland). An analysis, which aim to answer the question, which of those representations could serve as visualisation of deities or other supernatural beings.

Keywords. Western Slavs, Poland, Pomerania, Pagan, Religion, Idols

IN STUDYING THE PAGAN BELIEFS of Western Slavs, one of the most problematic questions relates to the figural representations identified as images of gods or supernatural beings. This arises inter alia from the fact that up until now the subject literature has not produced a satisfyingly precise definition of pagan idols, which could determine a theoretical basis for identifying material visualisations of gods. In general, it is intuitively accepted that they were images which represented the characteristics of human figures as accurately as possible.[1]

In the Pomeranian area, we know of around 15 artefacts identified as representing the pagan gods of Early Medieval Slavs.

In the 19th century a phallic shaped statue carved from red granite was still to be found at the summit of a burial mound in Gliśno Wielkie near Bytów. The meter high statue depicted a schematic (maybe incomplete) human figure.[2]

The subject literature usually describes it as stylistically related to the so called Prussian "baba" statues and connects with a cult of the dead. The latter observation is additionally supported by the original (?) location of the sculpture at the summit of a burial mound.[3] Without prejudging the validity of this point of view, the fact is that the artefact which interests us here does not find any analogies in Western Slavic figurative art. Neither is there much that we can say about the actual grave. Lacking information about its morphological features and possible contents, the question of the cultural provenance of the person (or persons) buried beneath the mound, remains open. In other words, we don't know if the

---

1. The issue of anthropomorphising figural images was aptly addressed by David Freedberg (2005: 60) stating that as a rule, to comprehend a concept of godliness one gives it specific characteristics resulting from the need to visualise transcendental forces. For this reason also supernatural beings were most commonly shown in a from closest to the human. In other words, by definition abstract subject matter, was given attributes allowing it to be familiarised and thus included in the world of a particular society's recognized meanings and system of symbols (Hume 1962: 150). A separate problem remains the issue of the features which a particular object must posses for it to be deemed anthropomorphic. It appears that the requirement was not always an accurate mirroring of human body features. At times it could simply relate to the form alone of a particular object, whose natural shape suggested a human form only in outline, this alone leading to discerning in it some manifestation of a supernatural being (Margul 1987: 182; Kowalski 2013: 244).
2. Łęga 1929: 266–267; Łuka 1973: 56–57.
3. Hoffmann 2004: 68.

mound was built for a newcomer[4] or for member of the local community or how the sculpture came to be in Pomeranian territory, and whether it could have played some kind of role in valorising the local community's funerary grounds.

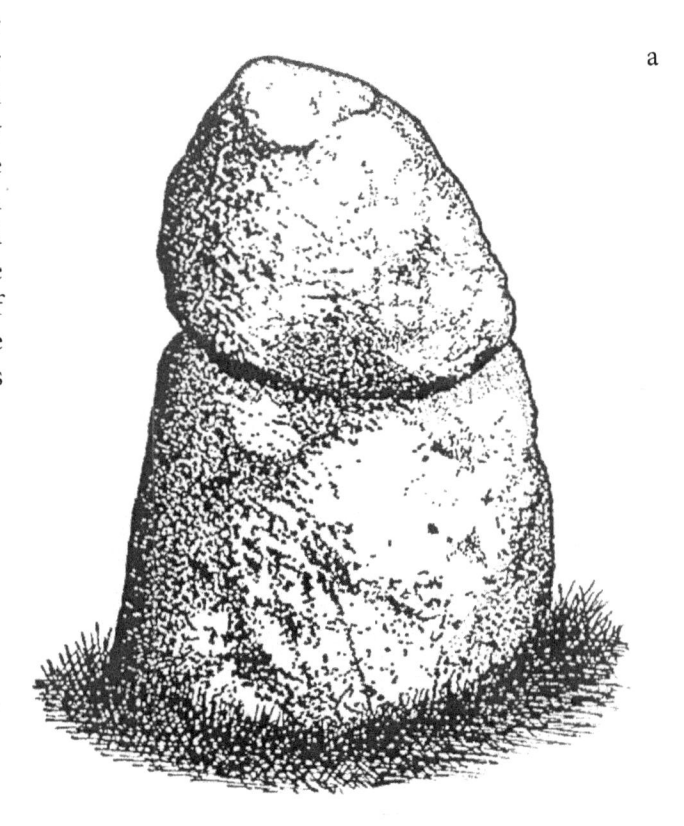

Fig. 1.
Gliśno, Bytów county
Granite sculpture.
After Łbik 1998: 127.

Connection with a pagan cult is also attributed to a sculpture found in Karnice.[5] A sculpture, set into the wall at the base of the south west corner of the 15th century church tower, depicts a human head, next to which is shown another, difficult to identify, figure.

Local legends link both the object itself as well as the stone font found on this site, with the missionary activities of St. Otto of Bamberg. However, it does appear that the artefact should be connected to an earlier Christian sanctuary which

---

4. It is worth noting that one of the concentrations of stone "babas" is found on the northern frontier of the Lubawska region (*Terra lubovia*) bordering Pomerania. This area, being in the 10th-12th century a zone where Slavic and Prussian influences intermingled, is deemed by some researchers to be bound up with Slavic life (Grążawski 2012: 50, 52).
5. Kajkowski, Kuczkowski 2010: 104.

stood on this site before the present one was built. It is difficult to determine whether the way in which it was embedded in the wall resulted from a need to depreciate its ancient (pagan) character. Nevertheless, I think it more likely that the sculpture under discussion may be deemed a re-cycled element of Romanesque architecture forming the interior décor of the church.

Fig. 2.
Karnice, Gryfice county
Stone carving depicting a human head.
Photo K. Kajkowski.

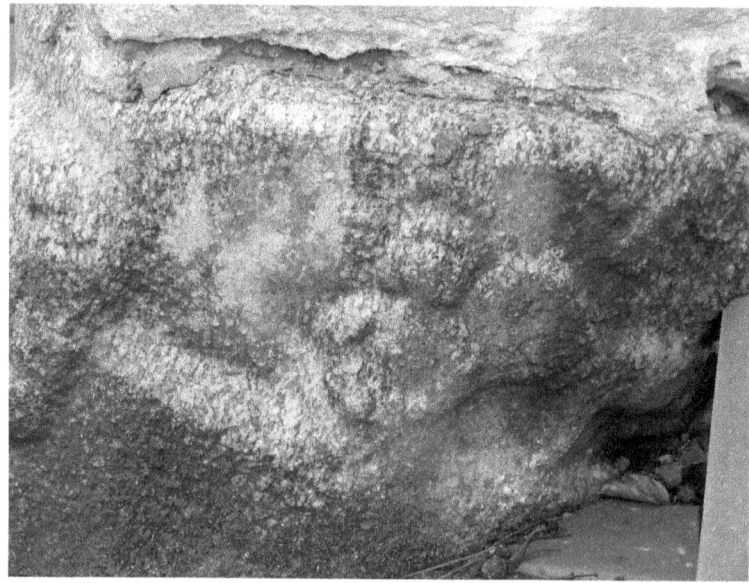

Fig. 3.
Karnice, Gryfice county
Detail with anthropomorphic figure.
Photo K. Kajkowski.

From information provided by Philip Heinhoffer. we know of a further artefact identified as depicting a pagan god.[6] According to this source, an image (which Heinhoffer described as a representation of the god Triglav), was apparently kept in the Cistercian monastery in Kołbacz. The sculpture was supposed to have been removed from the Abbot's House in 1754 and sent to a Berlin museum. Unfortunately, no details are known regarding the circumstances under which this artefact was acquired and placed within the monastery walls.[7]

Fig. 4.
Kołbacz, Gryfice county
Graphic representation of the statue.
After Brzustowicz, 2006: 21, fig. 10.

Another artefact frequently referred to by researchers into Slavic beliefs, is the carving in Leźno. A granite stone reaching 80 cm in height and about 60 cm in width is decorated on three sides with reliefs depicting figurative engravings. On one of the surfaces there is a schematic image of a horse, on the other a human figure in a long gown with a horn shaped object in its right hand, and on the third a man whose stance suggests that his hands are placed on his hips.[8]

Hitherto, the artefact described above has been subject to various attempts at interpretation which locate it in the religious beliefs of Prussians or Pomeranians and also link it to the beliefs of Celts and Scandinavians.[9] After one or other classification of the artefact had been made a usually fairly superficial analysis was undertaken, always, however, relating it to religious belief.

---

6. Heinhoffer 1834: 21.
7. It is worth adding that one of the claims pertaining to the sculpture link it to the Szczecin statue of *Triglav* whose silvered heads were sent by Saint Otto to Rome, after the idol was destroyed (Kajkowski 2008: 187).
8. Sokołowska 1928: 147; Gieysztor 2006: 237.
9. Łęga 1930: 267-269; Filipowiak 1993: 41; Błażejewska 1999.

Fig. 5.
Leźno, Kartuzy county
Stone sculpture with relief carvings.
After Sokołowska 1928: 146, fig. 22.

The figures visible on the sides of the stone were identified by names known from the pantheon of the society to which the object was ascribed. As the iconographic motifs placed on this artefact could in fact be ascribed to the art of all four of these societies, it is difficult to unequivocally claim any one of them as the stone's creators. Symptomatic in this context is the image of the figure whose stance one could interpret as showing it with its hands resting on its hips. We know of an analogous image connected to religious belief from the territory of the Western Slavs[10]. It is also worth noting that this artefact must have been located in a place which allowed for access from all sides, as this is essential to view the whole of the iconographic program being presented. We assume therefore that the stone from Leźno could have been located in a public place. It is not inconceivable that as a carrier of mythic-religious program it could have been part of a larger

---

10. I am thinking here i. a. of the copper-alloy fittings on the scabbard of the dagger from Oldenburg (Gabriel 2000), the analogous artefact from Ostrów Lednicki from Wielkopolska (Greater Poland) (cf. Biermann 2014), the bronze figure of a man from Schwedt which is moreover suspected of having a Pomeranian provenance (Filipowiak, 1993: 34) or also the staff/sceptre and hanger from Novgorod (Russia). Some researchers interpret these last objects as images of Perun (Milošević 2011: 57-58). It may be that one can include here some of the (anthropomorphic?) wooden laths originally decorating the temple buildings. If it is assumed that they were covered with paintings, it is worth noting that beneath the artistic images of supposed heads there is a surface which could suggest just such a figure (with hands on hips). In this context it is worth noting, that according to Saxo Gramatticus (Saxo XIV, 39) an analogous positioning of one hand was a characteristic of the statue of the famous Arkona *Svantevit* figure.

whole (an idol?) and/or the sacred topography of a cult site. However, there are no convincing proofs for this, in which case such an interpretation must remain solely in the sphere of difficult to verify hypothesis.

Analogous difficulties arise when characterising a further sculpture, found in Nowy Wiec not far from Kościerzyna. Accidentally uncovered in a peat deposit, the granite artefact measured about 30 cm in height and depicted the bust of a figure with two faces. The whole composition was placed on a base whose both sides display decorations which the literature connects with a form of Latin script or runes.[11]

Fig. 6.
Nowy Wiec, Kościerzyna county
Double faced granite bust.
After Łuka 1973: 73, fig. 52.

---

11. Antoniewicz 1957: 379.

This fact has lead to some researchers questioning the authenticity of the carving.[12] On the basis of fairly contentious arguments, Jan Leon Łuka considered it to be a Slavic cult image and tried to link it with the cult of the god *Svarožic*.[13] Some researchers do not exclude the possibility that we are dealing here with a figure from the period of Roman influence in the area. According to Tadeusz Waga it could be an image of *Janus* and have reached Pomerania as a result of trade or war.[14] Unfortunately, lacking knowledge of the context and circumstances of the sculpture's discovery, a more detailed interpretation is impossible. It is also difficult to decide whether (if we assume its prehistoric pedigree) it could have played a secondary role in Pomeranian observances in the Early Middle Ages. This is all the more possible as in the opinion of some researchers "One can't (…) exclude the existence of certain cultural similarities present in the archetypal substrate of Indo-European symbolism".[15]

A severely damaged stone statue conventionally known as "Belbuk", was discovered in the 19th century. This sculpture, retrieved from the bottom of Rakowskie Lake not far from Szczecinek city[16], embodying distinctly anthropomorphic qualities, measures 120 cm in height and was carved from sandstone. Its upper portion depicts a schematically carved male head with clearly marked eyes, nose, mouth and chin. According to existing information this artefact was found not far from a bridge crossing, near the early medieval microregion settlement situated around the lake. The supposition that a cult site could have functioned on an island in this lake has become the basis for suggesting that the statue might be the image of a god worshiped there. The sculpture itself was to be evidence of a functioning pagan sanctuary. So an interpretive vicious circle has been created. On the one hand, the artifact we are interested in is supposed to be evidence for the existence of a cult site and on the other hand, the area where it was discovered near a sanctuary is held to be evidence of its cult nature.

As a result, the chronology of the sculpture, assigned to the early medieval period on the basis of the context of its discovery and connected to the drowning of pagan cult images during the Christianization mission, remains uncertain.

---

12. Szafrański 1979: 368; Gieysztor 2006: 237.
13. Łuka 1973: 74-76.
14. Waga 1934: 102.
15. Dzieduszycki 1995: 19.
16. Skrzypek 1998/1999.

Fig. 7.
Rakowo, Szczecinek county
*Stone statue,
the so called* Belbuk.
Photo F.J. Lachowicz.

According to oral information provided by Ignacy Skrzypek, a statue stylistically similar to *Belbuk* stood in the vicinity of the Białogard railway station until the 1960's. In later years the statue was cut up into pieces. Its origins and later fate are unknown.

Another anthropomorphic figure interpreted by German researchers as being the "statue of a pagan god" was on display in the regional museum in Regenwalde (today Resko) before the second world war. It was claimed to have been found in Ornshagen (today Żerzyno). Unfortunately nothing else is know on the subject of this find.[17]

An intriguing artefact can still be seen next to the presbytery of the 13th century church in Sadlno not far from Białoboki. It is a granite sculpture of a human head stylistically related to images know from Rügen. The outline of a face with marked eyes, nose and three curls of hair on the left side of the head is legibly preserved on this stone.

---

17. Skrzypek 2001: 426.

Fig.8.
Sadlno, Gryfice county
Stone carving of human head.
Photo K. Kajkowski.

It appears that the way it was shaped is closely analogous to other objects which have been interpreted as pagan images. Unfortunately, the artefact's original location in the church grounds is unknown. However, it is possible to make the cautious assumption that during the church's alterations in the 19th century, the knocking through of a second door necessitated excavating the foundations. Maybe the statue under discussion was discovered during this work. If this speculation is correct, we can suppose that at an earlier time it was embedded in the foundations of the building, which would put it in the same category as other pagan images (or those deemed to be pagan) placed in a similar fashion within the precincts of Christian churches. In pre-war German literature the sculpture from Sadlno was linked to the presence in Western Pomerania of Otto of Bamberg or else directly linked to pagan beliefs.[18] However, one can't

---

18. Schulz 1928: 252.

be perfectly certain that it was not originally an architectural element, possibly from the monastery in nearby Białoboki.

One of the Pomeranian artefacts most frequently mentioned in the literature as being linked to pagan beliefs, is the relief discovered at the end of the 19th century under the stairs in the tower of St Peter's church in Słupsk. The image on its surface is an engraving of a human figure with long arms positioned along the sides of its body and an oval head. The arrangement of the legs suggests that the sculpture most probably intended to show it in a sitting or crouching position.

To date there have been two attempts at interpreting the above object. The first of these posits a Christian grave stone, the second, an artefact connected to pagan beliefs. The Christian nature of the slab may be negated by two conditions. Both concern the form in which the image on it is portrayed, which does not find a reflection in Christian eschatology according to the rules of which the dead were generally buried on their backs with straight legs. The observation that the slab itself does not find an analogy in Romanesque art seems equally pertinent. In addition, the method by which the relief was formed does not allow the possibility of deciphering any kind of information about the person whose supposed grave the slab was to cover.

Fig.9.
Słupsk. Słupsk county
Stone slab portraying a human figure.
After Kajkowski, Kuczkowski 2010: 103.

We also know that creating such an element as part of a sarcophagus was quite costly,[19] so it is doubtful that such a depiction of the deceased person would satisfy the patron paying for it. I am convinced that the engraving of an image of a cross on the reverse side of the slab (it remained invisible to potential observers) is insufficient evidence to allow for an unequivocal interpretation linking it with Christian eschatological beliefs,[20] and even less so with activities connected to evangelization.

An analogous stone slab with an engraving depicting a standing human figure was also located at one time in a place called Słup not far from Szczecin.[21] Unfortunately, we do not have access to any additional details relating to this artefact or its history.

According to folk tradition, the stoup found in the porch of Saint Mathew's church in Starogard Gdański was purported to be part of a pagan idol. Legend states that the present day church was built on the site of a pre-Christian cult, where a statue of *Svarog* was said to have been located. After Christianisation the statue was thrown into the Wierzyca river where it broke in half. After some time one of its parts was recovered and transformed into a receptacle for holy water. Unfortunately, the lack of any research into the stoup does not allow a position to be taken on the information provided by the legend. It seems, however, that it can find confirmation in another artefact – the font standing in the porch of the 15th century Church of the Holy Trinity in Łobżenica, Wielkopolska (Greater Poland). It is worth adding here that making stoups and fonts out of pagan sculptures is registered in the canon of cleansing rituals undertaken with the aim of desacralisation.[22] It is impossible to determine whether this was so in the case of the Starogard antiquity.

A stone engraved with a pair of human hands arranged in the gesture of prayer was embedded in the southern wall of the 13th century church in Uniradz. It is difficult to ascertain when the stone came to be in its present location. Pre-war pictures show the building to be plastered, which makes any kind of observation additionally difficult. Lack of information about any renovations or building work undertaken on a wider scale before this period suggests that it was already in place before the plastering was carried out. It is also difficult for a

---

19. Kalaga 2014: 134.
20. *Cf.* Błażejewska 2002; Wałkowska 2014: 12, 14.
21. Łuka 1930: 56; Gieysztor 2006: 237.
22. Kajkowski 2008.

direct analogy with the engraving in Uniradz, If one assumes that the stone with the engraved hands was used during the building of the church, one can try to connect it to the Early Medieval period and possibly it can be included in the body of relics regarded by local clergy as pagan.

Fig.10.
Uniradz, Kołobrzeg county
Stone bearing an image of human hands.
Photo K. Kajkowski.

An attempt to interpret the image of the hands remains a separate issue. Engravings of this part of the human body convey a rich symbolic meaning both in pagan and in Christian beliefs[23] which does not exclude the stone had some kind of function within the Catholic liturgy. Unfortunately, we will most probably never discover what role the stone under discussion fulfilled – whether it was part of a greater whole, or with what ideological system it should be linked to. One can only add that images of hands are often associated with the cult of the dead.[24]

---

23. *Cf.* Forstner 1990: 353; Jagla 2009: 19.
24. Szafrański 1981: 35-36; Jagla 2009: 19-20.

As a relic of pagan idol, one also interprets a fragment of a supposed wooden sculpture depicting as human leg, discovered in Wolin near the building characterised as a pagan temple and carefully dated to the 11th century.

Fig.11.
Wolin, Kamieński county
Fragment of a „leg" carved from oak.
After Filipowiak 1993: 28, fig. 8.

According to Władysław Filipowiak the dimensions of this artefact suggest that it might have been part of a statue originally measuring from 2 to 3 metres.[25] However, this researcher does not provide any metrical details for the described object. There are also doubts arising from the circumstances and place of its discovery. According to documentation preserved in Institute of Archaeology and Ethnology of Polish Academy of Sciences (delegacy in Wolin)[26] it turns out that it occurred in a place unconnected with archaeological exploration. From

---

25. Filipowiak 1993: 25-26.
26. Inventory card nr 3049. Unfortunately, the artefact itself has been lost.

this it can be supposed that it was only assigned to a layer of dig number 6 dated to the second half of the 11th century, on the basis of its closeness to the excavations area. The cult interpretation of the "leg" from Wolin seems to be negated by two further circumstances. On the one hand no traces were noted which could be evidence of the presence of an idol in the area surrounding the temple remains, and on the other hand, we don't know of any material remains of artefacts of this sort, modelled in a similar way or of similar dimensions, from the territory of Western Slavs. Without definitively rejecting the train of thought presented by Filipowiak, we should ask here whether the object which interests us is not perhaps an architectural feature of a local building?

A relief carving depicting a human figure was discovered about 600 m to the south west of the early medieval fort in Żydowo near Sławno. Władysław Łęga published a detailed description of this artefact, referring to a publication by the German researcher Robert Behla.[27] According to this researcher's description, the figure portrays the bust of a woman carved from a grey sandstone slab. The problem, however, lies in the fact that Behla doesn't know anything about it, mentioning only the site in Żydowo, which in turn he refers to on the basis of a paper by Hugo Schumann.[28] But Schumann's work deals with a different part of Pomerania, not engaging at all with the problem of this fort.[29] Where Łęga obtained information pertaining to both the carving itself and to the place of its discovery remains a puzzle. The idol's description rich in detail suggests that he may have known it from an autopsy (or at least from a source not cited in his deliberations). However, these are solely suppositions. Even if we accept the likelihood of such a series of events we still don't know the basis on which the carving was deemed to belong to the Early Middle Ages. According to Łęga it was supposed to have been discovered in a fortified settlement located near a mill in Żydowo. The site described by the researcher matches only one edifice whose use however links it to the Lusatian culture[30]. In these circumstances we do not have a basis for linking the site of the carving's discovery with the remains of the fort in Żydowo or a nearby Stare Borne. The problem of its dating must also remain unsolved.

From the above survey it follows that not one of the Pomeranian artefacts has a well documented archaeological context. On the basis of narrative sources (Ebo

---

27. Łęga 1930: 527.
28. Behla 1888: 138.
29. Schumann 1887.
30. Archive of Provincial Heritage Monuments Protection Heritage in Koszalin. File no. 18-26.

III, 1; VP II, 12) it has become accepted that anthropomorphic images of gods should be directly linked to sacred territory, in this primarily to sacred buildings (in this case Wolin and Szczecin). The problem however lies in the fact that we do not have at our disposal any evidence from archaeological excavations which would prove the functioning of temples in the localities which interest us. The link between such constructions know from the hagiography of Otto of Bamberg, with the organisation of the ceremonial-cult space of early medieval Pomeranians also remains unclear. This stems from doubts which surface regarding the tribal affiliations of these centres in the later stages of the Early Middle Ages. Some researchers place their genesis in northern Polabia.[31] Irrespective of the outcome of this discussion, the fact remains that both Wolin and Szczecin belonged to places unique in the scale of Pomerania. Places whose organizational form it is difficult to ascertain in the structure of sites lying far from the Baltic coastline. Therefore if we were to link the supposed images of gods known from the area we are interested in with an area validated as sacred, it must be an area with quite a different character. We must therefore ask here where the Pomeranian idols could have stood? It seems that clues to this can be found in a passage from the 12th century *The Book of Miracles of Monk Herbert*. The author of this work, created in the Clairvaux abbey, describes among others events, those connected to the journey of one of the Cistercian monks from Fontenay, who set out to the land of the pagans to trade. There he found a statue of a pagan god hidden by the local people, which he burnt – an act for which mentioned god is supposed to have punished him with an eye malady.[32] From the pages of this source we also find out that the wooden idol, standing next to three trees, was distinguished by its abnormal size and black colour resulting from its surface being covered in tar. According to the research results of Maria Szacherska the details contained in this description indicate that it may pertain to the Pomerania lands lying near to the abbey of Darguń.[33] Assuming that the story written about in the source finds its reflection in the context of real events, it is worth paying attention to the author's observations relating to the hiding of the statue. Such a situation would be explained in the context of a Christianisation mission, a process which in the first instance encompassed the capital forts of identifiable territorial communities. Could the idol interesting us here have originally been found within the fort's ramparts? This possibility can't

---

31. Piskorski 2002: 93 nn.
32. Szacherska 1968: 83; Miś 1997: 120.
33. Szacherska 1968: 85.

be excluded. Or the more so because this hypothesis finds a reflection in the text of Ebo (III, 1), who directly mentions statues standing within the fortifications of Wolin. A further clue in our search may be information provided by another chronicler. Helmold (I, 84), describing a grove dedicated to the Wagrian god *Prove (Prone)* states that "... apart from house gods and idols of which there were large numbers in the various towns, this place was sacred to the whole land". In this he seems to validate that beyond the borders of settlements there were no statues, or at least such information had not reached him. The monk confirms this observation in another place, adding that the gods residing in groves and forests were not represented in sculptures.

In the context of the records quoted above, the observation that all the known artefacts so far discovered in the Baltic Slavic territories and interpreted by some researchers as idols, relief images of gods or their anthropomorphic representations, were located near or directly within human settlements[34], seems pertinent. Leaving aside from the present deliberations a discussion about the ethno-cultural attributes of some of them, it should be noted that a connection of the carvings with a ceremonial-cult sites hasn't been proved in any of the cases. This may indicate – if we acknowledge the validity of the hypothesis about the lack of anthropomorphic images in so called natural hierophany – that we should search for their localisation in the area surrounding or close to residential area. In this context it is worth noting the series of Pomeranian fortified settlements indicating a purpose not connected with military functions. Unfortunately, the state of research relating to early medieval settlements, in particular the extent of identification of the spatial organisation of the strongholds and their supply base, does not allow far reaching conclusions in this area. In connection with this, at least at the present time, we are not in a position to answer the question whether the idols could have stood directly within the ramparts or in an additional distinctly sacred space beyond them.

As we can see, the picture emerged from the archaeological sources is not clear cut and is difficult to interpret. It transpires that in the region of Pomerania, we know of hardly more than twenty carvings which one can attempt to link with the ideological system of the early medieval inhabitants of this region.

---

34. Apart from some artefacts from Pomerania, images from Polabian Altenkirchen, Altfriesack, Behren-Lübchin, Bergen, Braak, Fischerisnel, Stolpe, Wolgast, Zadel should be indicated

Unfortunately, practically none of them posses professional archaeological documentation. What's more, some of them were discovered in "mysterious" circumstances. Consequently, we are denied not only the possibility of determining their chronology, but also their cultural attribution. This gives birth to certain doubts as to the authenticity of at least some of the artefacts. We note that most of them were discovered in the 19th and beginning of 20th centuries. This is significant in that there was a "fashion" at that time for souvenirs of the past, then colloquially referred to as antiquities. This is also a period when any remains linked to pagan beliefs were searched for with a particular intensity. At a time when the study of ancient religions was not particularly well developed, statues were regarded as the best and least controversial relics of the old beliefs and believers. This is why one should approach such artefacts with exceptional caution.

Literature

Primary Sources:

Ebo 1969: *Ebbonis vita Ottonis episcopi babenbergensis, in* K. Liman, J. Wikarjak (eds.), *Monumenta Poloniae Historica* 7(2). Warszawa: Państwowe Wydawnictwo Naukowe.

Helmold 1974: J. Strzelczyk (ed.): *Helmolda Kronika Słowian*. Warszawa: Państwowy Instytut Wydawniczy.

Saxo 2015: K. Friis-Jensen (ed.): Saxonis Grammaticus, *Gesta Danorum/The History of the Danes*. Oxford: Oxford University Press.

VP 1966: *S. Ottonis episcopi babenbergensis, in* K. Liman, J. Wikarjak (eds.) *Monumenta Poloniae Historica* 7(1). Warszawa: Państwowe Wydawnictwo Naukowe.

Secondary sources

Antoniewicz, W., 1957: « Religia dawnych Słowian », *in* E. Dąbrowski (ed.), *Religie świata*. Warszawa : Instytut Wydawniczy PAX, 319-402.

Behla, R., 1888: *Vorgeschichtliche Rundwalle in östlichen Deutschen*. Berlin: Asher.

Biermann, F., 2014: « Ein „Götterbildbeschlag" aus der Uckermark als Zeugnis mittelalterlicher Glaubensvorstellungen im nordwestslawichen Raum », *Praehistorische Zeitschrift*, 89(2), 390-403.

Błażejewska, A., 1999: « Skandynawski mit na kamieniu z Leźna k. Gdańska? Próba interpretacji treści oraz artystycznego rodowodu reliefów », *in* A. Błażejewska, E. Pilecka (eds.), *Argumenta, articuli, questiones. Studia z historii sztuki średniowiecznej. Księga jubileuszowa dedykowana Marianowi Kutnerowi*. Toruń: Fundacja Tumult, 265-290.

Błażejewska, A., 2002: « Głowa z Jankowa. Próba odczytania formy wczesnośredniowiecznego zabytku », *Teka Komisji Historii Sztuki*, 9, 15-37.
Brzustowicz, G.J., 2006: « Rycerze św. Katarzyny. Symbolika średniowiecznego herbu rodu von Wedel », *Przegląd Zachodniopomorski*, 21(2), 5-44.
Dzieduszycki, W., 1995: *Kruszce w systemach wartości i wymiany społeczeństwa Polski wczesnośredniowiecznej*. Poznań : Instytut Archeologii i Etnologii PAN.
Filipowiak, W., 1993: « Słowiańskie wierzenia pogańskie u ujścia Odry », *in* M. Kwapiński, H. Paner (eds.), *Wierzenia przedchrześcijańskie na ziemiach polskich*. Gdańsk : Muzeum Archeologiczne w Gdańsku, 19-46.
Freedberg, D., 2005: *Potęga wizerunków. Studia z historii i teorii oddziaływania.* Kraków : Wydawnictwo Uniwersytetu Jagiellońskiego.
Forstner, D., 1990: *Świat symboliki chrześcijańskiej*. Warszawa : Instytut Wydawniczy PAX.
Gabriel, I., 2000: « Kosmologisches Bildprogramm als Messerscheidenbeschlag », *in* A. Wieczorek, H.-M. Hinz (eds.), *Europas Mitte um ⊘ Katalog*. Stuttgart : Wbg Theiss in Wissenschaftliche Buchgesselschaft, 139.
Gieysztor, A., 2006: *Mitologia Słowian*. Warszawa : Wydawnictwo Uniwersytetu Warszawskiego.
Grążawski, K., 2012: « 'Terra lubovia' na północno-wschodnich rubieżach Słowiańszczyzny », *in* K. Grążawski, M. Dulinicz (eds.), *Pogranicza kulturowe w Europie średniowiecznej. Słowianie i ich sąsiedzi*. Brodnica – Warszawa – Olsztyn: Instytut Archeologii i Etnologii PAN, 43-56.
Heinhoffer, P., 1834: «Reise-Tagebuch enthaltend Schilderungen aus Franken, Sachsen, der Mark Brandenburg und Pommern in Jahre 1617», *Baltische Studien A.F.* 2(2), 1-181.
Hoffmann, M.J., 2004: « The Prussian Transition from Paganism to Christianity: Material Relics of the Transformation of Beliefs », *in* J. Gąssowski (ed.), *Christianization of the Baltic Region*. Pułtusk : Wyższa Szkoła Humanistyczne im. Aleksandra Gieysztora w Pułtusku, 64-74.
Hume, D., 1962: *Dialogi o religii naturalnej*. Warszawa : Wydawnictwo Naukowe PWN.
Jagla, J., 2009: *Wieczna prośba i dziękczynienie. O symbolicznych relacjach między sacrum i profanum w przedstawieniach wotywnych z obszaru Polski Centralnej*. Warszawa : Neriton.
Kajkowski, K., 2008: « Desakralizacja czy rewaloryzacja. Przejawy nieliturgicznych praktyk religijno-magicznych w murach średniowiecznych pomorskich kościołów », *in* M. Bogacki, M. Franz, Z. Pilarczyk (eds.), *Kultura ludów Morza Bałtyckiego*, t. I, *Starożytność i średniowiecze. Mare integrans. Studia nad dziejami wybrzeży Morza Bałtyckiego. Materiały z III międzynarodowej Sesji Naukowej Dziejów Ludów Morza Bałtyckiego, Wolin ⊘ 𝟸 ipca ⊘* . Toruń : Adam Marszałek, 175-194.

Kajkowski, K., Kuczkowski, A., 2010: *Religia Pomorzan we wczesnym średniowieczu*. Pruszcz Gdański : Wydawnictwo Jasne.

Kalaga, J., 2014: « Groby z płytami na cmentarzysku przy kościele pod wezwaniem św. Mikołaja w Wiślicy. Aspekt archeologiczny i społeczny », in T. Kurasiński, K. Skóra (eds.), *Grób w przestrzeni, przestrzeń w grobie. Przestrzenne uwarunkowania w dawnej obrzędowości pogrzebowej* (=Acta Archaeologica Lodziensia 60). Łódź : Łódzkie Towarzystwo Naukowe, 131-136.

Kowalski, A.P., 2013: *Mit a piękno. Z badań nad pochodzeniem sztuki*. Bydgoszcz : Epigram.

Łbik, L., 1998: « Wczesnośredniowieczny ryt kamienny z krajeńskiego Glesna », *Materiały do Dziejów Kultury i Sztuki Bydgoszczy i Regionu*, 3, 125-131.

Łęga, W., 1930: *Kultura Pomorza we wczesnem średniowieczu na podstawie wykopalisk*. Toruń : Towarzystwo Naukowe.

Łuka, J.L., 1973: *Wierzenia pogańskie na Pomorzu Wschodnim w starożytności i we wczesnym średniowieczu*. Wrocław – Warszawa – Kraków – Gdańsk : Zakład Narodowy im. Ossolińskich.

Margul, T., 1987: *Religie jako święte przekazy. Repetytorium z teorii i fenomenologii religii dla studentów wyższych lat kierunku religioznawstwa*. Kraków : Wydawnictwo Uniwersytetu Jagiellońskiego.

Milošević, A., 2011: « "Slika „Božanskog Boja" – likovni ikonografski pogled na konjanički reljef iz Žrnovnice u Dalmaciji », in M. Kropej, A. Pleterski, V. Nartnik (eds.), *Perunovo koplje*. Ljubljana : Inštitut za archeologijo ZRC SAZU, 17-72.

Miś, A.L., 1997: « Przedchrześcijańska religia Rugian », *Slavia Antiqua*, 38, 105-147.

Piskorski, J.M., 2002: *Pomorze plemienne. Historia – Archeologia – Językoznawstwo*. Szczecin : Sorus.

Schulz, H., 1928: « Die Kirche von Zedlin », *Unser Pommerland*, 13(5/6), 252.

Schumann, H., 1887: *Die Burgwälle des Randowthales*, "Baltische Studien", t. 37, 1887 (= Festschrift der Gesellschaft für pommersche Geschichte und Altertumskunde zur Begrüssung des XVII Congresses der Deutschen anthropologischen Gesellschaft in Stettin 1886).

Skrzypek, I., 1998/1999: « W sprawie „Belbuka" », in E. Choińska-Bochdan, M. Kwapiński, H. Paner, A. Szymańska (eds.), *Z Otchłani Wieków Pomorza Gdańskiego. Zeszyt okazjonalny dla upamiętnienia Tysiąclecia Gdańska. 997 urbs Gyddanyze – 1997 Gdańsk*. Gdańsk : Muzeum Archeologiczne w Gdańsku, 166-173.

Skrzypek, I., 2001: « Heimtamuseum Regenwalde (Resko) i jego zbiory (1929-1945) », in E. Wilgocki (ed.), *Instantia est mater doctrinae. Księga jubileuszowa prof. dr. hab. Władysława Filipowiaka*. Szczecin: SNAP, 419-429.

Sokołowska, J., « Wczesnohistoryczne posągi kamienne odkryte na ziemiach Polski », *Światowit,* 13, 113-151.

Szacherska, M., 1968: *Rola klasztorów duńskich w ekspansji Danii na Pomorzu Zachodnim u schyłku XII wieku,* Wrocław – Warszawa – Kraków ; Zakład Narodowy im. Ossolińskich, Wydawnictwo PAN.

Szafrański, W., 1979: *Pradzieje religii w Polsce.* Warszawa : Iskry.

Szafrański, W., 1982: « Rodowód motywu Chrystusika Frasobliwego (przyczynek do badań nad przedchrześcijańskim kultem zmarłych przodków) », *Euhemer. Przegląd Religioznawczy,* 26(3/4), 17-26.

Waga, T., 1934: *Pomorze w czasach przedhistorycznych.* Toruń : Ludowa Spółdzielnia Wydawnicza.

Wałkowska, J., 2012: « O rzekomych posążkach słowiańskich z Pomorza. Próba reinterpretacji », *Nasze Pomorze. Rocznik Muzeum Zachodniokaszubskiego w Bytowie,* 14, 11–24.

Slavic deities of death
Looking for a needle in the haystack

Stamatis Zochios

EPHE (Les Patios Saint-Jacques, 4-14 rue Ferrus 75014 Paris)

stamzochios@gmail.com

Abstract. Although the notion that Slavic mythology included an afterlife that was geographically distributed through an otherworld has occasionally been questioned due to the lack of necessary sources, this article aims to cast light on a set of gods that scholars have tended to associate with death – Nija, Morana, Černobog, Karačun, Veles, Triglav and Černoglav – in order to clarify a series of specific points. Namely, do they really belong to the category of death deities? Can they be considered as rulers of the otherworld, or do they have something to do with dualistic fertility rites involving death and the regeneration of nature? By answering these significant questions, this article will seek to determine whether we can speak of Slavic death deities, not in terms of hypotheticals and theoretical reconstructions, but with a certainty stemming from source analysis - unless lack of evidence ultimately makes any conclusion prohibitive.

Keywords. Death, Otherworld, Underworld, Dualism, Prosperity, Fertility

IT IS A FACT that most mythologies in the world give us clear evidence of the gods who reign in the realm of the dead. In the southern part of the European area, for example, the Greeks are led after the end of their life to the misty and gloomy Hades[1], which is under the control of the homonymic god or Pluto, while in the northern part Hel presides over the Norse otherworld Hel

---

1. Rayor 2004: 33. Greek underworld's descriptions are explicit enough to form a quite definite topography. The available literature on this subject is particularly extensive. See for example: Albinus 2000; Edmonds 2004; Wheatcroft 2014.

or Helheim (a name mostly used in secondary sources), that it is described in detail: according to Gylfaginning, the first part of Snorri Sturluson's 13th century *Prose Edda*, the threshold over which people enter is a pitfall called *Fallandaforad* ("Falling to Peril"), Hell's bed is named *Kor* ("Sick-Bed"), and her bed curtains are named *Blikjandabol* ("Gleaming Disaster")[2]. In fact, the sources referring to Slavs' afterlife beliefs, as well as practices that prepare and allow the deceased to pass from earthly life to life after death, are few and we cannot in any case talk about a clearly defined region such as in Greek or Norse sources. However, even under these circumstances, the existence of a an afterworld, cannot be rather disputed even if Thietmar, Prince-Bishop of Merseburg, in his *Chronicon* composed between 1012 and 1018 and including the earliest accounts of idolatry among the Western Slavs, mentions that *Slavs* believe all things come to an end after death[3]. Moreover the *Russian Primary Chronicle* informs us that:

> Vladimir summoned together his boyars and the city-elders, and said to them, "Behold, the Bulgars came before me urging me to accept their religion. Then came the Germans and praised their own faith; and after them came the Jews. Finally the Greeks appeared, criticizing all other faiths but commending their own, and they spoke at length, telling the history of the whole world from its beginning. Their words were artful, and it was wondrous to listen and pleasant to hear them. They preach the existence of another world. 'Whoever adopts our religion and then dies shall arise and live forever. But whosoever embraces another faith, shall be consumed with fire in the next world.[4]

It is possible that the chronicler implies that the Greeks (representing Byzantine orthodoxy), preaching the existence of another world, believed, unlike the Slavs, in an afterworld. Leger believes that both Thietmar, being a bishop, and Nestor the Chronicler, judge on the basis of Christian prejudices and he contrasts these views to the one of Cosmas of Prague. This priest, writer and historian who lived between 11th and 12th centuries, in his *Chronica Boemorum* (*Chronicle of Bohemians*), refers to a pagan worship of the dead:

> So also the superstitious practices which the villagers, still half-pagan, observed on the third or fourth day of Pentecost, offering libations over springs, offering sacrifices, and making offerings to demons; the burials they made in forests and fields; the play they performed over according to the pagan rites at crossroads and crossroad temples as if for the suppression of spirits; and the profane jests,

---

2. Young 1966. See also: Davidson 2013.
3. Thietmarus Merseburgensis 1807: 11.
4. Cross, Sherbowitz-Wetzor 1953: 110.

which they performed over the dead rousing useless ghosts, wearing masks on their faces, and reveling.[5]

The existence of these popular beliefs and practices, reminiscent of old practices and folk beliefs of the European region and more specifically of those who include veneration of the dead (called useless ghosts by the religiously militant chronicler), undoubtedly requires an afterworld, a place of residence of the dead[6], which should reasonably be ruled by some deity[7]. But what is the information given by the sources on this subject?

Nya/Nija and Moranna

Nya/Nija and *nav*

The most unequivocal reference about the existence of an afterworld and a ruler-deity seems to be found in Jan Długosz's magnum opus *Annales seu cronicae incliti Regni Poloniae* (*Annals or Chronicles of the Famous Kingdom of Poland*) written between 1455-1480:

> It is known about the Poles that since the beginning they were idolaters and that they believed and honored a number of gods and goddesses, namely Jove, Mars, Venus, Pluton, Diana and Ceres, and fell into the delights of other peoples and tribes. [...] Pluto called Nya, was considered as the god of the underworld and the guardian and protector of the souls when they were leaving the body. They prayed to him in order to be put into better subterranean settlements after death. To those souls was built in Gniezno a significant sanctuary.[8]

Długosz parallels the name Nya with the ancient Greek Pluto, forcing Leger to wonder if he is really a deity or the place of residence of the dead called in Polish *nyja*[9]. Bruckner calls it *shadowy existence* (in German *Schattendasein*) in which one can see a similar deity to the Greek Hades and Teutonic Hel. However the Polish philologist calls into question Długosz's sources arguing that he formed his

---

5. Wolverton 2009: 148.
6. According to Andrzej Szyjewski already in 15th century sources it is mentioned that on Holy Thursday the souls of the dead come to warm themselves at graveyards. See: Szyjewski 2010: 208.
7. Very interesting information can be also drawn by the works of the Arab travelers Al-Masudi (9th century) and Ahmad ibn Fadlan (10th century) commenting on funeral rites and ceremonies among the Rus. See Boskovic 2013, available at : http://etudesslaves.edel.univ-poitiers.fr/index.php?id=395.
8. Matusiak 1908: 2-3.
9. Leger 1901: 203.

Polish pantheon by interpreting freely old ritual texts, especially refrains of ritual songs, and on the basis of folkloric tradition; this view has generally prevailed.[10]

Długosz is not the first though to mention Nya/Nija. The Polish theologian Lucas de Magna Cosmin (d. 1412/15), in his postil points out that a man cannot be saved in the name of Lado, Jassa, and [Quia], Nija, which are otherwise names of idols here worshiped in Poland, but only in the name of Jesus Christ[11]. The 1420 "provincial" statutes *Statuta provincialia breviter* forbids clapping and singing, followed by the calling of the names of the idols Lado, Yleli, Yassa, Tija during the Pentecost[12]. We have every reason to believe that behind the name Tija, accompanied by the deities Lado and Yassa, lies the goddess Nya, accompanied in Lucas de Magna Cosmin's postil by the same idols-goddesses. In addition to the above, Jakub Parkoszowic, the Polish linguist, grammarian and author of the first treatise on Polish orthography, defines the name Nya as that which *is an idol* (*quod fuit idolorum*). Consequently, according to sources that precede the one of Długosz, Nya is a Polish goddess that is worshiped through pagan practices including clapping and singing, without being evidently presented as a death deity (and much less as a underworld ruler), but being connected to the period of Pentecost, as indicated by *Statuta provincialia breviter*. Her name seems to derive from the Proto-Slavic **navъ-* and initially the Indo-European **nāw-*[13], a root of which since its early Slavic variants seems to be related to the dead and sometimes to revenants. The mention of *navja* as evil dead is found in the *Russian Primary Chronicle*, where an epidemic in Polotsk is attributed to the *navjam* galloping around the city on invisible horses[14], a reference that is undoubtedly connected to the fact that revenants can cause fatal diseases and more specifically the plague[15].

---

10. Brückner 1892: 161-191. See also Znayenko 1980: 32-33.
11. Sieradzki 2017: 205; Kolankiewicz 1999: 416-417.
12. *Item prohibeatis plausus et cantalenas in quibus invocantur nomina ydolorum lado yleli yassa tya que consueverunt fieri tempore festi penthecosten.* See: Niederle 1911: 115.
13. On this Pokorny and Vasmer agree. Dictionaries available at http://starling.rinet.ru. See also Dukova 1997: 8, 36-38, 63 and Cooper 2005: 251.
14. The original "Tem i čeloveci glagolahu: jako navie b'jut' poločany" (Šahmatov 1916: 271-272) in Likhachov's translation is becoming "Potomu ljudi i govorili, chto jeto mertvecy b'jut polochan", where *navie* is replaced by *mertvecy*, meaning the dead. For the English translation see: Cross, Sherbowitz-Wetzor 1953: 173. See also: Rybakov 2013: 484 and Tolstoj, Agapkina 1995: 351.
15. In Bulgarian spells "Twelve nawi" are blood-sucking evil spirits, importing the

In addition, the *Chronicle of Dalimil* (*Dalimilova kronika*), the first chronicle in the Old Czech language written by an unknown author at the beginning of the 14th century, mentions the phrase: *Potom Krok jde do navi* ("Then Krok went to the *nav*"), that for Leger this *nav* refers to the country beyond the grave[16]. Therefore, the name *nav* and its various Slavic variants (Polish: *nawia* or *mawia*, Czech: *nav*, Slovene: *navje*, Serbian: *nav*, Ukrainian: *mavka* or *njavka*) denote the souls of the dead and, less possibly, the afterworld[17].

Linguistically related, moreover, seems to be the set of Russian festivals that includes sacrificial offerings of food and drinks to the dead, which is called the day of the dead (*navij den'* (or *nav'i provody* ["farewell to the dead"], *nav'skij Velykdjen'* ["the great day of the dead"]). Among eastern Slavs, this day corresponds to Radunitsa[18], sometimes is celebrated on Thursday of Easter week, at others on Thursday after Trinity, and is associated with the appearance of rusalki, the famous *Rusalii* - a holy ceremony in memory of the dead and the ancestors[19]. All these pre-Christian ceremonies that also existed under different forms in western Slavic countries, were taking place during Christian Pentecost without being only connected to the commemoration of the dead, whose role is not unequivocally negative as Pócs underlines[20], but to nature's rebirth and fertility as well. Under these circumstances, Nya could be indeed a deity of death, connected to the death and fertility festivities of the Pentecost period. This in no way means, though, that Nya was in parallel a ruler of the Slavic underworld, as Długosz believes. It is not unlikely, however, that Długosz did know, albeit vaguely, of Nya's connection to death-fertility ceremonies, considering this, in a simplistic way of thinking, as a reason to link her to Hades' ruler, Pluto. But this is only an hypothesis that cannot be verified with certainty.

Morana, death and fertility

Another family of language types associated with the notion of death, which also seems to denote a deity, poses equally important problems. It is a family of

---

plague. Szyjewski 2004: 206. About of this type of revenants causing the plague, see: Lecouteux 2001: 238-242.
16. Leger 1901: 202.
17. See Vinogradova 1995: 186-188.
18. Commemoration of the dead realized on the second Tuesday of Easter or in Southwest Russia on the second Monday of Pascha.
19. Dal' 1881: 397; Tolstoj, Agapkina 1995: 351.
20. Klaniczay, Pócs 2005: 130.

names deriving from the Indo-European root *mer- (die), appearing in several languages like the Greek *vrotós* 'mortal' <* *mvrotós*, or the latin *morior* (die)[21]. It is a very wide-spread verbal root in Proto-Indo-European languages[22] and from it apparently comes a series of demonic beings that exist already in European medieval folk beliefs (the French *cauchemar*[23], the English *nightmare*, the Slavic and Greek *mora*[24]), but also some more specific figures such as the Irish goddess connected to war, fate and death Mórrígan (or Morrígu), the famous enchantress of the Arthurian legend Morgan le Fay, and, finally, the figure that we which we will analyse below, Morana (Marzanna in Polish, Marena in Russian, Morana in Czech, Bulgarian, Slovenian, Serbian, Bosnian and Croatian, Morena in Slovak and Macedonian, Mara in Belarusian and Ukrainian), and that is usually defined as a Slavic goddess associated with death.

The first reference to this obscure figure is supposed to be done in the medieval encyclopaedical dictionary written in the Latin language around 1240, *Mater Verborum* (or *Glosa Salomonis*) where the name Morana is explained like this: *Ecate, trivia vel nocticula, Proserpina*[25]. If this gloss is authentic, it would mean that Morana was identified early on with the goddess of death Persephone-Proserpina and was also associated with magic. However, Leger does not consider the source to be authentic and, as it is characteristically stated, all the *Mater Verborum*'s glosses on Slavic mythology were constructed in the 19th century, poisoning the relevant studies for a long time[26]. The same view is shared by Niederle considering that Morana, the deity of death, owes her existence to the false glosses of the lexicon of the *Mater verborum*[27]. Despite Niederle's apparently wrong view, which is based on Leger's seemingly justified argument for a later superposition of the glosses, the early existence of Morana must not be disputed.

Długosz in his *Annals*, and specifically in his juxtaposition between Slavic and Greek gods to which we referred above, identifies Morana to Ceres, considering them both goddesses of agriculture and fertility[28]. This reference means firstly

---

21. Rix 2001: 439-440.
22. Boisacq 1916: 134. See also Mallory 1997: 150.
23. Zochios 2012.
24. Zochios 2018: 310-316; Furlan 2009: 101–112.
25. Kulišić 1979: 198.
26. Leger 1901: 44.
27. Niederle 1926: 152.
28. Matusiak 1908: 3. See also : *Mara; Marena* in Ivanov, Toporov 1988: 110, 111.

that Morana existed already since late Middle Ages and secondly that she was interfering into agrarian customs of prosperity. It seems that Church tried unsuccessfully to fight the ritual of drowning or burning Morana. During the synod of Poznań in 1420, bishop Andrzej Łaskarz forbade this superstitious custom[29]. Długosz's identification seems to be that was adopted by the Polish Renaissance scholar and Jagiellonian University professor, Maciej Miechowita, who mentions in his *Chronica Polonorum* (*Chronicle of the Poles*): "*Cererem uocarunt Marzana* (Ceres that they call Marzana)"[30]. Of course other scholars connected Morana to other goddess such as Kromer (*De origine et rebus gestis Polonorum libri XXX*, 1555) to Venus[31] and Marcin Bielski's son Joachim (*Kronika polska Marcina Bielskiego*, 1597), secretary of Sigismund III Vasa, to Mars ("Marzana, I would say that was the god Mars")[32].

Earlier Marcin Bielski in 1551, in an important passage refers to Morana's worship (in the original Marsá, Marzá, Marze or Márzáne) and to her famous drowning in the water[33], locating the customs to Gniezno, the same place where Nya was worshiped according to Długosz. This indirect connection of Nya with the place of worship of such a strongly rural divinity as Morana, may mean that Nya herself belonged to the same category of deities. These sources were however used by J. Grimm in order to consider Morana a deity of death:

> So it is not everywhere that the banished idol represented Winter or Death in the abstract ; in some cases it is still the *heathen divinity* giving way to Christianity, whom the people thrust out half in sorrow, and uttering songs of sadness. Długosz, and others after him, report that by order of king Miecislaus all the idols in the land were broken up and burnt ; in remembrance of which the people in some parts of Poland, once a year, singing mournful songs, conduct in solemn procession *images of Marzana* and *Ziewonia*, fixed on poles or drawn on drags, to a *marsh or river*, and there *drown* them; paying them so to speak, their last homage. Długosz's explanation of Marzana as 'harvest-goddess' seems erroneous; Frencel's and Schaffarik's 'death-goddess' is more acceptable.[34]

---

29. Kowalik 2004: 62.
30. *Ibid.*
31. *Ibid.*
32. *Ibid.*
33. The rite in its Silesian version was described by Aleksander Gwagnin in 1578 *Kronika sarmacji europejskiej*. From the (Chronicle of the European Sarmacia). See Rusinowa 2002: 59.
34. Grimm 1983 (1844): 773.

Indeed, almost one century earlier, in 1719, the Sorbian Lutheran clergyman and historiographer Michał Abraham Frencel, in his important (even if it contains many serious errors) treatise on Slavic mythology *Commentarius philologico-historicus de diis Soraborum*, dedicates a chapter to Morana depicting her as a goddess of death. The chapter's title is: *De Marzava, Dea Morte seu Mortis*[35], but according to him the name Marzava is a result of typographical error, as the correct popular type is Marzana and Morzana[36]. In 1826 the Slovak philologist Pavel Jozef Šafárik considers in his turn Morjana, Morena (Marzana) as a death goddess (Todesgöttin)[37].

But is Morana a deity of death of the same type as Hell or Pluto, that is, a ruler of the underworld? The answer is sooner negative as no extant source –early or late– depicts her that way. On the contrary, Morana is mostly connected to the death and the rebirth of nature, and we could mostly consider her as a goddess of the harvest rather than as a goddess of death, which however manages to combine that bipolar nature. Moreover, the association of a villainous-charitable character, a rebirth/fertility - death/destruction function within a deity (or an integral pair of deities) is a common place in the Indo-European mythology in general and more specifically in Slavic mythology. An example of such a dyadic Goddess and duotheism among North-Western Slavs is Živa (Siwa), who, as Helmold of Bosau notes, figures as the supreme Polabian goddess –*Siwa dea Polaborum* (Helmold I, 52)[38]–, and that was later used by the Croatian politician, historian and university professor Natko Nodilo in order to reconstruct the Southern Slavic Pantheon[39].

More specifically, Nodilo wonders if Vida and Živa are two names for the same supreme goddess, or if they are two personages, two great ladies, answering that he would not categorically state one way or the other but that he would definitely incline towards the second view, considering that way Vida, the Empress of the Heavens[40] (her name comes from the root **vid* or **vit* that refers to "sight", "vision"[41]), and

---

35. Frencel 1719: 85.
36. Frencel 1719: 223.
37. Šafárik 1869: 12.
38. Rosenwein 2018: 292.
39. Nodilo 1981 (1885-1890). For a good analysis of this work and Nodilo's reconstitution, see: Marjanic 2003: 181-203.
40. Marjanic 2003: 194.
41. This is not the only etymology proposed. See for example Pisani's rapprochement with the Gothic *heiwa*, family (Pisani 1950: 65).

Živa the two opposed sides of a single dyadic Goddess[42]. And, going further, he believes that Vida represents the celestial side and Živa the terrestrial one. Finally, following the cosmological day/night and summer/winter dualism, he matches Živa to winter, and furthermore to the hags that are connected to customs of spring's dominance over winter; the latter is represented as a malevolent and annihilating old hag, a Slavic baba[43]. According to S. Marjanić, Nodilo "found confirmation for driving out the Winter Hag in the Spring customs (in March) among the western and South-Western Slavs, when they carried a puppet out of the village which personified Morana/Death (Mora, Morana, Morena – the goddess of Winter and Death; (cf. Nodilo 1981:59) in the figuration of the old hag when they drowned her or sawed her up (ibid.: 286). [...] The Vida/Živa – baba (the aged Goddess's aspect) dichotomy also opens up the "dualism" between the Great Goddess and her nyctomorphic aspect (the Terrible Goddess) who evades the ethical categorization (Good-Evil) due to the fact that the Goddess's terrible aspect follows the cosmic seasonal changes"[44].

Consequently, Nodilo connects the dualistic and terrestrial/chthonian deity Živa to night/winter and furthermore to baba/hag and to all customs representing spring's rebirth and winter's death through the personification of Morana. His theory, was repeatedly used as a reason to name Živa as a death deity and, worse, as an underworld ruler[45]. It is evident, though, that the theory is mostly an hypothesis attempting to reconstruct the foundations of the Slavic religion, and it is based on too few sources in order to be secure. However what we can isolate is the fact that Morana is associated with the above dualistic scheme.

In fact his theory suffers from the ever-re-emerging and highly problematic interpretation of a myth hypothetically and without sources, or in a somewhat better case based on linguistic arguments. Such an example is the view of the linguist Mathieu-Colas, who considers Živa as the opposite facet of Morana, the goddess of death[46]. This argument, which is in sharp contrast to that of Nodilo, seems based on a simplistic etymological interpretation of the names: in the first case the name Živa refers to life, and in the second case the name Morana, to death. This theory is obviously problematic because it may be the etymology

---

42. Nodilo 1981: 264.
43. Nodilo 1981: 142-143.
44. Marjanic 2003: 198.
45. Such an example in : Dixon-Kennedy 1999: 320.
46. *Zivena* in Mathieu-Colas 2017. Accessible at : https://halshs.archives-ouvertes.fr/halshs-00794125v7/document.

of names is often a helpful means in the analysis of a myth, but it is clearly inadequate, and sometimes it can lead to the wrong conclusions. A mythological name, as a general rule, is one-dimensional (the name is associated with a particular feature), unlike a mythological entity that is mostly multidimensional (such as Nodilo's Živa which combines opposing features and functions)[47].

Consequently, in Morana's case we can only rely on the existing sources: on Polish chronicles that consider Morana and its variants as an agricultural goddess, and on the recorded customs about Morana. These are attested since quite early but they are unfortunately briefly described in medieval chronicles. In order to have a more complete picture we need to take for granted the unaltered continuity of folk traditions and to resort to the numerous folk references of the modern period: Morana participates in a set of magic practices aimed at the regeneration and fertilization of nature and, given the reports in Polish chronicles, it is very likely that these practices did not appear out of nowhere during modern times but that they were recorded in earlier times very sporadically.

The custom, which is performed in central and eastern Europe and is precisely the one mentioned analytically by J. Grimm, is based on a solemn procession and a sacrificial rite where the central role is played by Morana (or its geographically dependent variants Marzanna, Marena, Morana, Morena, Mara etc.), the straw mannequin wandering in a funeral procession in order to be finally sacrificed and thus ensure that way a good harvest in the upcoming year. This custom, which reminds us of the drowning or the burning of Maslenitsa and Rusalka in Russia[48], is common across the European area with significant similarities[49], while Frazer insists on the fact that the spirit is regarded as old, or at least as of mature age[50].

In central and eastern European area it is a hag, a *baba* and usually bears such a name: the Russian Baba Yaga, Baba Gorbata and Požinalka, the Slovak Jezibaba (Jenzibaba, Endzibaba, Jazibaba), the Carpatho-Ukrainian Ižužbaba, Indžibaba, the Polish Jedsi Baba ou Baba Jaga, the Sorbian Wjerbava, Wurlavu

---

47. This linguistic uncertainty becomes more important in the case of Siwa given the fact even her name's main form is not insured. The variant Synna that can be found in a manuscript copied at Stettin may imply just a copier's error or may complicate things even more proposing another –existing and maybe prevailing– version of the name. See: Meyer 1931: 44 and Moszyński 1992: 86.
48. The bibliography on these customs is extensive. See Krukova 1947: 185-192.
49. Stangé-Zhirovova 1998: 108, 1026-128.
50. Frazer 1925: 399-411.

(ou Worawy), Připolnica (Přezpołnica ou Poludnitsa), the Serbian Sumska Maika, Baba Korizma and Gvozdenzuba, and so on[51]. In the West-European area it is also a hag called Cailleach (old woman in Scotland), a wrach (hag in Wales), Harvest-mother or Corn-mother, Grandmother and Oldwoman in Sweden, Prussia, North Germany[52]. Based on this data, we can safely consider that Morana belonged since early on –at least since the end of the Middle Ages as evidenced by the Polish chroniclers' report, and which we have no reason to question as inaccurate– in the shape of binary, chthonian deities depicted as hags associated with winter and night, and combining the opposing elements of destruction and fertility, of death and (nature's) rebirth.

Černobog, Tribog, Černoglav
Černobog and the winter deity Karačun

Therefore, this dualistic character, devastating but at the same time fertilizing, should not surprise us, since many divinities are simultaneously malicious and beneficious. A typical case in Slavic mythology – although, as we shall see, it has occasionally provoked intense disputes – is the pair Belobog, the White god, and his dark counterpart Černobog, the Black god, which are the two sides of the same coin and were considered as a pair already by German chroniclers and then Slavic mythographers, such as Tatiščev and Čulkov, who included both Belobog and Černobog in their works on Slavic mythology[53]. However, as in the above cases, the information provided by our sources is not sufficient to be able to come up with safe conclusions about Černobog's nature and role. The first and more important reference is made in Helmond's *Chronicle of the Slavs* (12th century) where it is mentioned that:

> The Slavs, too, have a strange delusion. At their feasts and carousals they pass about a bowl over which they utter words, I should not say of consecration but of execration, in the name of the gods –of the good one, as well as of the bad one– professing that all propitious fortune is arranged by the good god, adverse, by the bad god. Hence, also, in their language they call the bad god Diabol, or Zcerneboch, that is, the black god.[54]

---

51. Johns 2004: 55-58; Caillois 1936: 20-22; Zochios 2016.
52. Many more examples in Frazer 1925: 399-411, 447-463.
53. Tatiščev 1962: 100; Čulkov 2016 (1987): 36. Černobog is also mentionned by Karamzin in his famous *History of the Russian State*: Karamzin 1892: 54.
54. Rosenwein 2018: 292.

The origin of the god is generally not disputed despite any contradictory attitudes that ignore the clearly Slavic etymology of the name. Such an example is the English poet and mythologist Gerald Massey, according to whom Czerny-Bog of the ancient Sclavonians "was also the dark Deity of the Anglo-Saxons called Zernebok"[55]. For this "particular" opinion, Massey based himself on Scott's *Ivanhoe* where is erroneously mentioned that Mista, Skogula, and Zernebock are gods or fiends of the ancient Saxons[56]. The name Černobog is, however, certain to denote the black (from Proto-Slavic *čьrnъ) god (from Proto-Slavic *bogъ). Because of this property, he has been associated with negative functions (such as misfortune and sterility) and even death itself[57]. At the same time, he is related to deities of death (if we can really consider them as such) like Karačun, to which we need to make a short reference here.

In fact, the word Karačun and its different variants has multiple meanings. First of all, it seems to denote Christmas, the period called *svjatki* in different Slavic languages (in Slovenian it is Krakun, in Bulgarian Kračun, in Transcarpathian Ukrainians Kerečun, in Romanian Craciun, and in Magyar Karacsony)[58]. The word can be already found in the old Russian language, namely in the *Novgorod First Chronicle*, where it is mentioned that during the year A.D. 1143, A.M. 6651, "all the autumn was rainy, from Our Lady's Birthday to Koročun warm, wet"[59]. At the same time, without being certain when and under which circumstances, the word obtained the meaning of death – where for example we find it in the phrases: *prišel emu karačun* (to die), *ždi karačuna* (wait for death), *dat' komu karačun, zadat' karačuna* (to kill) or even the verb *karačunit'* (to kill) etc.[60]. It is likely, though, that this significance of death is linked to the next meaning of Karačun, which in this case is a name and implies a god of winter, with dark qualities. Ivanov regards him as a deity of death[61], Sedakova agrees[62], Sobolev refers to an ancient belief according to which Karačun wakes the dead in the month of December, scattering their bones, and they come out of their coffins[63]

---

55. Massey 1883: 485.
56. Scott 1822: 16.
57. Ivanov, Toporov 1988: 452; Petruhin 1995: 8-9.
58. See Pigulevskaja 2011: 188.
59. Michel, Forbes 1914: 18.
60. Vološina 1996: 153; Dal' 1881: 92.
61. Ivanov 1998: 120.
62. Sedakova 2004: 141.
63. Sobolev 1999: 135.

and Tokarev adds the following: "All this (he means the different meanings of the name) suggests that Kračun, Karačun, represented a part of the Slavic tribes, represented the deity of winter and death, in whose honor the holiday around the winter solstice was celebrated. It is very likely that the name of this deity goes back to the same root "*krt*", the derivative of which is the "devil". But did this ancient Slavic deity represent a demon of evil, was it opposed to bright and kind deities? In other words, did the ancient Slavic pagan religion have a distinct dualism of light and dark beginnings, good and evil spirits? The era was marked, at least among the Western Slavs. This is indicated by the opposition, albeit not quite reliable, by Belboga and Černoboga"[64].

This dualism to which Tokarev relates Karachun, and which reminds us of the dualism through which Nodilo connected Živa (and in an expansive manner Morana), culminates in the archetypal duality of Belobog-Černonog. Indeed, Černobog is usually examined by experts in connection with Belobog, within a dualistic system of good-evil, rebirth-destruction, fertility-sterility, spring-winter, life-death. However, the varying point of views diverge considerably and this for two main reasons.

Initially, because many specialists, most notably Nehring[65], questioned the existence of Belobog that is not attested in any primary source, considering it as an unverifiable hypothesis and a creation of the compiler of the 17th century *Historia Carmensis*, who relied on the name of Černobog attested by Helmond in order to create the opposite pole, Belobog. This argument is not valid since Sebastian Münster's *Cosmographiae* –that was published in 1544– gives us a reference that precedes the 17th century *Historia Carmensis* mentioning that:

> In general they (i.e. the Rugian Slavs) worshipped two gods, namely Belbuck and Zernebuck, as if a white and black god, a good and evil genius, God and Satan, as the source of good and evil, according to the error of the Manicheans.[66]

Even earlier, the chronicler in the Duchy of Pomerania, Thomas Kantzow, refers to Belobog in his 1538 (but published in 1835) *Chronik von Pommern in niederdeutscher Mundart*, thus proving that Chernobog's counterpart already existed at least in the 15th century:

> They also worshipped the sun and the moon and two gods to whom they assigned a higher value than to other gods. One they called Bialbug - that is the white

---

64. Tokarev 1957: 109.
65. Nehring 1903: 66-73. For more information, see: Znayenko 1993: 177-185.
66. Münster 1554: 772.

god, believing him to be a good god, the other Zernebug - that is the black god, believing him to be a god who did harm. Therefore, they honored Bialbug so that he should do them good, and Zernebug so that he should not harm them...[67]

In any case, the question of Belobog's existence does not deeply affect the question of Černobog's existence and it does not concern us directly, since what we are really interested in is the participation of Belobog or not in a dual system, regardless of the name borne by its other end, the one that is not named by Helmond. But this dualism was also disputed, and considered not as an inherent feature of Slavic paganism, but a result of Bogomil-Manichean influences or of an *Interpretatio Christiana*[68].

For other theoreticians, though, such as Jakobson[69], Gimbutas[70] or Gieysztor[71], dualism is present here and originates from the Indo-European reservoir, without being associated with Bogomil influences[72]. In addition, for the supporters of this view, within Slavic mythology this dualism, which is in our case incarnated by Belobog-Černobog, lies at the very centre of religious beliefs and is associated with the highest gods in the hierarchy, and hence with the pillars of the religious system. Thus, according to Gimbutas:

> Three divine archetypes of the Indo-European religious tradition are clearly represented in the Slavic pantheon: the god of heavenly light, the god of death and the underworld, and the thunder god. The first two stand in opposition to each other, but the relationship of the three deities is triangular, not hierarchical. The god of heavenly light, also known as the white god, and the god of death and the underworld, also known as the black god, form a fundamental polarity in the Slavic religious tradition. This opposition of mythological figures is reflected in the semiotic system of Slavic languages, based on the arrangement of oppositions such as day and night, light and dark, life and death, good and evil.[73]

---

67. Böhmer 1835: 283.
68. Such as by Mochul'ski 1889: 153-204; Brückner 1929-1930: 340-351; Niederle 1924: 159-164; Máchal 1918: 288; Wienecke 1940: 276-280; Unbegaun 1948: 420-422; Nedo 1963: 5–18; Łowmiański 1979. For more details, see: Znayenko 1993: 177-178, 183. The idea of Manichean influences was thoroughly refuted, for reasons that we cannot expose here, by I. Ivanov in his work *Bogomilski knigi i legendi* (Sofia, 1925). See also : Obolensky 1948: 68-69.
69. Jakobson 1949: 1026.
70. Gimbutas 1987: 353-361.
71. Gieysztor 2018 (1982): 77-87.
72. Eliade 1970 : 83, 93-94. See also: Smith 1993: 99-102.
73. Gimbutas 1987: 356.

Furthermore, this supreme heavenly god, who is in opposition to his underworldly enemy, is considered to be Perun, and the God to whom he is opposed through a cosmic battle, who according to the dualistic scheme must be the god of death and the underworld, is Veles. Given these correspondences, Znayenko believes that Černebog echoes the existence of an old chthonic god, that is possibly the same as Volos/Veles, and needs no longer to be expelled from the Slavic pantheon[74].

Veles

Véles or Volos[75], known as *skotij bog*, the cattle god, was widely worshiped by Western Slavs, but his veneration was mostly established among the steppenland Slavs of the East and the North East, with some toponyms indicating the presence of his worship in the Southern Slavic regions as well. As his main title (*skotij bog*) betrays, he was connected to the pastoral lifestyle and agricultural prosperity[76]. But at the same time, he is often considered by specialists as a chthonian deity and a ruler of the underworld. Once again, the process of confirming this complementary nature through written sources is extremely complex since there are no texts (or archaeological monuments) to endorse it. The available relevant studies are few (for example, Jacobson in his article on Veles does not make any reference in this regard[77]), and we must basically turn to the reconstruction by Ivavov and Toporov of the famous controversy between Veles and Perun in order to have some clues.

Although different etymologies of Proto-Indo-European roots have been proposed for the name Veles such as *wel-, "wool"[78], *woltus, "meadow"[79], *wel, "see"[80], or a connection to the adjective *velij (velikij)*[81], Ivanov and Toporov believe that it derives from the Indo-European root *vel-, meaning the dead, such as in the cases of Old Icelandic *valr* 'the dead on the battlefield', the Old High German, Old English *wal*, as well as the Old Icelandic *valhall* (the abode of

---

74. Znayenko 1993: 182-183.
75. We will not raise here the issuer of the relationship between Veles-Volos, considering them as two different versions of the same name.
76. Hoddinott 1963: 83.
77. Jacobson 2010: 33-48.
78. Belaj 2007: 81.
79. Katičić 2008: 171.
80. Jacobson, R., *op.cit.*, p. 24-25.
81. Vasmer 1987: 287-288.

the warriors fallen on the battlefield), the *valkyrja* (a maid that has to choose the hero among the dead and to transfer him to Odin), the Old English *wœl* (a man who was left on the battlefield, a corpse), the Tocharian *wäl* (to die) and *walu* (the dead), and many others[82]. The root can be also found in a series of Lithuanian funeral songs (in the formula *atkelk vėlių vartelius*[83] that means "open the gate of souls"), and in Balto-Slavic customs associated with the dead (*navi*)[84]. Even more illustrative is the use of the root in names of evil spirits, such as in the 15th century Old Czech novel *Tkadleček* where we read : *"Ký jest črt, aneb ký veles, aneb ký zmek?"* ("What devil or what veles or what dragon incited you against me"[85]) as well as in Vélnias' name, that means in Lithuanian the devil[86]. In some cases, this spirit can be transformed into an horned animal of the cattle.[87] On this point, Ivanov and Toporov specify that the connection between the god of the cattle and the realm of the dead can be explained by the Common Indo-European concept of the nether world as a pasture. This view is not enough, in our opinion, to explain the connection of death and pasture, which in reality should not be surprising because in Indo-European mythology there are cases of pastoral customs connected to death (such an example is the East Slavonic rite burial rite of the *Death of the Cows* on the Day of Vlasiy, the saint who is a later equivalent of Veles-Volos due to the substitution of the pagan gods by corresponding Christian saints in the Russian tradition) or even cases of pastoral demons also connected to death. Such an example is the Byzantine-derived pastoral demon *smerdaki*, who accompanies the livestock, causes diseases and sometimes kills the farm animals, whose name undoubtedly originates from the Slavic root *smьrdъ* (from which the Russian word for death *smert'* comes) and the Proto-indoeuropean **smerd-* meaning to bite, to damage, to destroy[88].

---

82. Ivanov, Toporov 1973: 21-22.
83. Ivanov, Toporov 1973: 20.
84. Ivanov, Toporov 1973: 18-19.
85. Jacobson 2010: 36.
86. Ivanov, Toporov 1973: 16.
87. As Gimbutas points out, some two hundred years ago Vélnias was one of the most important pre-Christian Baltic deities: the god of the dead and of cattle (wealth and fertility). Sources do not neglect Vélnias' dreadful properties. Such an example is 1783 Lange-Stender's Latvian grammar where Véls is described as god of the dead and Veli as "days of the god of the dead". For more information concerning the Baltic god Velnias, Véls, etc. see: Gimbutas 1974 87-92.
88. Malingudis 1990: 89; Vasmer 1987: 684.

Consequently, it is likely that Veles, like Morana, is a deity associated with the known shape of death and rebirth of nature, destruction-fertility, but since the sources do not prove the opposite we are not in a position to assume with certainty that Veles is a ruler of the underworld, as is mentioned very often and with unnecessary ease in contemporary literature, even by scholars who are particularly meticulous, such as L. P. Słupecki[89]. Interpretations like the one of Gruel-Apert who considers Veles as a ruler of the hellish world because in Kiev his idol was not situated on the height near Perun and the other gods, but in the low quarter near the river[90], are hypothetical and precarious. We consider the representation of both Simargl, the enigmatic deity or creature with the quite vague functions, and Lada, the goddess of beauty and fertility, as gods of death and the otherworld to be equally precarious. Unlike the case of Veles, where the existing language base can lead us to reasonable assumptions, in the cases of Simargl and Lada, neither the ancient sources nor the language itself allow us to claim anything equivalent.

Coming back Gimbuta's triangle according to which the god of the heavenly light, also known as the white god, and the god of death and the underworld, also known as the black god, formed a fundamental polarity in the Slavic religious tradition, Veles could possibly be the last (and darker) term of this equation, of this tripartite shape that reminds us of the well-known Triglav.

Triglav and Černoglav

This particular deity, as its name implies (*tri* that means three, and *glav*, that means head), has three heads and thus is represented in statues in honor of him in Pomeranian cities like Wolin, as well as in written testimonies. In the *Dialogus de vita Ottonis epsicopus Babenbergensis*, composed by Herbordus, one of the three biographers of the Otto of Bamberg, the bishop and missionary, who converted a great part of medieval Pomerania to Christianity, it is mentioned that:

> Now there were in the town of Stettin four temples, of which the principal one was built with marvelous care and skill. [...] Into this temple the people brought, in accordance with the ancient custom of their ancestors, the stores and arms of their enemies which they captured, and whatever spoils they took by land or by sea, as they were directed to do by the law relating to the giving of a tenth.[...]

---

89. Leszek Paweł Słupecki in his thorough treatise on Slavonic pagan sanctuaries considers that Veles ruled the underworld. See Słupecki 1994: 9.
90. Gruel-Apert 2014: 30.

> Now there was a three-headed image which had its three heads on one body and was called Triglav. This with its three small heads adhering to part of the body was the only thing that he took ; he carried it away with him as a trophy and afterwards sent it to Rome as a proof of the conversion of this people […].[91]

According to the second biographer, Monachus Prieflingensis, his three heads were silver-plated. Similar information is provided by the third biographer of Bishop Otto, Ebo, in his work *Vita Ottonis Bishops Bambergenis*:

> When the temples and the idol images had been destroyed by Otto, the sacrilegious priests carried the golden image of Triglav, who was chiefly worshipped by the people, away by stealth outside the province and committed it to the care of a certain widow who lived in a small country house where it was not likely to be looked for.[92]

At another point of the text the details concerning this deity are much more specific:

> Stettin, their most extensive town, which was larger than Julin, included three hills in its circuit. The middle one of these, which was also the highest, was dedicated to Triglav, the chief god of the pagans; its image had a triple head and its eyes and lips were covered with a golden diadem. The idol priests declared that their chief god had three heads because it had charge of three kingdoms, namely, heaven, earth and the underworld, and that its face was covered with a diadem so that it might pretend not to see the sins of men, and might keep silence".[93]

The above texts were repeatedly analyzed, because Triglav is considered by some experts a *summus deus* as Ebo states explicitly, a type of god that, in the symbolic system, plays the role of a cosmological node and a mediator between the three levels, the three spheres or realms of the world[94], while for others it corresponds to the triple-headed deities of the Indo-European mythology, such as the Tsar Zmijulan and Aži Dahāka[95], or the Thracian Horseman[96]. As for the connection between Triglav and the otherworld, it is clearly mentioned by Ebo but it is

---

91. Robinson 1920: 78.
92. Robinson 1920: 88.
93. Robinson 1920: 110.
94. Dynda 2014: 58. This function as mediator of three realms of the world is also commented by Abraham Frencel in his 1719 *Commentarius philologico-historicus de diis Soraborum* and more specifically in the chapter dedicated to Trigla (sic) (p. 203-205).
95. Trkanjec 2013: 13, 19.
96. Dynda 2014: 67.

also indicated in other parts of the related narrations. Thus, it is mentioned by Monachus Prieflingensis and Ebo that a black horse was consecrated to him and used for divinatory proposes, and that a decorated horse saddle hung on a wall of his sanctuary. The horse is one of the most mythologically charged animals, often represented as a solar beast[97] but also associated with the otherworld as an image of Death, the incarnation or mount of revenants or as a guide to the soul (psychopomp).[98] Its sacrifice in a funeral context seems to have a Proto-Indo-European origin, and it was interred with the deceased, a practice called *horse burial*. Moreover, Dynda adopting Erben's opinion according to which Triglav is identified to the "Neptunus of three natures" of Adam of Bremen[99], where the the three coloured sea around "Neptunus" from Wolin, is an allusion to three realms over which Triglav reigns, finds in it another proof about Triglav's death proprieties: the water is a metaphor for the underworld[100].

Based on these accounts, Triglav, despite the general view of the theoreticians regarding a unity of three deities, a divine triad –a part of which corresponds to the ruler of the underworld–, was also considered by Čajkanović[101] and Chausidis[102] as a chthonic deity, and was considered by Gieysztor[103] as the northwestern variant of Veles. Moreover he was related to Černoglav, a deity that is mentioned in *Knýtlinga saga*.

Knýtlinga saga, the Saga of Cnut's Descendants, written in the 1250s, deals with the kings who ruled Denmark since the early 10th century and covers the history of the Danish rulers from the early 10th century until the 13th century. In it, we are informed that Tjarnaglofi was worshiped at Rügen, an island located off the Pomeranian coast in the Baltic Sea:

> There was also Tjarnaglofi (Černoglav), their god of victory who went with them on military campaigns. He had moustache of silver and resisted longer than the others but they managed to get him three years after.[104]

---

97. Jacobson 1992: 34; Wagner 2005: 39.
98. Wagner 2005: 89. See also the chapter "The the pig and the horse" in Lecouteux 2011 (ebook).
99. Adamus Bremensis 1846: 62.
100. Dynda 2014: 60-64.
101. Čajkanović 1994: 79-80.
102. Chausidis 2005: 448.
103. Gieysztor 1982: 125.
104. Pálsson, Edwards 1986: 169.

The name Tjarnaglofi is apparently a corrupted version of the Slavic Černoglav, where *tjarna* corresponds to *cherno* and *glofi* to *glav*.[105] The etymology of the name Černoglav is indisputable and means the one with the black head. Brückner believes the name is just a deformation of Triglav[106], and Ivanov-Toporov identify him to Černobog[107], while Schmittlein, inspired by Unbegaun, considered Triglav, Černobog and Černoglav as simple epithets[108]. Kalik and Uchitel, being based on the fact that in the saga he is named as a god of victory who went with them on military campaigns, consider him as a god of war[109]. For our research, this could mean that the god had some death-related characteristics given the fact that in some cases gods of war were connected to death[110]. Moreover, according to Pestalozzi, Chernoglav's silver moustache provides "an interesting monumental parallel"[111] between him, Perun's idol in Kiev that according to the *Russian Primary Chronicle* had a silver head and a golden moustache[112]. Finally Černoglav's name appears in toponyms, just like Triglav's[113] but also those of other gods', and mainly of Perun[114]. These are the elements we possess for Chernoglav and are in no way sufficient, firstly, to consider him with certainty to be a parallel of Triglav and Černobog (and from there of Veles), and, secondly, to characterize him as a death deity.

Conclusion

All these connections between Černobog-Veles-Triglav-Černoglav and again Černobog would have been of great interest and great significance if there were sources to confirm them. Any argumentation is based on linguistic assumptions,

---

105. The philologist Wilhelm Blum proposed another etymology according to which the first part of the name is Slavic, the second Germanic: in this case, the suffix "glofi" would mean "the claw", and consequently the name of the god would mean "the one with the black claw".
106. Brückner 1985: 128–129.
107. Ivanov, Toporov 1965: 56-57.
108. Schmittlein 1960: 183-184. See also Lajoye 2015: 14.
109. See chapter "Pizamar and Chernoglav" in Kalik, Uchitel 2019.
110. Such an example is Mórrígan, the fearsome goddess of battle and prophesy. See: Freeman 2017: 90, 134.
111. Pettazzoni 1967: 162.
112. Sinjavskij 2007: 100.
113. In both cases it is not sure that the toponyms are connected to gods' local worship.
114. Boskovic 2006: URL : http://journals.openedition.org/mimmoc/174. See also Lajoye 2015:44-46.

etymologies that seem reasonable but not sufficient, with few sources presenting some of the above deities as rulers of the otherworld: namely one, which is also written by a Christian biographer -Ebo- who quite possibly reshaped and modified the incomprehensible non-Christian beliefs. Most of the deities examined by this article seem to be actually linked to death, but mainly in the context of the nature's cycles of death-rebirth, destruction-fertility, which in no way implies the qualities of an underworld ruler.

In addition, the gods we have investigated, but also the gods of Indo-European as well as world mythology more generally, have multiple properties (with some predominant ones) and these can vary from community to community because there is no doctrine imposing certain constants, defining a well-fixed religion of a large scale. They can therefore display a multitude of features, attributes and names. This is not a rule only in the case of minor mythology[115] (where a rusalka for example may be a villain or charitable, an agent of devastation or prosperity, to be described as beautiful or ugly etc.), but in the case of major mythology as well, where gods and deities can be associated with agriculture, fertility, sickness, destruction or death. Therefore, we consider that of the above-mentioned deities are possibly related to the central in pre-Christian religion's central scheme of death- (nature's) rebirth / destruction-prosperity cycles, but that in no case (or almost none, if we exclude one in the case of Triglav and on in the case of Nya) do the sources refer to an otherworld ruler, such as Hel and Hades. The problem becomes more acute if we consider that we basically do not have any information about the underworld, so that some theorists, as we said at the beginning, have claimed that the Slavic underworld did not exist.

All this uncertainty resulting from the lack of sources has forced and still forces those involved in the study of Slavic mythology to resort in many cases to simplistic schematizations as we showed above, or even to seek easier solutions in order to satisfy the necessity of a death god's existence. Such an example is Koshchei the Immortal[116] who in some cases has been surprisingly enough considered as the ancient Russian lord of death[117]. Koshei is a character of Russian fairy tales and not of folk beliefs, but Rybakov insists on his name's origin from the old Slavic

---

115. The minor (or small) mythology is the one which concerns the gods, the genii, the spirits and in general the supernatural beings considered as minor. Régis Boyer summarizes his main ideas in: « Petite mythologie : qu'est-ce à dire ? », in Bayard, Guillaume 2010 : 63-74.
116. See in "Kashhej Bessmertnyj" in Ivanov, Toporov 1990: 278.
117. Leonard, McClure 2007: 204.

kosh'noe, that cannot be found in old Russian dictionaries but only in the phrase of *The Chronicle of Novgorod* "*i ply (idol Peruna) iz sveta vo kosh'noe, sirech' vo tmu kromeshnuju*". For Rybakov this *kosh'noe* has undoubtedly an infernal meaning, connected to the Slavic kingdom of the dead[118]. Gruntovskij[119], Lydko[120], Haney[121], Baranov[122] and others find the theory plausible but it is understood that we cannot come to a safe conclusion based on a word's single appearance in a chronicle.

Another, even more complicated example, is the name Pekla-bog, the god of *peklo*, a name that is used in Slavic languages for the Christian Hell. It comes from the church Slavic пькълъ and old Slavic пьцьлъ, originating from Proto-Slavic **pъkъlъ*, from Proto-Indo-European **pik-* ("pitch"), and is already used in 11th century[123]. However in 1842 the Czech philosopher and expert on Slavic mythology Ignatius Jan Hanuš, pointed out in his book that Pekla-Bog (a compound formed by the word *peklo*), corresponds to the death judge Schiwa (Živa). For this he was quite possibly based on Frencel, who dedicates a whole chapter to this infernal God, as he calls him (*De Picollo, deo inferorum*)[124]. This Picollo or also Peckols, Pockols, Patollo corresponds to deities or spirits worshiped by the Old Prussians. They are mentioned in quite a lot of sources in 15th-16th century[125] but it is certain that the origin of the name is not Slavic but Baltic[126]. Consequently the name has nothing to do with the Slavic пькълъ and *peklo*, as was thought by the scholars of that period. The name Pekelnybog was quite possibly a creation of the people that added the Slavic bog next to the Baltic *pekelny*. What is even more interesting is the name Peklabog that seems to be a pure invention by Hanuš, who considered *pekelny* as Slavic, and explained *Peklabog* as the Slavic god of hell. What is finally even more interesting than all these, is that the name Peklabog re-appears in Korn's *Populäre Mythologie* published

---

118. Rybakov 2013: 264-265.
119. Gruntovskij 2002: 47.
120. Lydko 2002: 111.
121. Baranov 2002: 76.
122. Haney 1998: 120.
123. Mel'nyčuk 1982: 328.
124. Frencel 1719: 232-234.
125. Such as in a letter of Bishop of Warmia to the Pope (1418), in the *Sudovian Book* (1520s) or in the *Preussische Chronik* (1529) of Simon Grunau. See Balsys 2010: 223-231.
126. In Lithuanian *piktas, piktasis, pikta dvasia, piktis, pikis, pikulas* means evil. See Valencova 2016: 79.

three years after Hanus' book, and then in 1854 Ipolyi's *Magyar mythologia*[127] (and from there in certain Hungarian dictionaries), as well as in an article called *About historical sources issued from etymologies* in 1863 *Revue trimestrielle*[128]. Hanuš' creation that was based on a very insecure mythological reference from the 18th century, became a commonplace and entered the unlimited uncanny space formed and recycled by the Internet's ouroboros. Thus, today we can find the name Peklabog in a Wikipedia list of deities of the Slavic religion, identified to Nya, as well as in an important number of related sites. This final step is the definitive one, the way false information becomes established.

Reality is less satisfying and does not meet the needs of a broad audience because of its uncertainty. The lack of sources severely hampers the situation and, in our opinion, does not allow us to draw clear conclusions. Neither Morana, nor Karačun, Černobog, Černoglav, nor Veles, and not even Nya and Triglav, about whom we have two specific testimonies, cannot be qualified as rulers of the otherworld, even if they all seem to be connected to death, mostly through the death-rebirth scheme. In our opinion, research should continue under the sole condition of strict faithfulness to the sources. This is the only way to remain optimistic in terms of solving a problem that is not insignificant since it concerns an important part of the Slavic worldview. It is certain, however, that optimism and the expectation of finding a needle in a haystack, cannot be equated with finding it.

References

> Albinus, L., 2000: *The House of Hades: Studies in Greek Eschatology*. Oxford, Aarhus University Press.
> Balsys, R., 2010: *Lietuvių ir prūsų dievai, deivės, dvasios: nuo apeigos iki prietaro*. Klaipėda, Klaipėdos Univ. Leidykla.
> Baranov, D. A., 2002: *Jetnicheskoe edinstvo i specifika kul'tur: materialy Pervyh Sankt Peterburgskih jetnograficheskih chtenij*. Sankt Peterburg, Rossijskij jetnograficheskij muzej.
> Bayard, F., Guillaume, A. (dir.), 2010, *Formes et difformités médiévales, en hommage à Claude Lecouteux*. Paris, PUPS.
> Belaj, V., 2007: *Hod kroz godinu: mitska pozadina hrvatskih narodnih vjerovanja i obicaja*. Zagreb, Golden marketing - Tehnička knjiga.
> Böhmer, W. (ed.), 1835: *Thomas Kantzows Chronik von Pommern in niederdeutscher Mundart sammt einer Auswahl aus den übrigen ungedruckten*

---

127. Ipolyi 1854: 381.
128. *Revue trimestrielle* 1863: 36.

Schriften desselben. Stettin.

Boisacq, E., 1916: *Dictionnaire étymologique de la langue grecque, étudiée dans ses rapports avec les autres langues indo-européennes*. Heidelberg, Winter.

Boskovic, S., 2013: « Les survivances du paganisme slave dans les rites funéraires serbes », *Revue du CEES, Numéro 2 - L'imaginaire slave dans la culture, la société et le langage*. URL : http://etudesslaves.edel.univ-poitiers.fr/index.php?id=395

Boskovic, S., 2006: « Une figure de l'exclusion : la mémoire mythique dans la topographie des Balkans », *Les Cahiers du MIMMOC* [online], 1. URL : http://journals.openedition.org/mimmoc/174

Brückner, A., 1929-1930 : "Fantazje mitologiczne", *Slavia, casopis pro slovanskou filologii*, vol.8, 340-351.

Brückner, A., 1985: *Mitologia słowiańska i polska*. Warszawa, Państwowe Wydawn.

Brückner A., 1892: "Mythologische Studien III", *Archiv für Slavische Philologie*, vol. 14, 161-191.

Caillois, R., 1936: « Les spectres de midi dans la démonologie slave : les faits », *Revue des études slaves*, t. 16, fasc. 1-2, 18-37.

Čajkanović, V., 1994: *O vrhovnom bogu u staroj srpskoj religiji*. Beograd, Srpska književna zadruga.

Chausidis, N., 2005: *Poganska religija Slavena u svjetlu ranosrednjovijekovnih materijalnih nalaza s područija Balkana*. Pula, Histria Antiqua.

Cooper, B., 2005: "The Word "vampire": Its Slavonic Form and Origin", Journal of Slavic Linguistics, Vol. 13, No. 2 (summer—fall 2005), 251-270.

Cross S.H., Sherbowitz-Wetzor O.P. (ed.), 1953: *The Russian Primary Chronicle: Laurentian Text*. Cambridge, Massachusetts, Mediaeval Academy of America.

Čulkov, M. D., 2016 (1987): *Peresmešnik, ili Slavenskie skazki*. Moskva, Direktmedia.

Dal', V.I. (ed.), 1881: T*olkovyj slovar' živogo velikorusskogo jazyka: sovremennoe napisanie : v četyreh tomah, Vol. 2*. Sankt Peterburg, Izdanie knigoprodavca-tipografa M. O. Vol'fa.

Davidson, H., 2013 (1943): *The Road to Hel: A Study of the Conception of the Dead in Old Norse Literature*. Cambridge, Cambridge University Press.

Dixon-Kennedy, M., 1999: *Encyclopedia of Russian & Slavic myth and legend*. Santa Barbara, ABC-Clio.

Dukova, U., 1997: *Die Bezeichnungen der Dämonen im Bulgarischen*. München, Verlag Otto Sagner.

Dynda, J., 2014: "The Three-Headed One at the Crossroad: A Comparative Study of the Slavic God Triglav", *Studia mythologica Slavica* 17, Institute of Slovenian Ethnology, 57-82.

Edmonds, R., 2004: *Myths of the Underworld Journey in Plato, Aristophanes,*

and the Orphic Gold Tablets: A Path Neither Simple Nor Single. New York, Cambridge University Press.
Eliade, M., 1970: *De Zalmoxis à Gengis-Khan : études comparatives sur les religions et le folklore de la Dacie et de l'Europe Orientale.* Paris, Payot.
Frazer, J., 1925: *The Golden Bough: A Study in Magic and Religion, Vol. 1 (abridged edition).* New York, Macmillan Company.
Freeman, Ph., 2017: *Celtic mythology : tales of gods, goddesses, and heroes.* Oxford, Oxford University Press.
Frencel, A., 1719: "Commentarius philologico-historicus de diis Soraborum aliorumque Slavorum, in quo Slavorum antiquitates, multaque hactenus obscura illustrantur, aut minus recte intellecta & scripta corriguntur" in *Scriptores rerum lusaticarum…*, T. 2. Lipsiae et Budissae, D. Richter.
Furlan, M., 2009: "Polisemija in homonimija slovanskega pridevnika *morьskъ", *Studia etymologica Brunensia 6*, ed. I. Janyšková, H. Karlíková, Praha, 101–112.
Gieysztor, A., 2018 (1982): *Mitologia Słowian.* Warszawa, Wydawnictwa Uniwersytetu Warszawskiego.
Gimbutas, M., 1974: "The Lithuanian God Velnias", in ed. Larson, G., Littleton, C.S., Puhvel, J., *Myth in Indo-European Antiquity.* Berkeley; Los Angeles; London, University of California Press, 87-92.
Gimbutas, M., 1987: "Slavic Religion", *The Encyclopedia of Religions*, ed. Eliade, M. vol. 13, New York, 353-361.
Grimm, J., 1983 (1844): *Teutonic mythology, Vol. 2.* New York, Dover Publications.
Gruel-Apert, L., 2014: *Le monde mythologique russe.* Paris, Imago.
Gruntovskij, A. V., 2002: *Potehi strašnye i smešnye : kniga o fol'klornom teatre, skomorohah, rjaženyh i kulačnyh bojah.* Moskva, Russkaja zemlja.
Haney, J., 1998: *An Introduction to the Russian Folktale.* New York; London, Sharpe.
Hoddinott, R.F., 1963: *Early Byzantine Churches in Macedonia & Southern Serbia.* New York, Palgrave Macmillan.
Ipolyi, A., 1854: *Magyar mythologia.* Budapest, Európa Könyvkiadó.
Ivanov, V. V., 1998: *Russkij mifologion: učebnoe posobie.* Petrozavodsk, KGPU.
Ivanov, V. V., Toporov, V. N., 1973: « A comparative study of the group of Baltic mythological terms from the root *vel- », *Baltistica*, IX, 1, 1973, 21-22.
Ivanov, V.V., Toporov, V.N., 1990: "Kaščej Bessmertnyj" in *Mifologičeskij slovar'*, red. Meletinskij, E.M., Moskva, Sovetskaja enciklopedija.
Ivanov, V. V., Toporov, V. N., 1988: *Mify narodov mira: enciklopedija v 2 t.*, gl. red. S. A. Tokarev, T.2, Moskva, Sovetskaja jenciklopedija.
Ivanov, V.V., Toporov, V.N., 1965: *Slavianskie iazykovye modeliruiuščie semiotičeskie sistemy*, Moskva, Nauka.
Jacobson, R., 2010: *Selected Writings V. 7: Contributions to Comparative Mythology. Studies in Linguistics and Philology.* Berlin; Boston, De Gruyter Mouton.

Jakobson, R., 1949: "Slavic Mythology", *Funk and Wagnall's Standard Dictionary of Folklore, Mythology and Legend*, New York, Funk and Wagnall, 1025-1028.

Jacobson, E., 1992: *The Deer Goddess of Ancient Siberia: A Study in the Ecology of Belief*. Leiden, Brill.

Johns, A., 2004: *Baba Yaga, The Ambiguous Mother and Witch of the Russian Folklore*. New York; Washington; Bern, Peter Lang.

Kalik, J., Uchitel, A., 2019: *Slavic Gods and Heroes*. New York: Routledge.

Karamzin, N.M., 1892: *Istorija Gosudarstva Rossijskogo, T.1*. Sankt Peterburg, Tipografija Zhe. Evdokimova.

Katičić, R., 2008: *Božanski boj : tragovima svetih pjesama naše pretkršćanske starine*. Zagreb, Odsjek za etnologiju i kulturnu antropologiju Filozofskog fakulteta, Ibis grafika; Mošćenička Draga, Katedra Čakavskog sabora Općine.

Klaniczay, G.; Pócs, É. (ed.), 2005: *Communicating with the Spirits*, Vol. 1. Budapest; New York, Central European University Press.

Kolankiewicz, L., 1999: *Dziady. Teatr święta zmarłych*. Gdańsk, DiG.

Kowalik, A., 2004: *Kosmologia dawnych Słowian: prolegomena do teologii politycznej dawnych Słowian. Kraków, Nomos*.

Krukova, T. A., 1947: "Vosdenie rusalki, v sele Oskine Voronežkoj oblasti", *Sovetskaja Etnografia* 1 (1947), 185-192.

Kulišić, S., 1979: *Stara slovenska religija u svjetlu novijih istraživanja posebno balkanoloških*. Sarajevo, Akademija nauka i umjetnosti Bosne i Hercegovine.

Lajoye, P., 2015: *Perun, dieu slave de l'orage: Archéologie, histoire, folklore*. Lisieux, Lingva.

Lecouteux, Cl., 2011: *Phantom Armies of the Night: The Wild Hunt and the Ghostly Processions of the Undead*. Rochester, Inner Traditions (ebook).

Lecouteux, Cl., 2001: « Typologie de quelques morts malfaisants », *Cahiers slaves* 3, 2001, 238-242.

Leger, L., 1901: *La Mythologie slave*. Paris, Ernest Leroux.

Leonard, S., McClure, M., 2007: *Myth and knowing: an introduction to world mythology*. Boston, McGraw Hill.

Łowmiański, H., 1979: *Religia Słowian i jej upadek*. Warszawa, Państwowe Wydawn. Naukowe.

Lydko, D., 2002: *Mater' Lada: božestvennoe rodoslovie slavjan : jazyčeskij panteon*. Moskva, Eksmo.

Máchal, J., 1918, "Slavic Mythology", *The Mythology of all races*, vol.3, ed. Gray, L. H., Boston, Archaeological Institute of America, 217-389.

Malingudis, Ph., 1990: «K voprosu o ranneslavjanskom jazyčestve: svidetel'stva Psevdo-Kesarija», *Vizantijskij vremennik*, T. 51, Moskva : Izd. Akad. Nauk SSSR, 1990, 86-91.

Mallory, J.P., Adams, D.Q., 1997: *Encyclopedia of Indo-European culture*. London,

Fitzroy Dearborn.

Marjanic, S., 2003: "The Dyadic Goddess and Duotheism in Nodilo's the Ancient Faith of the Serbs and the Croats", Studia Mythologica Slavica VI, 2003, 181-203.

Massey, G., 1883: *The natural genesis: or second part of A book of the beginnings*, Vol. 1. London, Williams and Norgate.

Mathieu-Colas, M., 2017: Dictionnaire des noms de divinités. Accessible at : https://halshs.archives-ouvertes.fr/halshs-00794125v7/document

Matusiak, S., 1908: *Olimp Polski : podług Długosza*. Lwów,-.

Mel'nyčuk, O. S., 1982: *Etymolohičnyï slovnyk ukraïns'koï movy: v semy tomakh, Vol.4*. Moskva, Nauk. Dumka.

Meyer, K., 1931: *Fontes historiae religionis slavicae*. Berlin, De Gruyter.

Michel, R., Forbes, N. (trans.), 1914: *The Chronicle of Novgorod*. London, Camden Society.

Močul'ski, V. N., 1889: "O mnimom dualizme v mifologii Slavian", *Russkii filologičeskii vestnik*, vol, 2 (1889), 153-204.

Moszyński, L., 1992: *Die vorchristliche Religion der Slaven im Lichte der slavischen Sprachwissenschaft*. Köln; Weimar, Böhlau.

Münster, S., 1554: *Cosmographiae universalis*. Basilea, apud Henrichum Petri.

Nedo, P., 1963: "Czorneboh und Bieleboh, zwei angebliche slawische Kultstätten in der Oberlausitz", *Lětopis*, Reihe C – Volkskunde 6-7, 5–18.

Nehring, W., 1903: "Der Name Belbog in der slawischen Mythologie", *Archiv für slavische philologie*, vol. 25 (1903), 66-73.

Niederle, L., 1926: *Manuel de l'antiquité slave. Vol.2, La civilization*. Paris, Champion.

Niederle, L., 1911: *Slovanské starožitnosti: Oddíl kulturní. Život starých Slovanů, Vol. 1-2*. Praha, Busík-Kohout.

Niederle, L., 1924: *Slovanské starožitnosti : Oddíl kulturní. [II], Zivot starých Slovanů*. Prague, Bursík a Kohout.

Nodilo, N., 1981 (1885-1890): *Stara vjera Srba i Hrvata (Religija Srbâ i Hrvatâ, na glavnoj osnovi pjesama, priča i govora narodnog)*. Split, Logos.

Obolensky, D., 1948: *The Bogomils: A Study in Balkan Neo-Manichaeism*. Cambridge, Cambridge University Press.

Pálsson, H., Edwards, P. (ed.), 1986: *Knytlinga saga: the history of the kings of Denmark*. Odense, Odense University Press.

Pertz, G. H. (ed.), 1846: *Adami Gesta Hammaburgensis ecclesiae pontificum*. Hannoverae, impensis Bibliopolii Hahniani.

Petruhin, V. (red.), 1995: *Slavjanskaja mifologija: enciklopedicheskij slovar' podgotovlen sotrudnikami Instituta slavjanovedenija i balkanistiki Rossijskoj Akademii nauk*. Moskva, Jellis Lak.

Pettazzoni, R., 1967: *Essays on the history of religions*. Leiden, E.J. Brill.

Pigulevskaja, I.S., 2011: *Istorija, mify i bogi drevnyh slavjan*. Moskva, Centrpoligraf.
Pisani, V., 1950: *Le Religioni dei Celti e dei Balto-Slavi nell'Europa precristiana*. Milan, Istituto Editoriale Galileo.
Rayor, D. J. (trans.), 2004: *The Homeric Hymns: A Translation, with Introduction and Notes*. Berkeley; Los Angeles; London, University of California Press.
[...], *Revue trimestrielle*, Vol. 37, Bruxelles, 1863, 36.
Rix, H., 2001: *Lexikon der indogermanischen Verben*. Wiesbaden, Dr. Ludwig Reichert Verlag.
Robinson, Ch. (trans.), 1920: *The Life of Otto Apostle of Pomerania 1060-1139 by Ebo and Herbordus*. New York, Macmillan Co..
Rosenwein, B., 2018: *Reading the Middle Ages : sources from Europe, Byzantium, and the Islamic world*. New York, University of Toronto Press.
Rusinowa, I., 2002: *Silva Rerum Pultusiensis*. Pułtusk, Wyższa Szkoła Humanistyczna.
Rybakov, B. A., 2013 (1987): *Jazyčestvo drevnej Rusi*. Moskva, Akademicheskij Proekt.
Šafárik, P.J., 1869: *Geschichte der slawischen Sprache und Literatur nach allen Mundarten*. Prag, F. Tempsky.
Šahmatov, A., 1916: *Povest' vremennyh let*. Petrograd, Imperatorskaja Arheografičeskaja Komissija.
Schmittlein, A., 1960: « Les noms des dieux des Slaves de la Baltique », *Revue Internationale d'Onomastique*, 3 (1960), 167-194.
Scott, W., 1822: *Ivanhoe*. Edinburg, Archibald Constable.
Sedakova, O., *Pojetika obrjada: pogrebal'naja obrjadnost' vostočnyh i južnyh slavjan*. Moskva, Indrik.
Sieradzki, A. 2017: "Teonim Perun w leksyce średnio- i nowopolskiej (na podstawie słowników)", Język. Religia. Tożsamość 1 (15) 2017, 199-211.
Sinjavskij, A., 2007: *Ivan the fool : a cultural history : Russian folk belief*. Moscow; Chicago; London, GLAS New Russian Writing.
Słupecki, L. P., 1994: *Slavonic pagan sanctuaries*. Warsaw, Institut of Archeology and Ethnology/ Polish Academy of Sciences.
Smith, J., 1993: *Map is not territory: studies in the history of religions*. Chicago, University of Chicago Press.
Sobolen, A.N., 1999: *Mifologija slavjan [Zagrob. mir po drevnerusim predstavlenijam*. Sankt-Peterburg, Lan'.
Stangé-Zhirovova, N., 1998: *Une autre Russie: Fêtes et rites traditionnels du peuple russe*. Paris, Peeters.
Szyjewski, A., 2010: *Religia Słowian*. Kraków, Wydawnictwo WAM.
Tatiščev, V. N., 1962: "Istorii Rossijskoj", in *Sobranie sochinenij*. V. 1, Moskva, Nauka.
Thietmarus Merseburgensis, 1807: *Dithmari Episcopi Merseburgensis Chronicon*. Norimbergae, Sumptibus I.L.S. Lechneri.

Tokarev, A.A., 1957: *Religioznye verovanija vostočnoslavjanskih narodov XIX-načala XX v.*. Moskva, Akademii nauk SSSR.

Tolstoj, N.I.; Agapkina, T. A (ed.), 1995: *Slavjanskie drevnosti etnolingvističeskij slovar' v pjati tomah / Vol. 3: K (Krug) - P (Perepelka)*. Moskva, Mezhdunarodnye otnoshenija.

Trkanjec, L., "Chthonic aspects of the Pomeranian deity Triglav and other tricephalic characters in Slavic mythology", *Studia mythologica Slavica* 16, Institute of Slovenian Ethnology, 9-25.

Unbegaun, B. O., 1948: «La religion des anciens Slaves» in Grenier, A., *Les religions etrusques et romaines*. Paris, Mana, 2, III, 387-445.

Valencova, M., "K issledovaniju balto-slavjanskoj demonologii", *Res humanitariae*, T. XX, 2016, 70-88.

Vasmer, M., 1987: *Etimologičeskij slovar' russkogo jazyka*. Moskva, Progress.

Vinogradova, L. N., 1995: *Slavjanskaja mifologija. Enciklopedičeskij slovar'*. Moskva, Jellis Lak.

Vološina, T.A., 1996: *Jazyčeskaja mifologija slavjan*. Moskva, Feniks.

Wagner, M.A., 2005: *Le Cheval dans les croyances germaniques*. Paris, Honoré-Champion.

Wheatcroft, A., 2014: "On the Topography of the Greek Underworld and the 'Orphic' Gold Tablets", Prandium - The Journal of Historical Studies, Vol. 3, No. 1 (Fall, 2014), URL: http://jps.library.utoronto.ca/index.php/prandium/editor/submission/21849/

Wienecke, E., 1940: *Untersuchungen zur Religion der Westlaven*. Leipzig, Otto Harrassowitz.

Wolverton, L. (ed.), 2009: *Cosmas Pragensis, The chronicle of the Czechs*. Washington, D.C., Catholic University of America Press.

Young, J.I., 1966: *The Prose Edda: Tales from Norse Mythology*. Berkeley; Los Angeles:, University of California Press.

Znayenko, M., 1993: "On the Concept of Chernebog and Bielbog in Slavic Mythology" *Acta Slavica Iaponica*, Vol. 11-12, Hokaido, Collegium Slavicum Academiae Hokkaido, 1993, 177-185.

Znayenko, M., 1980: *The gods of the ancient Slavs*. Columbus; Ohio, Slavica.

Zochios, S., 2012: *Le Cauchemar mythique : étude morphologique de l'oppression nocturne dans les textes médiévaux et les croyances populaires*, PhD, Université de Grenoble III.

Zochios, S., 2016: « Baba Yaga, les sorcières et les démons ambigus de l'Europe orientale », *Revue Sciences/Lettres*, 4, URL: https://journals.openedition.org/rsl/973

Zochios, S., 2018: « Interprétation ethnolinguistique de termes mythologiques néo-helléniques d'origine slave désignant de morts malfaisants », *Revue des études slaves*, 38/3, 2018, 310-316

Slovak mythological vocabulary on the Common Slavic background
Ethno-linguistic aspect

Marina M. Valentsova

Senior Research Advisor, Department of Ethnolinguistics and Folklore, Institute of Slavic studies, Russian Academy of Sciences, Moscow

mvalent@mail.ru

Abstract. In the all-Slavic ethnolinguistic studies, the Slovak tradition is still not sufficiently covered, first of all, the mythological vocabulary has not been compiled and analyzed in various aspects. This article, based on the earlier work of 2013, is an attempt to analyze Slovak demonological vocabulary among and against the background of other Slavic vocabularies: to determine the amount of common Slavic mythonyms in it (for example, *čarovnica, divá žena*); to examine its correspondence with other West Slavic (Moravian, Czech and Polish) terminological systems (the terms *rarášek, škriatok, permoník*); to analyze the Slovak-East Slavic (*rusalka*) and Slovak-South Slavic (*víla, moria noha*) parallels; to reveal the own Slovak vocabulary of demons (such as *futkač, molek, grgalica* etc.). Particular attention is paid to the analysis of the Carpathian features in Slovak demonological beliefs (beliefs about the «double-souled» men, flying dragons) and their vocabulary (*striga, bosorka, šarkan*, etc.).

Keywords. Slavic ethnolinguistics, Slovak demonology, Slavic mythological vocabulary, comparative mythological studies

FOLK MYTHOLOGICAL BELIEFS as an integral part of the traditional spiritual culture and vocabulary describing them are gathered and generalized for a number of Slavic traditions in monographs, dictionaries and encyclopedias[1], as well as in papers, studying this topic on a large Slavic scale[2].

---

1. E.g., Čerepanova 1983, Vlasova 1995, Pełka 1987, Baranowski 1981, Georgieva 1993, etc.
2. SD, Vinogradova 2000, Plotnikova 2004, etc.

At the same time, the Slovak tradition is not sufficiently represented in Common Slavic studies.[3] There are still no generalizing ethnographic sources on folk demonology or special works on mythological vocabulary. This subject and vocabulary are partly summarized in the *Encyclopaedia of Folk Culture of Slovakia* (*EĽKS*) and the encyclopedia *Slovakia* (*Slovensko*), which are, unfortunately, too generalized and do not present numerous details or exact localization for the information given. Meanwhile, the Slovak tradition has a special place in the culture of the Slavs, occupying the central area of the Slavic world, where the West, East and South Slavic languages and peoples meet each other and were meeting during long centuries[4], whereas the Slovak language, probably heterogeneous in origin, reflects the dialectal features of all three groups of Slavic languages. At the same time, "there is a particularly close connection between the South Slavic languages and the Slovak language, or more precisely, one of its dialects, which currently takes the central position and in the Middle Ages was spoken in most of present-day Southern Slovakia".[5] This connection is a constituent part of the isoglottic complex, which unites the West and South Slavic languages, for example, the Bulgarian language and the North Lechitic dialect group, Slovenian and Sorbian languages.[6]

Mythological vocabulary reflecting the archaic views of the Slavs is of utmost interest in this regard. Some lexemes of this group trace back to Indo-European roots and represent the pre-Slavic heritage, others characterize contacts, migrations, territory of ethnic groups' settlements. On the one hand, conclusions drawn for a particular language as a whole are also relevant for mythological vocabulary, on the other hand – in such vocabulary there are features determined by the "nature of the correlation of the word and the concept in the demonological system," and a "special semantic status". This refers to the unusual pattern of interaction of the name and the "reality" denoted by it.[7]

Identification of lexical and semantic links of the Slovak demonological system (as a subsystem of the mythological one) with other Slavic traditions seems promising. In this we rely on the theoretical views of N.I. Tolstoy on existence of not only

---

3. The two vast articles on the Slovak supernatural beings were published in French about a hundred years ago (I thank Patrice Lajoye for pointing to them): Polívka 1922a and Polívka 1922b (they are based on primarily folklore material and mainly fairy tales).
4. See Ivić 1957–1958, Bernštejn 2000, Avanesov 1977, Vendina 2008, etc.
5. Kurkina 1985: 67.
6. *Ibid.*: 66.
7. Vinogradova 2001: 16.

linguistic, but also cultural dialects, which are practically "the only source for the internal reconstruction of the earliest state of Slavic spiritual culture," including mythological ideas and the system of demonological characters.[8]

The main bulk of the Slovak mythological vocabulary in general and the names of mythological characters (hereinafter – MC) in particular, which are mainly considered in the article, is represented by **Common Slavic** units. It includes lexemes with the following roots: *bab-, *blǫd-, *bog-, *čar-, *div-, *gad-, *mar-/mor-, *sъmьrt-, *svět-, *věd-/*věšt-, *vьlk-, *vod-, *vorg-, *zna-: *baba, boh, blúdička, čarodejnica, čarovnica, veštica, vražka, vedma, (domovy, biely) had, mora /mara, vlkodlak, divá žena, vodník, smrtka, svetielka*, etc. Some lexemes still have their Common Slavic meanings (*baba* 'female demon of different qualities', *upír* 'vampire', *mora* 'nightmare', *vedma* 'witch', *vodník* 'water elf', *rusalka* 'summer female spirit'), and others have different ones that are characteristic of Slovak as well as other Carpathian dialects (*bohyňa* 'wise woman', *bohynka* 'wild forest woman', *čarnoknižník* 'black magician') or of all West Slavic dialects (*blúdičky, svetielka* 'wanderting lights'). The latter, together with mythonyms unknown in East and South Slavic languages (*rarášek* 'dragon of enrichment', *pikulík* 'demon of enrichment', *permoník* 'spirit of the mines', *škriatok* 'wealth giving spirit', etc.), form a group of specific West Slavic MC names. As will be shown below, the majority of Common Slavic mythonyms form lexical or semantic isoglottic lines, which combine dialect groups with separate Slavic languages and dialects in different ways.

A considerable number of Slovak mythonyms belong to the **Carpathian** (or only Slavic-Carpathian) vocabulary, that is, they are common to the Slovak, Carpathian-Ukranian, South Polish, Moravian (and often also Romanian, Moldavian and Hungarian) language areas (for example, *striga* 'witch', *bosorka* 'witch', *ďug* 'demon of malady, devil', *šarkaň* 'weather dragon', *chmurnik* 'cloud-breaker' etc.), and often have correspondences in South Slavic languages.

Specific Slovak MC names, that are not found to define characters with a similar set of attributes in other Slavic tradition, make up a small but interesting group.

Let us consider these groups in more detail (to save space, the main sources of the analyzed vocabulary for each tradition are listed at the end of the article).

Common Slavic vocabulary

Speaking about the common Slavic vocabulary in Slovak mythonymy, we mean the similarities at the level of the root composition of lexemes. Due to the fact that

---

8. Tolstoj 1995: 46, 47

the vocabulary of spiritual culture cannot have complete semantic identity, in some cases the term meanings are generalized, the semes (units of the meaning) that are not essential to the image are ignored, and in other cases, close attention is focused on the details of the MC images in view of their importance in genetic and typological sense.

Perhaps the only lexeme that has Common Slavic correspondences, both in terms of expression and in terms of content, is Slovak *čarovnica* 'sorceress' (*čarujú čarovnici* – Radava, dist. Nove Zamky).[9] The difference applies only to the forms of masculine gender in the meaning of 'sorcerer', that are absent in the Slovak and Sorbian languages (here they mean 'plant Circaea alpina').

The root **div-* is present in all Slavic languages (mainly in compound nouns and stem compositions). The image of a MC designated by it is not certain, often close to the other MCs common for each individual tradition, for example, to *boginka* for the West and *vila* for the South Slavs.[10] In Slovak *diva žena* (*diva zona*) 'a wild forest woman' is synonymous with both *boginka* and *vila*: it is an evil creature living in the forest, near the water, in holes in the ground, in the rocks'; *divak* 'boginka's child' (Zamagurie). The presence of the whole family of "wild" MC unites the Slovak tradition with the Moravian one: *divížena* 'wild forest woman', *divižák* 'wild forest woman's husband', *divúch, divoženče* 'wild forest woman's child, that she dumped off instead of a human baby'.

An absolutely different character (as well as another root **dikъ*, however, related to **divъ*[11], is represented by the East Slavs: Bel. *dzikija ľudzi* (дзікія людзі) "wild people" – 'single-eyed and large-eared, tailed mythical creatures that eat people'; Rus. *dikar', dikij, dikoj, diken'kij mužičok* (дикарь, дикий, дикой, дикенький мужичок) 'the forest master, spirit of the forest', usually called *lešуу (леший)*. He shows up as a small man with a huge beard and a tail (Saratov.); *dikij (дикий)* 'devil' (Kostrom.), *dikon'kij (диконький)* 'evil spirit, causing paralysis' (Vyat.). An intermediate character is Ukr.-Carpath. *dika baba (діка баба)*, having W.-Slavic traits: 'she is beautiful, moves with the help of seven-league boots, swaps children and drinks their blood, seduces young men'.[12]

Lexical items with the root **div-/dikъ* oppose <u>the East Slavic area to the West and South Slavic areas</u>.

---

9. For an exhaustive list of lexemes in other Slavic languages, see: ESSJa 4: 25
10. See SD 2: 92-93
11. See *ESSJa* 5: 30, 36.
12. SD 2: 93.

In all Slavic languages, one can find lexical and character correspondences with the Slovak **mara, mora,** nora, mura, mor, zmor 'half-demon–half-human, who at night in the form of an animal, an object or a shapeless heaviness chokes and strangles, sucks milk or blood from the sleeping'; 'personified cause of diseases', 'materialized lovesickness'; 'the soul of a double-souled person' (Zamagurie); *mora, morka, saňimorka, zmora, múra, kaňimura, mur, mara, slepá mara* 'night butterfly; nightmare'; *mura, noční mura* 'butterfly'.[13]

In W.-Slav. and S.-Slav. languages the roots *mor-* is mainly represented, in Slovak - equally *mor-* and *mar-*[14], in E.-Slav. – mainly *mar-*, with almost no derivatives. The lexeme with the formant *z: zmor(a)* is a West Slavic isogloss (present only in Slovak, Czech and Polish). Isoglottic lines already stated by the researchers to connect the Sorbian and Bulgarian languages should be added with one more: L.-Sor. *morawa, murawa* 'mora, something falling heavily on and tormenting in a dream', 'personification of night suffocation' – Bulg. *Marava, murava* (марава, мурава) 'nightmare', 'personification of a disease', 'invisible night spirit, falling heavily on and tormenting sleeping people'.[15] The root **mar-* is also widely represented in Germanic languages, in Romanian and Lithuanian.

In different Slavic traditions, this character specifies and develops various aspects of the image. In Slovaks, Poles, Moravians, the main function of *mara* is to choke at night and suck out blood and milk which exemplify lifeforce. The same image is characteristic of the South Slavs. Belarusians and Carpathian Ukrainians give *mara* the features of a walking dead. In North-West and South Russian dialects, *mara* transforms into a dreadful creature that lives in the house, into *kikimora* (кикимора). Lexeme *mara* also has the meaning 'butterfly' (in mythology, a butterfly corresponds to the soul), recorded in Slovak, Czech, Polish and South Slavic languages and apparently absent among East Slavs, where *mara* became a home spirit.

Slovak *mara/mora* has various ethno-linguistic parallels. For example, the motif of the internal organs (*mora* leaves the insides, the guts in front of the door when it enters the house through a keyhole – Šumjac, Brezno dist.[16]) draws the Slovak tradition closer to the Belarusian (*mara* has no skin, so all her internal organs are visible[17]). The idea of *mara* as a little girl with the face of an old woman and

---

13. For more information, see SD 3: 178–179; ESSJa 19: 211–214.
14. See more in Valencova 2013.
15. *Cf.* also ESSJa 19: 214
16. AT ÚEt, inv. Č. 168, etc.
17. BelM: 303.

uncombed hair (p. Kravany, Poprad.[18]) reminds of Russian *kikimora*.

Considering this MC, we can talk about semantic <u>opposition of the Eastern Slavic areas to the Western and Southern Slavic areas</u>.

The character functionally similar to *mora* is **nočnica** 'an MC sucking milk from a newborn baby's chest'; 'mora, night choking'; 'a night butterfly'; *nočnica* (*polnočnica*) 'a character that prevents a child from sleeping' (Kysuce, Gemer); 'mora that strangles at night'; *nočnica* 'a creature that falls heavily on a person and sucks on him at night' (region Mountain Spiš); *noclica, noclička* 'night butterfly' (Košice dist., E.-Slovak).

In various meanings, this lexeme (including variants with *pol-/polu-* (*пол-/полу-*) (prefix 'half-') is known in many Slavic languages: E.-Slav. *polunočnica* (*полуночница*) 'a night demon, mainly attacking children and depriving them of sleep' and 'a disease caused by it (insomnia and cries)'; Ukr. *nočnica, nička* (*ночница, нічка*); Carp-Ukr. *noclica* 'night butterfly', Hutsul. *ničnici* (*нічниці*) 'an MC, which takes away sleep and causes insomnia; diseases, night dreams'; 'an evil spirit that sucks on children and breastfeeding women'; Bel. *Načnica, načnicy* (*начніца, начніцы*) 'an MC, in which a cursed woman who never had children turns into after her death', 'personified childhood illness', Rus. *nochnitsa, nochnaya* (*ночница, ночная*) 'insomnia; child's disease and its personification'; *polinočnica, polinoč', polinoč'nik* (*полуночница, полуночь, полуночник* 'spirits of midnight; a disease and its personification').

In the South Slavic area: Serb. *nočnica* (*ноћница*) 'a night demon who enters a house where the light is on'; these demons beat children (N.-E. Bosnia), suck on children's breast (Levach – Shumadia) and adults; similar to *mora*; S.-Cr. *nočnica* 'night butterfly'; Sloven. *nočnine* (= *mora*) and others, 'an MC, taking a child's sleep'; *nočnina* or *mračnina* 'night spirit that prevents children from sleeping'.[19]

The lexeme *nočnica* <u>unites Slovakia with the East Slavic</u> on the one hand, and the Slovenian and Serbo-Croatian dialectal areas on the other hand and contraposes to the Western Slavic area (cf. lexically and semantically different: Morav. *nocuľa* 'a monster to frighten children walking at night'; Czech *noční poluda* 'evil spirit', 'midnight field spirit'; L.-Sorb. *nocnice*, pl. 'night wanderings of feverish patients'; Pol. *nocnica* 'wandering night lights'). Single Pol. *nocznica, nocnica* 'mora, zmora', 'wandering light', 'night butterfly' seems to be a loaned character and requires additional checking.

---

18. Michálek 1989: 283.
19. See for more information: SD 3: 436-437.

A certain parallel in the method of protection against *nochnitsa* makes up a Slovak-Belarussian isodox: "old women made knots from rags for protection against the night demon, and put them under a blanket for the day and outside the hut window for the night, then the night demon sucked the knot but not the baby" (Slov. – Dobšinský 1880: 115). To protect children from the night demon ... they made several puppets of dirty rags and put them in windows with the words: Глядзіце, лялечкі, каб мой маленькі спаў (Look, dolls, that my baby sleeps, i.e. take care of the sleeping of my baby), it was thought that the puppets would chase the night demon away.[20]

The terms with the root **vešt-** also show dialectal cultural differences in various Slavic languages.

Slovak *veštica* 'wisewoman, witch' (Orava); 'fortune-teller (on the mirror), sorceress' (Liptov); 'cuckoo', 'fortune-teller' (B. Bystrica, Turč., central Slovakia); 'fortune-teller, pythoness' (Turiec); also a male character: *veštec* 'person with supernatural abilities – wiseman, soothsayer, healer'; *věštík (-šč-)* 'wiseman', E.-Slov. *veščec, veščuch*. *Veštec* and *veštica* could both break or cast a hex (*odrobiť* and *porobiť*) (Orava). Babies who were born "in a cap" – *v čepci* (i.e. "in a shirt", 'with a silver spoon in one's mouth') or with teeth – *veštci* – could find treasure troves (Zvolen – Tekov, central Slovakia). A Common Slavic "etymological" meaning of the words with this rout, found in all Slavic dialects and represented in Old Slavic – 'witch, prophetess, wisewoman' – is, apparently, the original one. Negative connotations of the character prevail on the periphery of the Slavic area: in Northern Poland and especially among Kashubians – transformation of a wisewoman into a 'vampire': Pol. *wieszczy* – obs. 'witcher' (*wieszczek, wieszczka, wieszczycz*, even 'ghoul'), Kashub. *vešba* 'prophetic child born with a silver spoon in his mouth, or with teeth, who will grow and become a vampire', *vešči* 'vampire'. South Slavs have a witch as an image close to *mora*, a vampire: *veshtitsa* (вештица) 'a witch turning into a bat or a black bird and eating the hearts of children and young people at night, putting them to death'; Sloven. *vešča, veša* 'witch'; Bulg. *veščitsa, veščerica, veščer, veščik, veščernik*) (вещица, вещерица, вещер, вещик, вещерник) 'a witch whose soul flies away in the form of a black bird or a butterfly while sleeping to drink the blood of children and domestic animals; a sorceress who uses magic to throw the Sun and the Moon off the sky, rules the nature elements; predicts the future, opens secret thoughts, cures diseases'. The Moravians had a shift to the meaning of "forest woman": *věščica, věštka* 'wild woman'. The Russian population of the Urals and Southern Siberia

---

20. BelM: 340.

have the motif of "extraction" and eating of a fetus from a pregnant woman's body: *veshitsa* (вещица) 'sorceress, fortune-teller'; 'witch, werewolf eating babies, taking them from the womb of a pregnant woman' (Sib., Perm.), 'evil, forest spirit in the form of a squirrels or magpies' (Perm, Ufim., Tobol.), which is probably associated with beliefs of those (North-Russian) territories where people migrated from when making settlements in Siberia.

It is believed that the most archaic and "blurry" implicit features are characteristic of the areal center,[21] while with the spread of the phenomenon, new values and changes in the original semantics arise. It can be assumed that such center (rather, a range) was located within the <u>Sorbian-Slovak-Carpathian-Ukrainian territory</u>, including the Western Belarussian regions (here, only positive connotations of the term are registered – 'wisewoman', 'prophetess, soothsayer'). This idea is also supported by the absence of terms with the meaning of 'butterfly, night moth' in that area, which would indicate the character's witchcraft nature (whereas in Slovak, for example, there is a wide variety of "demonological" folk names for butterflies: *striga, bosorka, bohiňa, mora, černokňaznik*, etc.[22]). At the same time, in the Slavic South, the 'butterfly' meaning and corresponding beliefs are widely presented, cf. S.-Cr. dialect *vjěštica, viščica, věščica* 'moth, especially night moth'; Sloven. *veša, véšča, věška* 'night butterfly', *véščec* 'evening butterfly', Bulg. *veščica* (вещица) or *veščerica* (вещерица) 'night butterfly'. "Entomological" meanings of the considered root are also presented on the Russian territory: Transbaik. *vedin'* (вединь) 'horse-fly',[23] Don. *ved'ma* 'dragonfly', 'species of locust'.[24]

Slovak **vlkolak**, *vlkodlak, vrkolak, vilkolak* – 'a person able of turning into a wolf, werewolf'; 'half-man – half-wolf, harming people and domestic animals'; *vrkolak* (Gemer, Malogont); *vlkolák, vlkodlák* 'the soul of a witch or witcher', 'a walking dead, the soul of a deceased who was carried away headfirst' correlates with ideas about a werewolf in other Slavic (as well as Lithuanian, German, Romanian, etc.) traditions, which are, however, characterized by a certain variability of the term, its semantics and the different content of the image. The meaning of 'man-wolf, werewolf' is found in all Slavic languages, but in West and East Slavic languages, it prevails, while in Serbian and Bulgarian it is represented marginally, and the main meaning is 'vampire'.[25]

---

21. Trubačev 1985: 8.
22. See Vážný 1955.
23. SS: 70.
24. Serdjukova 2005: 40.
25. See more in SD 1: 418–420

Some plots of Slovak mythological stories about *vlkodlaks* are related to the plots found in Ukrainian, Belarussian and Polish traditions, for example, about the thread of the wife's skirt stuck in her husband's teeth. No less important are the motifs of legends and beliefs connecting the *vlkodlak* with the moon phases, with the sun, including the motif of the wolf eating the moon and the sun. These motifs apparently exist as echoes of ancient mythologems. Another important aspect is the mythological connection between the *vlkodlak* and the vampire.

According to the Slovak data, a person born from a woman and a vampire (*upír*) could become a *vlkodlak*; a child of a *vlkodlak* and a witch becomes a vampire, as well as a child that was born on a new moon or with his feet foremost. Most often a *vlkodlak* turns into a wolf at the periods of the summer and winter solstice.[26] The soul of a witch (witcher) or of an improperly buried deceased comes back home ... to choke and strangle young women ... Turning into a wolf, it chokes sheep, but does not eat them.[27] A specific dependence of a person transformation into a wolf on the full moon is either an echo or a modification of an ancient "wolf - moon" relation, widely represented, for example, in the Carpathian-Ukrainian tradition. According to a Hutsul legend, some people turned into wolves at new moon time. An euphemistic name for *vovkun* (вовкун) 'werewolf' is *misichnik* (місічник), the main meaning of which is 'lunatic', 'a person changing his gender under the influence of the moon'.[28] Compare similar stories in Orava: *vlkoláci* are such people as lunatics (*namesačníci*), who turned into wolves at the full moon (Bobrov, dist. Namestovo). The motif of eating the moon, found in the Hutsul tradition,[29] has correspondences in Romanian (*vîrcolács* live on the moon, in the sky; eating the moon and the sun, they cause solar and lunar eclipses[30]) and South Slavic beliefs (Bulg. and Serb. beliefs, explaining the lunar and solar eclipses by *v'rkolak* (върколак) having eaten or swallowed the moon or the sun). The whole complex of "astronomical" motifs associated with werewolves should be attributed to the Carpathian–South Slavic group, although in the Carpathians the considered motifs are less pronounced, and among the Romanians there are significant semantic deviations compared to South Slavic beliefs.

The mythonym **poludnica** ("Lady Midday") 'an anthropomorphic MC, appearing at noon, controlling the abidance by prohibition to work at noon' can

---

26. EĽKS 2: 309.
27. Dobšinský 1880: 116–117.
28. Hobzey 2002: 72–73.
29. *Ibid*.: 77.
30. Svešnikova 1979: 212–215.

be referred to the West Slavic–Russian isogloss. "According to K. Moszyński, it is known to almost all West Slavs – the Sorbs, the Czechs, the Slovaks and the Poles (it seems only the Kashubians and the Masurians have no idea about it)"[31] and to a number of Russian traditions. The term is marginally found with the Slovenes: "*polednica* is a woman who comes for a baby at noon"[32], which should also be referred to as the West Slavic–Slovenian isogloss. The *poludnica*'s habit of stealing and changing children is well developed in the Middle Slovak local tradition (Horehronie).[33]

The abovementioned isoglosses and isodoxes are consistent with the conclusions of Lyubov' V. Kurkina, made in the study of S.-W. groups of South Slavic dialects: "The general part of the vocabulary units of the north-western area is greatly represented by lexemes with limited separate connections with dialects of the Czech-Slovak region, some isoglosses of this type appear in Lechitic and Sorbian dialects.[34]

West Slavic Lexemes

This group includes mythonyms that are not found in East and South Slavic languages; it presents both Slavic roots and those borrowed, mainly from the German language.

The terms derived from **rarogъ* were studied by Václav Machek[35] and Oleg N. Trubachev,[36] who proved its Iranian origin. Slovak **rároh** 'prince of evil spirits', 'hawk', old-Czech and Slovak *rároh* 'bird of prey of Falconidae family'; Czech 'bird of prey', 'devil'; old-Czech *raroch* 'a huge bird with fire sparks', rare 'demon'; Czech dial. *rarach* 'flying fire demon', Czech, old-Czech *rarach* 'god, bringing wind', 'devil'. Also Morav. *rarach* 'flying fire pillar', 'devilkin', Pol. *raróg* 'bird', 'crank, monster, marvel, devilkin' and Ukr. *rarig* (*papiz*) 'the same'.

Lexeme *rarog/rarach* is also associated with Slovak **rarášek, rarášok** 'a demon – angry and cunning, but giving happiness'; *rarášek, rarách* 'evil spirit, demon, devil, witch's partner', he appears as a fiery chain, a fire serpent or a ball and flies in through the pipe into the witch's house for a sexual affair, giving her

---

31. Pełka 1987: 99.
32. Kropej 2008: 327.
33. See more about *poludnica*: SD 4: 154–155.
34. Kurkina 1985: 69.
35. Machek 2010: 508.
36. Trubačev 1967: 64–71.

supernatural power and bringing money. It is also 'the personified evil essence of a witch', sometimes 'the witch herself, flying over the village'[37]. In a number of stories this character is combined with another one – *zmok* (змок) (White Carpathians, W.-Slovak).

Czech *rarášek* 'home spirit in the form of a white dwarf (mid.-Czech); 'whirlwind, an evil spirit teasing and harming people' (dist. of Plzeň, Chodsko); *randášek* 'devilkin', *rarášek, rarašík* 'home godkin'; 'demon'; 'god bringing wind'; old-Czech 'a huge fiery bird, commanding witches'; 'spirit bringing whirlwind', 'devil', *rarášek, rarášík, rarach* old-Slav. 'god creating wind', 'godkin of happiness and unhappiness', 'devil, evil spirit', *jerášek* 'povětroň', i.e. 'wind spirit' (Vsatsko, Morav.), *radášek* (S.- Czech). The Moravians give it the meaning of 'a huge fiery bird', 'a huge fiery dragon-like creature, guarding treasures'; as well as *raška* 'little home godkin, gobbling people' or 'demon's wife *raráška*' (Luhačoviské Zalessie). Cf. also random Slovenian lexical units: *rarašek* (West. Pannonia[38]); *rarášek* 'spirit of the wind, whirlwind (=*veter, veternik*), servant of Pechtra Baba, who has winds locked in a barrel'.[39]

The marginality of ideas about devil *rarashek* among Slovenes and their intertwining with other contexts suggest that they came from the West Slavs, which confirms O.N. Trubachev's opinion: "West Slavic *rarogъ* was undoubtedly one of such elements, never known to other Slavs, and we interpret it as pre-Slav dial. **rarogъ*".[40]

Slovak. **škriatok** 'wealth giving spirit', hatched from an egg carried for 9 days under the arm' appears as a wet chicken at daytime, and as a fiery chain flying into the chimney of the house at night. He brings wealth, for which the owner must give him food from each dish or sign a contract in blood where he promises to give him his soul or the soul of "his pregnant wife's" yet unborn child. He is also called *zmok* (Bošácka Valley, W.-Slovak); *škrat* 'devilkin', *škrata* 'home godkin; monster', *škratek* 'devilkin; home godkin'.

Czech beliefs about the wealth giving spirit *skřítek* are almost identical to Slovak. Polish beliefs are similar in their basis and demonstrate a greater development and enrichment of the image, preserving the main identifying features: it is a wealth giving spirit; it brings material wealth in exchange for the soul; it is hatched from an egg; at daytime – an unsightly hen/chicken (or another bird), at

---

37. Bužeková 2009: 37–38, 40.
38. Machek 2010: 508.
39. Kropej 2008: 327.
40. Trubačev 1967: 66.

night – a fiery flying serpent; it is difficult or impossible to get rid of it. However, the origin of this character from the souls of the dead is more explicit here; instead of a fire serpent coming at night, a fire bird appears: "*płonącą drapaka – bird with a big flamy tail*"[41] (*cf.* the Firebird from Russian fairy tales). Pol. *skrzat* 'home watcher spirit', *ziemscy skryatkowie* (form of XVI cent.), *skrzaty, skrzaki* (Great-Pol.), *skrzaciki* (Siles.), *skrzek, skrzak* (Helm.) 'spirit bringing people grains and money'. In Warmia and Masuria a version of finding this demon in the form of a black wet hen after the rain is very common; if it is dried and fed, it starts bringing wealth to its owners – a plot identical to that of Slovak.

A Slovenian character *škratec, škrat, škret, škratelj, škrabec*, etc.,[42] despite a similar name differs considerably from the MC described above, at the same time having certain features in common (e.g., guise of a fiery chain).

Extralinguistic material lets us see the contamination of the borrowed from German term *(Schrat)* with the Slavic verbs, e.g.: Slovak *kryť* 'coat, cover, hide, keep', Czech *krýti* 'conceal, hide, keep, coat'.[43] The belief, recorded by F. Bartoš, is illustrative from the point of view of implementation of these ideas: *skřítek* is a devilkin hiding from thunder (lightning) in a person's armpit (*skřítek, ten čertík, před hromem sa kryje a kryje, a fuk člověkovi pod pažu, a hrom ho zabije*[44]).

West Slavic languages are also characterized by common mythonym borrowings from German: *vaserman, hastrman, fras, pikulík*, including:

Permoník 'anthropomorphous MC, watchman and keeper of fossils and treasures' (Liptov; Horehronie), *permoník, permúňik* 'spirit of mines in the guise of a dwarf' (mid.-Slovak), *perkmaníček, permonik* (Orava), *permoučik, permočnik*. Cf. Czech *permon* 'spirit of mines' < Germ. *Bergmann* or *Berggeist* via *perkman* and *perkajst*. These also include Ostrava-Silesian *pěrun* 'demon', *pěrunek* 'spirit of mines', secondarily approximated with Perun.[45]

Slovak *nelapší* 'vampire' and *pikulík* 'home wealth-giving spirit', their W.-Slavic parallels and possible etymology were discussed in another article.[46]

---

41. Pełka 1987: 142.
42. Kropej 2008: 331.
43. ESSJa 13: 71.
44. Bartoš 1883: 219.
45. Zubov 2010: 116.
46. See Valentsova 2016, however, an adjustment should be done: the etymology of the Slovak *nelapší* should, apparently, be derived from all-Slavic **lap-*, old-Rus. лапь (lap') 'simply', 'anyhow', and the word *nelapší* thus has to be understood as "not simple, not

Carpathian vocabulary

In the Slovak mythological system carpathian vocabulary contains: *striga, strigôň, bosorka, bosorkaň, šarkan, d'ug, dvojdušnica, dva duchy (dva srdcia) mat', čiernokňažník, chmarnik* and a number of others. Specific Carpathian features have also the beliefs associated with these characters.

Lexical item ***striga / стрига*** (< Lat. *strīx, -gis* < Greek στρίγγλα, old-Gr. στρί(γ)ξ[47] is spread on a single area, including Slovakia, Eastern Moravia, Southern Poland (Silesia, Kraków Voivodeship, Podlasie, etc.), sporadically – in Northern Hungary (dial. *sztriga* 'boszorkány'[48]), found almost everywhere in Romania and Moldavia, further in Slovenia, Croatia, Montenegro, marginally in the South Slavic range – in Istria and to the north of it, on the Croatian Mediterranean coast and near the Serbian-Albanian border.[49]

In the Carpathian-Ukrainian, the word is sporadically found and has semantics far from the main meaning. The lexeme thus forms the Carpathian–South Slavic isogloss.[50]

The root ***bosor-*** (< Hung. *boszorkány*, initially 'spirit of the dead, ghost', later 'witch' and so on, which is from Turk. **basyrkan* 'mora', from *bas-* 'strangle'[51]) is wide-spread in West and East Slovak dialects, also known in the Middle Slovak regions, but feels bookish: *bosorka* 'witch', 'wicked woman', *bosorka, bosurka* 'sorceress' (W.-Slov.); 'some types of night butterflies' (Novograd, S.-W.-Slov., S.-Zemplin); rare 'big toad' (dist. Považská Bystrica); 'whirl, whirlpool' (W.-Slov.). Lexemes of masculine gender are also wide-spread: *bosorák, bosorkáň, bosor, bosor(k)oš, bosurkoš* 'sorcerer', 'witcher', *bosorák, bosorkáň* 'night moth or dark-coloured butterfly' (S.-W.-Slov.), *bosorča, bosurče* 'bosorka's child' (E.-Slov.); *bosorča* 'a child who after weaning was fed with lactation again' (Detva, mid.-Slov.).[52]

In Czech the following examples are considered borrowings from Slovak: *bosorka, bosorkyně, bosořice* (Slovak, earlier from Hung.), folk 'witch'; Morav.

---

ordinary", i.e. 'he who knows', sorcerer or witch.
47. Klepikova 1994: 94–95.
48. Vážný 1955: 89.
49. Plotnikova 2004: 220–221, 646–650.
50. For more details, see Valentsova 2012.
51. Machek 2010: 61.
52. For more on *bosorka* see SD 1: 241–242.

bosorka, bosora 'wild woman, wicked sorceress', *bosorák* 'evil sorcerer', 'person who stays up late at night'; *bosorča* 'bosorka's child, which she abandoned in a cradle'. Pol. *buosorka, baśorka, basorka, bąsorkyńa; bisurkania* 'witch' (Sanocke-Krośnieńskie).

A large number of variants are represented in Ukrainian and especially Carpathian-Ukrainian: *bosorka, bosorkan'a* (босорка, босорканя) 'witch, sorceress', 'toad'; *bosirka, bisurka, bisurkan'a, borsukan'a, bosurgan'a, bos'urkan'a, busurkan'a, poshurkan'a* (босирка, бісурка, бісурканя, борсуканя, босурганя, босюрканя, бусурканя, пошурканя) 'wisewoman, witch', *bosorkan'a* (босорканя) 'night moth', 'toad'; *bosorkun* (босоркун) 'ghoul', Russin. *Bosorkan'a* (босоркáня) 'witch, sorceress'; *bosorkun* (босоркун) 'sorcerer, turnskin; witcher'; *bosorak, bosorosh* (босорак, босóрош), Carp.-Ukr. *bosorkána* 'witch, sorceress', 'dragonfly (childish)', *bosorkún* 'sorcerer, witcher' and so on.

Single Sloven. *bosaruna* 'witch'.[53]

The area of terms with the root *bosor-*, including Hung. *boszorka*, Romanian *bosorcáic* gives grounds to speak of them as typical Carpathian mythonyms.

The **double-souled** is in general a Carpathian character, known in West Ukrainian, Slovak and Polish traditions, although ideas about double-soulness are also present in Polessie, in Belarussian and South Slavic traditions (for example, the Polessian motif of a double-souled witch (Volyn., Bryan.); *double-soulness* of sorcerers and sorceresses that are not even trusted by demons, by whose power they act (Bel.).[54]

According to the Slovak beliefs, *striga, bosorka*, as well as *mora, upír, vlkodlak* are the double-souled, that is, demonic incarnations of people who were born with two souls. Such a half-demon strangles sleepers at night, suffocates them, drinks blood, spoils livestock, sucks milk and blood from cows, causes loss of cattle and devastation in the village (E.-Slov., mid-Slov.). In Zamagurie, the double-souled are shepherds, witches, healers and those who have not been anointed. The Slovaks and the Poles, do not have a term for idea of the double-souled, they mostly use a phrase like "a person with two hearts, with two souls": *dve srdcia* (dist. Sobrance, Snina, Michalovce; dist. B. Bystrica, Horehronie), *dvoje srcov má* (Orava), *dva duchy mať* (dist. Sobrance, dist. Stará Ľubovňa, E.-Slovak); *má dvoch duchov* (dist. Čadca, W.-Slov.).

---

53. Kropej 2008: 315.
54. For details see SD 2: 29–31.

Only sporadically the terms are found: *dvojdušník* and *dvojdušnica* (dist. Dolný Kubín in Orava) 'a demonic creature, which strangles at night',[55] *dvojdušňicä* 'double-souled, that is a witch or a mora' (Revišné, dist. Orava[56]), Ruthen. *двадушні, двадушникьи* 'vampires', who can let their soul out when they want, and after death they roam among the living; *дводушник* 'turnskin', [*dvodušnik*] (Verchovina), *d'v'idúšnik* – a person which has two hearts, 'witch, turnskin' (L'vov dist.).

In Slovakia, beliefs about the double-souled are more widespread than the term itself. In the field of beliefs, as an <u>all-Carpathian and Balkan parallel</u> a "cloud-breaker" can be considered, an aerial demon controlling dark clouds, rain, hail and storm. Common lexemes in the Carpathian region denoting this MC, are: *chernoknizhnik, planetnik, chmarnik (chmurnik)* (*чернокнижник, планетник, хмарник (хмурник)*) 'warlock'.[57]

Slovak **čiernokňažník** (*čarnokňažník, černokňižník*), *černokrižník* (with a black cross over the nose – dist. Kysuce and Trenčín), also called *chmurnik, chmarnik, planetnik, veterník* (Zamagurie, Spiš) – 'a demonic character controlling natural powers'; 'witcher/fortune-teller'. He is mainly known in the mountainous region: Orava, Horehronie, Mountainous Spiš and White Carpathians, there are also stories about him in Slovak regions Gemer and Malohont. In the Czech language the term has other semantics: *černokněžník*, m, *černokněžnice*, f – 'mythical character, doing evil sorcery', 'enchanter', 'sorcerer'; figurat. 'priest'.

In modern Hutsul dialects *чорнокнижник* is 'a person who drives away the rain and hail clouds' (*grad'anik, čornokniżnik* (*град'аник, чорнокнижник*) – those who are against the hail), according to ethnographic records, they are 'ghouls, who have sold their soul to the devil and got his "black books", which they use to send diseases, mutilation and death to people'.[58] In the dialects of Galician Lemkos, *čornokniżnik* (*чорнокнижник*) lets the hail fall or chases dark clouds away.

The meaning of 'a cloud-breaker' is then found in Polish: *czernokniżniki* 'people, who standing on the ground drove away the clouds with special spells'; *płanetniki* are black magicians, which originate from the souls of hangmen. The meaning of 'evil sorcerer, reading by black books' continues in Polessie: *čornokniżnik, čarodeinyk, volšebnyk* (*чорнокнижник, чародейнык, волшэбник*) 'sorcerer'

---

55. SSN 1: 418.
56. Habovštiak 2006: 274-275.
57. To read more about the genesis of this character, see: Valentsova 2018.
58. Khobzei 2002: 184.

– those who do harm (Brest.); *černokniżniki* (чэрнокніжнікі) 'sorcerers' (Gomel.), *černokniżnik* (чернокніжнік) treats or puts in a disease (Brest.).

Slovak lexemes **chmurnik, chmarnik** 'warlock' (Zamagurie, Spiš), *chmarňik, hmurňik* 'a tall man in a long cloak torn by lightenings, flying on a three-headed dragon (*smok*), who lives in the dark clouds' (Zamagurie) corresponds with Carp.-Ukr. *hmarnik* (хмарник) 'cloud-breaker, who can fight evil spirits when the hail cloud is coming, not letting hail come to the village fields'; Ruthen. *gonihmarnik* (гоніхмарник) 'evil spirit', Pol. *chmarniki, chmurniki* 'demons, spreading hail clouds around the world', *chmurniki* 'spirits that live in the dark clouds – spirits of unchristened children, of the "nav" dead'. In general the term also characterizes the Slavo-Carpathian area.

Slov. **planetnik** 'warlock' (Zamagurie, Spiš); *planetňik* 'a tall man in a long torn cloak, flying on a three-headed dragon *smok*' (Zamagurie).

Lexemes with the root *planet-* in Belarussian-Polish-Ukrainian area show that the motivating for naming that character was the meaning 'dark cloud', cf.: Bel. *plameta* (пламета)[3] 'dark cloud, cloudiness', Ukr. (W.-Volyn.) *planita* (планіта) 'large thunder cloud', Pol. *plametnik* 'black cloud moving in the sky', Pol. dial. *planeta* 'migratory cloud', *planetnica* 'white cloud, flying in the sky', old-Pol. *planeta* '(dark) cloud'. This lexical connection is depicted in beliefs: *Planetnik* is a person who was born in a house at the time, when such a dark cloud (*taka chmara, taka planeta*) hung above it (S.-E.-Pol.).

A certain parallelism is found between the Slovak-Polish and South Slavic beliefs: according to Slovak belief from Zamagurie, there is one *planetnik* in the dark clouds over each region; according to Polish one, in each village there used to be several *planetniks* who protected the village from bad weather – and in South Slavic traditions it is known that every village has its own protector from hail and bad weather, called *zmay*.

Beliefs about the fight of two weather demons, good and evil, "defender" and "malicious serpent", are widely represented among the South Slavs and known also, for example, to Hutsuls, but were not encountered in the Slovak material, however the motive is present. The warlock (*černokniżnik*) serves as a defender here (he warns villagers about the storm; tells people who have done him a favour how to protect their fields from the storm and hail; commands the dragon *šarkan* to send hail not to the villages but to uninhabited mountains, lies to *šarkan* that those are not the bells ringing, but the dogs barking), and the malicious one is the *šarkan* dragon, in some areas called *smok* (cf. W.-Bulg. смок, смук – on the contrary, 'a snake-like demon, a dragon protecting the village' (fields, vinelands) from bad weather.

Slovak. *šarkan* (< Hung. *sárkány*), *Hriwaty Šarkan*; *šarkan* (E.-Slov.) 'mythical creature, bringing thunder and storm (in summer)', 'winged dragon'; 'domovoy (home spirit)' (Banská Bystrica), 'flying serpent, incarnation of the storm', *šiarkan preletel* 'about a storm with thunder'; *šarkaň* 'domovoy' (E.-Slov.); *žiarkaň* 'fairytale dragon' and 'domovoy'. Cf. Hung.: шаркань 'storm', 'dark cloud', 'a three-headed dragon, hitting the ground with his tail and killing seeds'; *šarkan flew over* 'about a storm' (North Hungary).

They used to say about laid wheat that is was beaten-down by a serpent (*šärkan chvostom ušluhau*) (Orava). In Liptov, it was believed that everything freezes out because of *šarkan-serpent* (*had-šarkan*). *Šarkan* has a wide strong tail which breaks the tops of the trees (Horehronie). It was thought that in a storm accompanied by a whirlwind, *šarkan* flies, who thinks the bells are the dogs barking, and flies away in fear (Gemer – Malohont).

Moravians have no lexeme, but it is believed that when a whirlwind rages, it's a warlock unleashes a dragon (reg. Rožnov pod Radhoštěm, Wallachia). Czech *šarkan* 'mythical dragon' is defined as a borrowing from Slovak.

The mythonym and related beliefs are known in Carpathian-Ukrainian: шаркань 'a 12-headed serpent, shooting out fire from the mouth', Zakarpat. *šarkan'* (шаркань) 'a flying serpent, eating the sun, which gets smaller', Lemk. *šarkan* (шаркан) 'strong wind, storm'. Beliefs say that the serpent *sharkan* guards water and does not give it to people; *šarkan* originates from a common whip snake which grows wings in 14 years and carries the storm and hail, but since he is blind, he is controlled by *vetryanik*. Warlock sorcerers saddle him up and lead him to where they want to beat the fields with hail.

Some of the Ukrainian beliefs have correspondence among Bulgarians: flying serpent шаркан drinks water from the sea, it goes to the clouds, and when two serpents fight each other, downpour begins (Banat).

Semantic Carpathisms also include lexemes formed from common-Slavic root ***bog-/bož***: Slov. *boh* 'healer, wizard' (Kysuce); *zemský boh* 'wiseman, wizard, healer' (Myjava); *bohyňa*[1] / *bohiňa* / *bogiňa* 'wisewoman, healer, fortune-teller; kind witch' (W.-Slov., E.-Slov.); *božica* 'sorceress'; *bohiňa*[2] 'bohinka, or a wild woman, who steals children and swaps human children for her ugly freaks' (Liptov, mid.-Slov.); *bohiňa*[3] 'butterfly' (W.-Slov.); *bohynka*[1] (*bohinka, boginka*) 'a forest woman, dangerous for expectant mothers and stealing human children' (Orava, Spiš, Zamagurie); *bohinka* (*boginka*) 'a witch, double-souled, leaving cows without milk, strangling sleeping people at night' (Orava, mid.-Slov.); *bohiňár* 'bohinka's husband' (Orava, Spiš); *bohiň* 'bohinka's child' (Orava), *bohynča, bohíňča* 'bohinka's ugly child' (Orava), 'a child stolen and brought up by bohinka' (Horehronie); *boginče* 'changeling, bohinka's child' (Zamagurie); *buožik, buožiček domovy* 'home spirit'. Traditions closest to the Slovak one are Moravian, Carpathian-Ukrainian and South Polish, characterized by lexemes, similar externally and/or internally: Morav. *boh, bůh* 'sorcerer-conjurer', *božec, božek, bůžek* 'good sorcerer', *bohoň* 'the one who charms diseases away', *bohyně* 'wisewoman', *bohyňář* 'wiseman'; *bohynník* 'sorcerer, fortune-teller', *božice* 'fortune-teller (woman)', Morav. Val. *božec* 'diviner, soothsayer'; 'healer'. In Carpathian-Ukrainian area: Hutsul, Boyk. *Bog zemniy (zem'linij, zemnij), zemsk'i bogi* (богземіний (землʹіний, земний), земскʹі боги) 'person with a special gift, with the help of which he can do good or do harm', 'sorcerer, wiseman, fortune-teller' and so on. Sporadically in Hutsul and Boyko dialects – *bogi* (боги) 'fortune-tellers, wisewomen', and in Hutsul and Pokuttye – *božok* (божок); Ukr. *big, bog* (біг, бог) 'forest deity', 'wiseman', *boginja* (богиня) 'mermaid', Ukr. *bogyni* (богині), *bohynja* 'bohinka'.[59] Partially in Pol.: *boginki* (Kraków, Pińczów regions), *bogienki, bogunki, boginie* (Chęciń.), *ubogini, ubogenka* (Pol. Górov) *ubyhyna* 'witch'.[60]

The survey of mythonyms allows considering the terms *bohyňa / bohynka* and their derivatives in the meanings of 'bohinka, forest woman' and 'wisewoman, sorceress' <u>Slavo-Carpathian</u> (together with the corresponding MC of masculine and neuter genders). Of special note is the coincidence of the local meaning of 'fortune-teller' in W.-Slavic and Slovenian languages.

Particularly Slovak mythonyms

Particularly Slovak mythonyms are not numerous and the lexemes seems not to be known in other Slavic traditions. Moreover, specific can be both the name and the MC (*runa, grgalica*), only the name of the MC, while the character is recognizable (*slnečnica, futkač*) or typologically similar to other Slavic MCs (Slovak *Pondelníča, Štvrtnica* – mid.-Rus., Ukr. *Pjatnica* (Пятница), Poles. *Sereda* (Середа):

Futkač 'MC that strangles a person who sleeps soundly' (Riečnica, reg. Čadca[61]). *Molek* 'water spirit',[62] *molok (-ek)* 'water spirit',[63] compare to Cz. *molek* 'drunk', Siles. *mola* 'some bogeyman', Slov. *molok* 'water spirit', *molek*, most likely from Germ. *Molch*, i.e. *mlok*.[64]

---

59. Khobzei 2002: 105.
60. On *boginka* see.: SD 1: 215–217.
61. AT ÚEt, inv. č. 578B.
62. ČL I 1892: 52; Kott 7: 1328.
63. Kálal: 340.
64. Machek 2010: 373.

Pondelča (pondelníča) – '"Spirit of Monday", MC, punishing for violation of a ban on certain household chores on Monday'. According to the mythological narrative, a little girl would fly through the chimney to spinning women and malevolently say: *Ja som dievča-pondelča a nepradiem kúdelča* [I am a Monday girl and I don't spin flax], then she would turn round three times, spit over women, stamp her feet and disappear. Soon all women would get sick (Brezno reg., Horehronie). E. Horvatová assumed, that initially the character was associated with a ban on baking bread on Monday morning.

Monday is also special in other traditions: mid. Ukr. custom of married women not to work on Mondays (*понеділкуванне*) and the character *Святый Понеділок* (Holy Monday 'a gray old man, who meets the soul in the afterlife and asks about sins'), as well as the Czech ideas about the non-working "blue Monday" (*modrý pondelok*), though of later origin.

Štvrtica (Štvrtnica) '"Spirit of Thursday", keeping an eye on spinning and following the ban on spinning on Thursday'. It would appear in front of a spinstress and say: *Ja som štvrtok-nieštvrtok, ja nepradiem vo štvrtok* [I am Thursday-nonThursday, I don't spin on Thuraday]. In the 19th century the character disappeared,[65] as well as *štvrtočná víla* (Kysuce). Thursday was believed to be the happiest day of the week, wholesome for all kinds of work, however spinning was forbidden on Thursday (Horehronie). Cf. in Polessie spinning was forbidden on Friday, so Friday was personified as *St. Friday* and Wednesday, when it was forbidden to shuttle, as *St. Wednesday*.

Slnečnica 'a creature that walks in the fields at noon, and if it finds someone sleeping, it pricks him on the ear or throat and they will get inflamed' (Gemer, Malohont[66]); 'personification of the summer sun', cf. *slnečnica ho opálila* [Slnečnica burnt him].[67] The character can be identified with *poludnica* (*полудница*).

Samorac 'one of the names of *nočnica*' (Nižná Slaná); strangles people at night, sometimes seen in the form of a large fly (Gemer–Malohont[68]).

Umornica 'a soul of a dead sorcerer, coming back home and strangling, torturing his close people, till it exhausts them to death' (Vikartovce, dist. Poprad, Spiš[69]).

---

65. Horváthová 1986: 47; EĽKS 2: 62, 1: 371.
66. Michálek (ed.) 2011: 373.
67. Dobšinský 1880: 116.
68. Michálek (ed.) 2011: 371.
69. Michálek 1989: 283.

Bahorka 'anthropomorphous female MC, similar to *poludnica* and *runa*: an old woman with long uncombed hair'.[70] The image is vague, the term is local. Probably, the name is associated with roots **baxarъ, baxora, *bajati* (old-Czech. *báchora* 'fairy tale, fable, fiction', Slov. *báchorka* 'nursery rhyme, fiction'). Cf. Ukr. *baxoriti* (*бáхориmи*) 'tell fortunes, augur', Rus. dial. *baxora* (*бахóра*) 'the one who boasts, brags; wiseman, wisewoman', S.-Croat. *baxorica* (*бáхориц̌а*) 'sorceress, wisewoman', Sloven. *bahoríti* 'practise witchcraft'.[71] Considering phonetics, as well as the presence of a number of isoglosses between the Slovak and Slovenian languages, we can assume with high probability that Slovak word formation of *bahorka* was based on the Slovenian verb *bahoriti*.

Grgalica 'forest woman'. She was depicted as a huge woman with black legs, large hands, with uncombed hair and huge breasts slung over her shoulders. She shoved them into a trapped man's mouth until he's smothered. Her presence was signified by a prolonged whooping (dist. Zvolen, mid.-Slov). She lived in the mountains, and people heard only her whooping (dist. B. Bystrica, mid.-Slov.).[72] *Grgolica* 'wicked vila, luring people to the marsh' (Kálal).

Perhaps, due to the sound characteristics of the MC, the word can be related to **gъrgati*: Sloven. *gŕgati* 'bubble', 'curr'; Bel. dial. *gjargats'* (*гяргаць*) 'shout, gaggle', Rus. dial. *gorgat'* (*гóргать*) 'knock' (Volog.), *garkat'* (*гаркáть*) 'beat' (Arch.), *gurgat'* (*гýргать*) 'knock, thunder; rumble' (Volog.), *gărgat'* (*гыргать*) 'knock' (Volog.), 'hum, talk to oneself' (Perm.).[73] Such etymology is possible taking into account the presence of Slovak – Belarussian –North Russian isoglottic lines including the mythological vocabulary.

Runa, zemná pani (Spiš, Horehronie, Liptov, Gemer) 'a powerful woman with long golden hair and large breasts who lived underground with her husband and a lot of children'; or 'a golden haired woman in white clothes and with a golden key, who had a lot of children'; in Liptov – 'a forest demon, covered with hair'. *Runa* owned all the underground wealth, but showed the treasure only to those who promised to give her their child. Sometimes she stole human children. According to the mythological narratives, *runa* was stolen food from miners and wood-cutters.[74] She was a type of "a wild woman" (*divá žena*) with long breasts,

---

70. Horehronie: 336.
71. ESSJa 1: 135-136.
72. EĽKS 1: 155.
73. ESSJa 7: 208.
74. EĽKS 2: 131; Michálek (ed.) 2011: 371–372.

slung over to the back; she stole food from men and babies from women; lived underground; sometimes people managed to catch her (Mountainous Spiš[75]).

The name can be explained on the basis of lexeme *rúna*: Morav. 'boundary-strip between vineyards', Slovak *rúna*, Mor.-Slovac. *odrunek* 'one side of the boundary-strip (of runa)' < from Germ. *Rune (Rinne)*[76]; *run, run(a)* (<Germ.) 'groove, path in the vineyards' (Kálal); Morav. *rŭna* 'a path between one's and other's grapes'. Semantically it does not contradict the meaning of the image of *Runa* as *the owner of earthly wealth*. Cf. similar development: Slav. *čьrtъ* 'devil, evil spirit' < *čьrta* 'boundary-strip', 'line' with semantic analogy in Fin. *piiru* 'line, dash, boundary' – *piru* 'demon'.[77]

On the other hand, in the image of *runa*, attention is drawn to having many children, the ability to kidnap children, referring to excessive sexual energy and lust, common for many female MCs. In this sense, we can correlate the name *runa* with Morav. *rúňat sa: roby sa rúňajú* = run after men (Brodsko[78]). *Rúňat sa* is referred to old-Czech. *říjě* and *řuje* 'estrus in deer (in autumn)', primary *řuja* from *řváti* 'roar, cry'; deer estrus is accompanied by roar. The root *řu-* gives rise to *řuja*, and then *řuj-ьnъ*, Val. *řujný,* Lash. *řujny,* Morav.-Slovac. *rúňat' sa*.[79]

The article shows only a small fragment of the Slovak demonology in the context of the analysis of selected mythonyms. At the same time, it gives an idea of the system of MCs and mythological beliefs of the Slovaks in general, characterizes the type of the given cultural dialect. This dialect, although related to the West Slavic type, includes a considerable number of East Slavic and South Slavic ethno-linguistic facts. The study was mainly based on synchronous data from the 19th and 20th centuries, however, it can serve as a foundation for possible reconstruction of more ancient states, and further clarification of the causes and ways of changing the semantics of lexemes, ways of motivation, the direction of word migration, etc.

The basis of the Slovak mythological system is a Common Slavic stratum of beliefs and vocabulary describing them. Almost all ancient mythologems and most of the Proto-Slavic roots referring to MCs and their functions are reflected in Slovak dialects. Some of them are known in all or most of the Slavic languages

---

75. Horváthová 1972: 500.
76. Machek 2010: 525.
77. ESSJa 4: 165-166.
78. Bartoš 1903–1906: 368.
79. Machek 2010: 532.

and dialects (*čarovnica, smok, upír, mora*), others oppose the West Slavic area to the East and South Slavic areas (*škriatok, lútky, mamuna, nočnica*), and the third ones – the West and East Slavic areas to the South Slavic ones (*kúzliť, perún, ježibaba, čert*), etc. The areas outlined by mythological isoglosses and isodoxes do not always coincide with modern linguistic division – in this case, we can speak either of the Slavic areas of a later formation (for example, the Carpathian), or of the routes of ethnic migrations, or of the ancient Common Slavic dialectal division. A number of local but diagnostic features in the semantics of mythonyms (less commonly – in MC names) connect the Slovak demonological system with Sorbian and Belarusian (*mara, nočnica, veštica*), some of them extend to the North Russian and Siberian dialects of the Russian language (the last – apparently, due to the stream of migration from the Northern Russian territories). Some of the isoglosses (*zmiňa, poludnica, škrat, striga, vedomec*) and isodoxes (Slovak *moria noha* – Sloven. *morino taco*; Slovak *biely had* – Sloven. *bela kača*) connect the West and Middle Slovak dialects with Slovenian, and some of them – further – with Croatian and Serbian dialects. The East Slovak dialects have lexical connections with Polish Goral ones, on the one side, and Carpathian-Ukrainian dialects (*vražec, sotona*), on the other.

Most often, in the studied vocabulary, isoglosses are accompanied by isodoxes, that is, with the general (similar) name of the MC, the ideas about it are also generally similar (as far as we can speak about the coincidence of images of MCs in different traditions[80]). Sometimes isoglosses do not correspond with isodoxes (cf., for example, Slovak *černokňažník* means a completely different character than the Russian *chernoknizhnik* (черпокнижник) 'warlock'; Slovak *planeta* 'evil incarnate, bad person, demon' – and Ukr. Volyn. *planita* (планіта) 'big thunder cloud'). There are also isodoxes that are not associated with a corresponding isoglosses. That is explained by the dynamic nature and variable combinability of motives, features, the smallest semantic elements giving rise to creation of MC images (for example, a witch or a mora can be endowed with features of a vampire; beliefs about a wealth giving spirit can be reflected in different characters with various names).

The most vivid characteristics of Slovak demonology are associated with its Carpathian features. In the Carpathian region, innovative features and functions of MCs were formed while the names remained, sometimes with slight modification (*vlkolak, bog-*). The appearance of foreign names in Slovak

---

80. See Vinogradova, Tolstaja 1994.

mythonymy (*striga, bosorka, šarkan*) is also associated with Carpathian specificity. These terms of non-Slavic origin were superimposed on images already known in the tradition and dramatized them, giving, for example, a witch the features of a vampire, a cannibal, giving a serpent the features of a storm and a hail demon. At the same time, own Slavic terms (*veštica / vedma / vedomkyňa* and *had/smok*) received purely positive connotations or were driven out to the periphery. The Carpathian beliefs, often spreading to the Balkans, also include: "specialization" of witches and other MCs ("against rain", "against drought", "against people", "against cattle", "against milk", etc.), the motive of a demon eating the moon and the sun, the involuntary harmful effects of the "evil eye", the ability of a MC to change its height, etc. The latter motive is not typical for Slavic ideas and has correspondence in Finno-Ugric mythology[81] the impact of which on the views and the MC system of the peoples of the Carpathian area, especially the Slovaks, is promising for the study.

Slovak dialects have close ties not only with Carpathian-Ukrainian and the dialects of Minor Poland, not only with the north-west group of South Slavic dialects, but also with Sorbian, Belarusian and Polessian dialects, which is especially important for characterizing the Common Slavic dialectal status of the time of the Carpathian migration of Slavs. In the future, special attention should be paid to the study of these lexical ties. The absolute need is to map the results obtained, which is not yet possible due to insufficient data.

The considered isoglottic links of the selected Slovak mythonyms complement and specify the well-known isoglosses between Slavic dialects. At the same time, "mythological" isoglosses are qualitatively different from "language" ones, since, in the spirit of ethnolinguistics, they are considered in conjunction with isodoxes and characterize the cultural dialect as a whole. Mythological vocabulary, reflecting not only the language, but also ideological, philosophical concepts, is of great importance for the reconstruction of the linguistic and cultural history of the Slavs.

Abbreviations:

Arkh. – Arkhangel'sk region, N.-Russia
arch. – archaic
Bel. – Belorussian
Boyk. – W.-Ukrainian Boyko dialicts
Bryan. – Bryansk region, W.-Russia

---

81. See Petrukhin 2003.

Bulg. – Bulgarian
Carp.-Ukr. – Carpathian-Ukrainian
Chęciń. – Chęciny region, Poland, pow. Świętokrzyski.
dial. – dialectal
Don. – Don-river region
E.- – East-, Eastern
Gomel. – Gomel region, Belorussia
Great-Pol. – Great-Polish
Kostrom. – Kostroma region, Central Russia
L.-Sorb. – Low-Sorbian
Lemk. – Lemko dialects (north part of Russinian dialects)
mid. – middle
Mor.-Slovac. – Moravian Slovacko
Morav. – Moravian
N.- – North-, Northern
Perm. – Perm region, E.-Russia
Pol. – Polish
Rus. – Russian
Ruthen. – Ruthenian dialects in East Slovakia
S.- – South-, Southern
S.-Cr. – Serbian-Croatian
Saratov. – Saratov region, E.-Russia
Slov. – Slovak
Sloven. – Slovenian
Sorb. – Sorbian
Tobol. – Tobolsk region in W.-Siberia, Russia
Ufim. – Ufa region, Bashkir republic, RF
Ukr. – Ukrainian
Viat. – Viatka region, E.-Russia, now - Kirov
Volog. – Vologda region, N.-Russia
Volyn. – Volyn' region, W.-Ukraine
W.- – west-, western
Val. – Valašsko, Wallachia and its dialects in E.-Moravia, Czech Republic
Zakarpat. – Zakarpatie region, W.-Ukraine

References

AT ÚEt – *Archív textov Ústavu etnológie SAV*. Bratislava.
Avanesov, R. I., 1977: "K problematike Obšeslavjanskogo lingvističeskogo atlasa", *Zbornik radova – povodom 70. godišnjice života akademika Jovana Vukovića*. Sarajevo. 29-36.
Baranowski, B., 1981: *W kręgu upiorów i wilkołaków*. Łódź.

Bartoš, F., 1883: *Lid a národ. Sebrané rozpravy národopisné a literární.* Velké Meziříčí.
Bartoš, F., 1903-1906: *Dialektický slovník moravský.* V Praze. Část I. 1903. Část II. 1906.
BelM – *Belaruskaja mifalogija. Encyklapėdyčny sloŭnik.* Minsk, 2004.
Bernštejn, S. B., 2000: "Karpatskiy dialektologičeskiy atlas", *in* S. B. Bernštejn, *Iz problematiki dialektologii i lingvogeografii.* Moscow.
Čerepanova, O. A., 1983: *Mifologičeskaja leksika Russkogo Severa.* Leningrad.
Dobšinský, P., 1880: *Prostonárodnie obyčaje, povery a hry slovenské.* Turč.S. Martin.
EĽKS: *Encyklopédia ľudovej kultúry Slovenska.* [Bratislava], 1995. T. 1, 2.
ESSJa: *Etimologičeskij slovar' slavjanskikh jazykov. Praslavjanskij leksičeskij fond.* 1-33. O. N. Trubačeva, A. F. Žuravlev (dir.). Moscow. 1974-2007.
Georgieva, I, 1993: *B"lgarska narodna mitologia. Vtoro preraboteno i dop"lneno izdanie.* Sofia.
Habovštiak, A., 2006: *Oravci o svojej minulosti, Reč a slovesnosť oravského ľudu.* Martin.
Horehronie – *Horehronie. Kultúra a spôsob života ľudu.* Bratislava, 1969.
Horváthová, E., 1972: "Zo zvykoslovných a poverových reálií na Hornom Spiši", *Slovenský národopis,* 1972/3: 484-503.
Horváthová, E., 1986: *Rok vo zvykoch nášho ľudu.* [Bratislava].
Ivić, P., 1957-1958: "Značaj lingvističke geografije za uporedno i istorisko proučavanje južnoslovenskih jezika i njihovih odnosa prema ostalim slovenskim jezicima", *Južnoslovenski filolog.* Knj. 22. Belgrade.
Kálal – *Slovenský slovník z literatúry aj nárečí. Slovensko-český diferenciálny. Na základe slovníkov, literatúry aj živej reči spracovali Kar. Kálal a Mir. Kálal.* V Banskej Bystrici, 1923.
Khobzej, N., 2002: *Gutsuľs'ka mifologija. Etnolingvističnyj slovnik.* Ľviv.
Klepikova, G. P., 1994: "Motiv dviženija-poleta v semantike karpato-balkanskogo striga (štriga)", *Balkanskie čtenia 3. Lingvo-etnokuľturnaja istorija Balkan i Vostočnoj Evropy. Tezisy i materialy simpoziuma.* Moscow. 94-99.
Kott Fr. Št.: *Česko-německý slovník zvláště grammaticko-fraseologický.* D. 1-7. Praha, 1878-1893. (http://kott.ujc.cas.cz)
Kropej, M., 2008: *Od Ajda do Zlatoroga. Slovenska bajeslovna bitja.* Ljubljana, 2008.
Kurkina, L. V., 1985: "Praslavjanskie dialektnye istoki južnoslavjanskoj jazykovoj gruppy", *Voprosy jazykoznanija,* №4: 61-71.
Machek, V., 2010: *Etymologický slovník jazyka českého.* Fotoreprint podle 3. vydání z roku 1971. Praha.
Michálek, J., *a kol.,* 1989: *Ľud hornádskej doliny (na území Popradského okresu).* Košice.

Michálek, J. (ed.) 2011 – Gemer–Malohont. Národopisná monográfia. Ján Michálek *a kol.* [Martin].
Pełka, L. J., 1987: *Polska demonologia ludowa.* Wrocław.
Petrukhin, V. Ja, 2003: *Mify Finno-Ugrov.* Moscow.
Plotnikova, A. A., 2004: *Etnolingvističeskaja geografija Južnoj Slavii.* Moscow.
Polívka, J. 1922: "Du surnaturel dans les contes slovaques: les êtres surnaturels", *Revue des Études Slaves*, 2, 1-2: 104-124.
SD: *Slavjanskije drevnosti. Etnolingvističeskij slovar' (Slavic antiquities. Ethnolinguistic dictionary),* T. 1-5. Moscow, 1995-2012.
Svešnikova, T. N., 1979: "Volki-oborotni u rumyn", Balcanica. Lingvističeskie issledovanija. Moscow. 208-221.
Serdjukova, O. K., 2005: *Slovar' govora kazakov-nekrasovtsev.* Rostov-on-Don.
Slovensko, 1975: *Slovensko. Ľud.* II časť. Bratislava, 1975.
SS: *Slovar' govorov staroobrjadcev (semejskikh) Zabajkaľja,* T. B. Jumsunov (dir.). Novosibirsk. 70.
SSN – *Slovník slovenských nárečí. Ukážkový zväzok.* Bratislava, 1980. Red. I. Ripka. Bratislava. D. 1. 1994. D. II. 2006.
Tolstoj, N. I., 1995: *Jazyk i narodnaja kuľtura. Očerki po slavjanskoj mifologii i etnolingvistike.* Moscow.
Trubačev, O. N., 1967: "Iz slavjano-iranskikh leksičeskikh otnošenij", *Etimologiya 1965. Materialy i issledovanija po indoevropejskim i drugim jazyka.* Moscow. 3-81.
Trubačev, O. N., 1985: "Jazykoznanie i etnogenez slavjan. V", *Voprosy jazykoznanija,* №4: 3-17.
Valencova, M. M. 2012: "Iz karpato-balkanskikh skhoždenij v oblasti mifologičeskoj leksiki", *Slavjanskij mir v tretjem tysjačeletii.* Moscow, 345-362.
Valencova, M. M., 2016: "K issledovaniju balto-slavʼanskoj demonologii", *Res Humanitariae XX*, Klaipėda. 70-88.
Valencova, M. M. 2018: "Slavjanskaja mifologičeskaja leksika Karpatskogo regiona: genezis osobennostey (etnolingvističeskiy aspekt)", *Slavjanskoye jazykoznaniye. XVI Meždunarodnyy s"yezd slavistov. Belgrad. 20-27 avgusta 2018 g. Doklady rossiyskoy delegatsii / Otv. red. S.M. Tolstaya.* Moscow, ISl RAN, 417-435.
Vážný, V., 1955: O jménech motýlů v slovenských nářečích. Bratislava.
Vendina, T. I, 2008: "Karpato-južnoslavjanskiye jazykovyye kontakty (po materialam OLA)", *Karpato-balkanskiy dialektny landshaft. Jazyk i kultura.* Moscow. 58-124.
Vinogradova, L. N., 2000: *Narodnaja demonologija i mifirituaľnaja traditsija slavjan.* Moscow, 2000.

Vinogradova, L. N., 2001: *Slavjanskaja narodnaja demonologija: problemy sravniteľnogo izučeniya*. Dissertatsija v vide naučnogo doklada na soiskanije učenoy stepeni doktora filologičeskikh nauk. Moscow.

Vinogradova L. N., Tolstaja, S. M. 1994: "K probleme identifikacii i sravnenija personažej slavjanskoj mifologii", *Slavjanskij i balkanskij foľklor. Verovanija. Tekst. Ritual*. Moscow. 16-43.

Vlasova, M., 1995: *Novaja abevega russkikh suyeverij. Illjustrirovannyj slovar'*. Saint-Petersburg.

Zubov, M. I, 2010: "Kiľka etimologičnix zauvažen' do nazv slov'jans'kix mifologičnix personaživ", *Movoznavstvo*, № 2-3: 113-123.

Mythological triadism as the paradigm of princely succession in early Rus' according to the *Primary Chronicle*

Aleksandr Koptev

Helsinki

aleksandr.koptev.55@gmail.com

Abstract. The Old Russian Rurikid dynasty's foundation story of three brothers has many parallels in the early historical narratives of various nations. Three brothers as heroes of Russian fairy tales about three kingdoms resembles the Scythian origin myth as recorded by Herodotus. They divide the universe for three kingdoms of copper, silver and gold, the best of which always get to younger brother in the triad. The oral tradition preserved the memory of an archaic custom to divide the tribal country among three princely heirs, the youngest of whom was considered as the principal successor (minorate). The third son ruled a new town (Novgorod), built perhaps on the newly occupied territory. Pre-state society did not have tools to organize large territories, and therefore, in every compact region the same ternary structure was reproduced. The order was based on the mythological idea of a universe consisting of three worlds. The habit detects itself in the three groups of the Rus' (Kuyaba, Artania, and Slavia) and the three branches of Prince Vladimir's descendants in Polotsk (*Rogvolodovichi*), Kiev (*Yaroslavichi*) and Novgorod (*Rurikovichi*). The Russian country with the capital in Kiev was ruled by the brotherly triads in every generation: (1) Igor and his brothers Uleb and Volodislav; (2) Svyatoslav with Ikmor and Sfenckel (or Igor and Akun); (3) Yaropolk, Oleg and Vladimir; (4) Sudislav, Mstislav and Yaroslav; (5) Izyaslav, Svyatoslav and Vsevolod. Chroniclers extended the princely triadism back into the past, calling into existence the ruling triads of newcomers in Novgorod (Rurik, Sineus, Truvor) and Kiev (Oleg, Askold, Dir) and the triad of the founders of Kiev (Kiy, Shchek and Khoriv).

Keywords. Rurikid dynasty, Rus', triadism, *Primary Chronicle*, princely succession

> **6**368-6370 (860-862). The tributaries of the Varangians drove them back beyond the sea and, refusing them further tribute, set out to govern themselves. There was no law among them, but tribe rose against tribe. Discord thus ensued among them, and they began to war one against another. They said to themselves, "Let us seek a prince who may rule over us and judge us according to the Law." They accordingly went overseas to the Varangian Rus': these particular Varangians were known as Rus', just as some are called Swedes, and others Normans, English, and Gotlanders, for they were thus named. The Chuds, the Slavs, the Krivichians, and the Ves' then said to the people of Rus', "Our land is great and rich, but there is no order in it. Come to rule and reign over us." They thus selected three brothers, with their kinsfolk, who took with them all the Rus' and migrated. The oldest, Rurik, located himself in Novgorod; the second, Sineus, at Beloozero; and the third, Truvor, in Izborsk. On account of these Varangians, the district of Novgorod became known as the land of Rus'. The present inhabitants of Novgorod are descended from the Varangian race, but aforetime they were Slavs. After two years, Sineus and his brother Truvor died, and Rurik assumed the sole authority. He assigned cities to his followers, Polotsk to one, Rostov to another, and to another Beloozero. In these cities there are thus Varangian colonists, but the first settlers were, in Novgorod, Slavs; in Polotsk, Krivichians; at Beloozero, Ves', in Rostov, Merians; and in Murom, Muromians. Rurik had dominion over all these districts. With Rurik there were two men who did not belong to his kin, but were boyars. They obtained permission to go to Tsargrad with their families. They thus sailed down the Dnipro, and in the course of their journey they saw a small city on a hill. Upon their inquiry as to whose town it was, they were informed that three brothers, Kyi, Shchek, and Khoriv, had once built the city, but that since their deaths, their descendants were living there as tributaries of the Khazars. Askold and Dir remained in the city, and after gathering together many Varangians, they established their dominion over the country of the Polyanians at the same time that Rurik was ruling at Novgorod."[1]

This legendary story has attracted the attention of many scholars who dispute the origins of Rurik, tracing his genealogy either to Scandinavian chieftains, or to Slavic princes from the South Baltic sea region (Pomerania, *Pomorze*)[2]. The princely dynasty which ruled Rus' from 862 to 1598 is called 'Rurikids'

---

1. *Primary Chronicle* 1953: 59-60.
2. See Lowmianski 1985; Pčelov 2001; Fomin 2005.

(*Rurikovichi*, Rurik's descendants). There are no traces, however, of the rule of Rurik in Novgorod on the Volkhov, or his brothers in Izborsk and Beloozero[3]. After the death of the brothers, Rurik appears in the company of another two men, Askold and Dir, whose departure to the south unified Novgorod and Kiev under the rule of the same family. In former times, Kiev was supposedly also ruled by three brothers, Kyi, Shchek and Khoriv, who had founded the town.

Similar tales of three brothers, ancestors or founders, are numerous in the traditions of various peoples. In the biblical foundation myth, the ancestors of all nations are the sons of Noah - Shem, Ham, and Japheth (*Genesis* IX, 18-29). The *Primary Chronicle* develops this idea, stating that Shem, Ham, and Japheth divided the earth among them and lived each in his appointed portion. The tripartite universe was typical in Indo-European cultures. In Greek cosmography, the entire oikumene consisted of three parts - Europa, Asia, Africa, and the forefather Hellen had three sons, Aeolus, Dorus, and Xunthus, who became the progenitors of the Aeolians, the Dorians, and the Achaeans with the Ionians[4]. In Iranian tradition, at the end of his life the cultural hero Fereydun (Avestan Θraētaona) allocated his kingdom (universe) to his three sons Salm, Tur, and Iraj, who ruled in Rum, Turan and Iran[5]. According to the Scythian origin, referred to by Herodotus (*Hist*. IV, 6), Tarhitay, a son of Zeus, had three sons: Lipoksay, Aproksay, and Kolaksay, who were ancestors of the Scythian people. The Ossetian versions of the Nart epos depict the Nartic tribe as composed of three distinct clans who sometimes rival one another: the brave Æxsærtægkatæ (to whom the most prominent Narts belong), the rich Boræta, and the wise Alægatæ[6]. According to Jordan (*Get*. 180), the Hunnic empire was founded by three brothers, Octar (Optar), Ruga (Roas) and Mundzuk, the father of Attila. Three brothers from the Amal clan (Amelungen in the *Niebelungenlied*), Theodemir, Valamir and Vidimer, headed the Ostrogoths in the Battle of the Catalaunian Plains (Iord. *Get*. 199). Tacitus (*Germ*. II, 3) refers

---

3. The name *Rurikovo Gorodische* for a settlement nearby Novgorod on the Volkhov is an attribution of the 19th century, influenced by legends which identify this place with the capital of the state of Rurik. Izborsk and Beloozero signify the outskirts of the Novgorod lands in the west and east at the time of the *Chronicle* was compiled in the early 12th century, and they have nothing to do with the 9th century.
4. Herodot. *Hist*. I, 56; Thucyd. *Hist*. I, 3; Apollod. *Bibl*. I, 49; Pausan. *Hellad. Per*. VII, 1, 2; Plut. *Quest. Conv*. IX, 15, 747.
5. Molé 1952: 455-463; Raevskij 2006: 72-77, 107.
6. Colarusso 2002; Dumezil 2001.

to the origins of the Germanic people on the basis of the traditional songs of the earth-born god Tuisto, whose son Mannus had three sons who gave their names to three groups of tribes - the Ingaevones, the Herminones, and the Istaevones. Bede in his *Ecclesiastical History* (Bk I, 15), written around 731, identifies the Germanic migrants to Britain as belonging to three tribes, the Angles, Saxons and Jutes. Three brothers, Amelaus, Syttarachus, and Yvorus, founded the first three cities of Ireland, Dublin, Waterford and Limerick. An Armenian legend, recorded by Venod Glak or John Mamikonean in the 'History of Taron', tells of three brothers, Kuarh, Metley, and Khorean, each of whom built a city and named it after himself.

In the 'Saga of Didrik of Bern' (*Saga Điðriks konungs af Bern / Þiðreks saga af Bern, Niflunga saga* or *Vilkina saga*, ch. 22), the Russian king Gertnit had three sons, whom he divided his kingdom: Osantrix headed the Wilkinaland, Valdemar ruled Poland and Ilias ruled Greece (that is, Kievan Rus')[7]. The Russian Primary Chronicle under the year 898 refers to three princes of Moravia - Rostislav, Svyatopolk and Kotsel. According to the *Chronicle of Ioakim*, the prince Vandal was succeeded by three sons, Izbor, Vladimir and Stolposvyat. In the Helmold's *Chronicle of the Slavs* we read that at the time of the Polish king Boleslav, the Slavic tribe of Vinules or Vinites was ruled by three princes Mechislav, Hakon and Zederix, while the tribe of Obodrites was ruled by Anadrag, Gnaeus and Udo, who was especially committed to paganism[8]. According to the *Chronicle of Serbian princes*, after the archon Vlastimir dead, his power was inherited by his three sons, Muntymir, Stroimir and Goynik. Muntymir captured and issued his brothers to Bulgaria, and after his death he was similarly succeeded by his three sons, Prebyslav, Bran and Stefan[9]. The *Chronicle of Greater Poland* (*Chronicum Poloniae* ch. 1) tells us of the three sons of Pan, the lord of the Pannonians, - Lekh, Rus and Czech: "These three, multiplying in kin, owned three kingdoms: Lekhites, Russians and Czechs". Apparently, all these legends went back to the very ancient mythological archetype, described in the opening lines of the Serbian folk song: "The city is built by three brothers ... / The city has been under construction for three years, / Three hundred masters help them"[10]. V. Petrukhin considers these legends of three brothers to be a topos of literature

---

7. See Veselovskij 1906, 137-138.
8. Helmold *Chron. Slav.* I, 15; Adam. Bremen. *Gesta Hammaburg. eccl. pontif.* II, 26-27, 19.
9. Casebook 1987: I, 71-72.
10. *Serbian epos* 1960: I, 56.

and folklore, rather than anything with a historical foundation[11]. However, unlike his brothers, whose fictiveness is acknowledged, in scholarship Rurik is considered a historical personage[12].

***

B. Rybakov drew attention to a complex of fairy tales about the three kingdoms, of copper, silver and gold, in which three princes or three heroes act[13]. Yu. Sokolov calls the tale of three kingdoms the most widespread in the Russian oral tradition, which exists in 45 Russian variants alone (besides the Ukrainian and Belorussian versions)[14]. The basic scheme of such tales presupposes a campaign of heroes to search for the disappeared princesses or their own mother, who was carried away by the atrocious Serpent (*Zmey*), a Whirlwind or the evil Raven (*Voron Voronovich*)[15]. The hero of the fairy tale, together with his two brothers goes to the distant reaches of the earth and after long wanderings they find themselves by some kind of pass leading to the underworld. To perform their task, the heroes must descend into the depths to battle with a monster (Serpent) and to rescue the princesses. When the goal of the heroic campaign is attained, the brothers try to kill the main hero or leave him imprisoned in the darkness, cutting the rope by which he must rise from the underworld to his own kingdom (to the 'white (sunny) world'). Overcoming the cunning of his brothers, the main hero finally receives the golden kingdom and the most beautiful princess as a prize, and he endows his brothers with the silver and copper kingdoms. As shown by P. Sentiv and V. Propp, many fairy-tale motifs are derived from ancient myths and rituals, surviving as poetic vestiges of them[16]. The prototypes of the three fabulous heroes were the mythological heroes of the age of foundation - Manu 'man', *Yemo 'twin' and *Trito 'third'[17]. Each of the heroes served as a mythological model for one of the three main social groups (people, warriors, priests). Br. Lincoln traces two main elements in the Indo-European myth of *Trito[18]. This is the myth of the victory over the monster, usually three-

---

11. See Petruxin 1982: 143-158; 1995: 52-61.
12. See Mel'nikova 2000: 143-159.
13. Rybakov 1981: 528-596.
14. Sokolov 1941: 321.
15. Afanasiev 1957, № 559.
16. See Gilet 1998.
17. Lincoln 1976: 42-65. *Cf.* Elizarenkova, Toporov 1973: 65-70; Al'bedil, Misjugin 1984: 102-111.
18. *Cf.* Toporov 1977: 41-65.

headed, and the first cattle raid (cattle being the most valuable commodity of a pastoral society and thus the commodity by which other things were valued, approximating to archaic money). Lincoln emphasizes the connection of the mythical monster with the earth, its serpentine form, and its role as a stranger, the kidnapper and invader.

The fairy story about three kingdoms resembles the Scythian origin myth as recorded by Herodotus (*Hist.* IV, 5-6). The legend clearly had a mythological origin. Tarhitay, the son of the god Zeus and the daughter of the river Borysphen (Dneper), was the first human in the Scythian country and he had three sons: Lipoksay, Aproksay, and Kolaksay, the youngest. During their lifetime gold objects fell from the heavens to the Scythian land: a plough, a yoke, axes, and a goblet. The first to spot these objects was the oldest son Lipoksay. When he was approaching them, the gold objects began to glow, and he stepped back. When the middle son Aproksay tried to seize them, the same thing happened to them, and he stepped back. When the youngest of the brothers, Kolaksay, approached the gold, it stopped glowing, and he took all the objects to his home. After this his elder brothers decided to relinquish the entire kingdom to their younger brother. The brothers became ancestors of the Scythian tribes named *Skolotai*, that is, royal. V. Abaev and E. Grantovsky interpret the name of Lipoksay as 'Mountain-king', Aproksay as 'River-king' and Kolaksay as 'Sun-king'[19]. The name of the youngest brother thus has a similar association to that of the Russian fairy-tale hero 'Ivan Light-Bringer, Dawning, Sunrise' (*Svetovik, S'vitovyk, Ivan Zor'kin, Svetozar, Svetlanya, Zorjavoy Ivan*)[20].

To the same line also belongs the title of the 'Russian king' – *Swet* or *S.wit.m.l.k*, referred to by the Arabic and Iranian authors (Ibn Rustah, Gardizi, Hudud-al-Alam, Marvizi, Schukrulla, Mukhamed Katib, Khadji Khalif)[21]. The similar notion 'light princes' (*свѣтлые кнѧзн*) is known from the treaty of Prince Oleg with the Byzantine Empire in 911[22]. The 'light king' resembles the Slavic princely names Svyatoslav and Svyatopolk and the name of the solar god Svyatovit (Swentovit) by the Western Slavs. The author of 'The Song of Igor's Campaign' used the notion '*dazhbozhii vnuki*' ('grandchildren of Dazhbog'), which suggests that before the adoption of Christianity, the Russian princes were regarded

---

19. Abaev 1949: I, 243; 1965: 39-40; Grantovskij 1960: 7-9.
20. Rybakov 1981: 580-581.
21. See Novosel'cev 1965: 388-391, 396; Zaxoder 1967: 119-121; Kmietowicz 1976: 177; Mišin 2002: 59-60.
22. *Cf.* Rybakov 1993: 276-277.

as the offspring of the solar deity[23]. In the *Hypatian Chronicle* under the year 1114[24], the name of Helios from the Greek chronicle of Malala is translated as Dazhbog[25]. The word 'light' (*svyet, swiat*) is close to the Sanskrit श्वेत 'shveta' light, white, used as an epithet for the deity of the sun[26]. A similar epithet is used in the expression 'white day' and 'white light' in the sense of 'white world', that is, the world illuminated by heavenly light. Lithuanian *swietas* and Old Prussian *switai* are also used in both senses - as a world and as an element of light. It seems, therefore, that B. Rybakov correctly interprets the Arabic term *S.wit.m.l.k* as a translation of the Slavic 'light prince'. In fact, the last term probably meant something like 'red/beautiful, glorious Sun' or 'Sun-prince'. The folkloric nickname of Prince Vladimir – *Krasnoe Solnyshko* ('Red or Beautiful Sun' or 'Sun-prince') looks like a copy of his patronymic *Svyatoslavich* (son of Svyatoslav).

Rybakov also points to the name of the old hero Tarkh Tarakhovich of the fairy tales, who resembles the Scythian forefather Tarhitay (Ταργιταος)[27]. The advanced age of Tarkh Tarakhovich, his staying in the underworld, into which the hero needs to fly, falling 12 days and 12 nights through the earth, indicate that he is an ancestor figure, like Tarhitay. A similar figure occurs in the legends of early Rome, where Tarkhetius is the grandfather of Romulus and Tarquinius is the founder of the Etruscan dynasty. The Iranian hero of Traetaona (Fereydun) was considered the mythical forefather of the Persian kings. According to other myths, Iranian Traetaona and Indian Traitana (Trita) fought against a three-headed dragon and liberated captured women and herds of bulls[28]. Similarly, Vedic Indra overpowered the cosmic dragon Vritra, and the son of Zeus, Apollo Targelius, defeated the giant snake Python. On the territory of ancient Lydia, Zeus had the epithet *Tarhuenos*, obviously related to the Hittite *Tarhu* ('Powerful'). Tarhun, also spelled *Taru, Tarhu, Tarhunt, Tarhunna*, or *Tarhuis*, was the ancient Hittite and Luwian weather god, who slew a dragon during New

---

23. For the image of Sun-king as Khors or Khors-Dazhbog, see Vasil'ev 1999.
24. *Cf.* Rybakov 1981: 266–352, 434; 1987, 440–442; Sokolova 1995: 79-82.
25. *PSRL* II, 5 : "after [Svarog] his son with the name Sun reigned, he is named also Dazhbog... Sun-king, son of Svarog, that is Dazhbog, because is a man strong."
26. Ilovajskij 2002: 48-49; Toporov 1987: 184-252.
27. Tarkh Tarkhovoch was defeated by Baba Yaga and lived in his palace on the Bright Mount (*Siyanskoy gore*). See Novikov 1974: 161.
28. Raevskij 2006: 108.

Year rituals[29]. In iconography Tarhun's symbol was a three-pronged thunderbolt, which he usually carried in one hand while brandishing a club, ax, or other weapon with the other. Tarhunt was the Luwian form and Tarhun (Tarhunna) probably the Hittite, from the common root *tarh-*, 'to defeat, conquer'. The weather god was one of the supreme deities of the Hittite pantheon and was regarded as the embodiment of the state in action. He played a prominent part in mythology, although his name is sometimes to be read either Taru or Teshub (the Hattian and Hurrian weather gods, respectively). The Hurrian deity name Teshub appears in Luwian as *Tarhunzas*. Teshub reappears in the post-Hurrian cultural successor kingdom of Urartu as Teisheba. Taru was known as *Tarhun / Tarhunt- / Tarhuwant- / Tarhunta*. In Armenia, the god of fertility and vegetation was Tarku (Turgu), while the Ossetians named a similar deity Taranjeloz. The Celtc god Taranis (the name has the forms *Tanarus, Taranucno-* (son of *Taranis), Taranuo-*, and *Taraino-*) was a thunder god (all the Celtic languages retain the word *taran* for thunder: Irish *toirneach*, Welsh *taranu*, Breton *taran*, Gaelic *tàirneanach*), comparable to Jupiter[30]. It is difficult to say whether the Scandinavian Thor should be included in this series, but the similar features of both name and attributes are beyond doubt.

Obviously, Tarkh, Tarkhetius, Tarhitay, as well as Etruscan Tarkhon, Tarhunias, Tarquinius, Iranian Traetaona (Fereydun), Vedic Trita, not to mention many similar royal and divine names in ancient Anatolia, can be traced to the same ancient prototype[31]. The twelve-dimensionality of time-space on the way to the staying place of Tarkh Tarkhovich indicates the remnant of a mythological interpretation of the annual cycle. In the original version, the three sons of the first human symbolized three seasons - winter, spring, summer. Apparently, summer, as the most important annual season for pastoralists and farmers, received a symbolic reflection in the image of the solar king. This image became central in the ternary mythology of the ancient Indo-Europeans. In fairy tales, the brothers compete in various ways (they move the stone, the club, etc.), and the younger always wins, becoming the main hero after this competition. In the fairy tale 'On the Three Kingdoms', the rivalry of the brothers takes the form of hostility. After the victory over the monster (Serpent or Yaga) and the rescue of the three princesses, the older brothers cut the rope along which the younger is climbing from the underworld (winter or the dead-season). Magic wonderful

---

29. Ünal 2001: 99-121.
30. *Myths* 1982: II, 495-521.
31. Alföldi 1984: 181-216; Raevskij 2006: 36-37, 61-62, 72-101, 106-112.

forces save the hero, and he reigns in his golden kingdom. Of the three fairy kingdoms - copper, silver and gold - the best is always available to the younger brother, just as in Herodotus the sacred gold is placed in the hands of only the youngest of the brothers, Kolaksay or the Sunny king[32]. The calendar, which interpreted the annual cycle as a cycle of three seasons, began on September 1. The motive of enmity between brothers symbolises the misadventures of the sun at the exit / entrance from the winter period. In the Vedic hymns, Trita ('Third') acts as a brother thrown into the well, just like the younger brother in Russian fairy tales[33].

The motif of three kingdoms can be represented not only in the form of three seasons of the annual cycle, but also in the form of a vertical structure of the universe[34]. The trinity of the universe is demonstrated by the discovery of the so-called Zbruch idol[35]. B. Rybakov interprets three tiers of the Idol's stone tetrahedral pillar as symbolizing three worlds - heavenly, earthly and underground (otherworld). An image of the god ruling in each of the worlds is placed in each tier. The celestial and subterranean worlds are an imaginary reality, the place of the gods, while the middle terrestrial world is inhabited by the people and their ruler, who, despite his divine status, is shown as smaller than his divine 'brothers'. He is more like a hero, a demigod or a half-man. Such a view of the universe corresponds to the ritual of the burial of the prince described by the Christian compiler of the *Primary Chronicle* as the threefold revenge that Princess Olga inflicts on the Drevlyans. In the funeral ritual there is a triad of 'brothers': the two 'elder brothers' are the gods of the heavenly and underground worlds and the third younger brother is the hero, the ruler of the terrestrial world, the prince. Before the funeral ceremony (*trizna*) in honour of the deceased Prince Igor, his wife Olga sent ambassadors to the rulers of the worlds adjacent to the Russian land. The ambassadors burned in the bathhouse were sent to the heavenly god, and those buried in a boat in the earth went to the underground kingdom. The physical nature (that is, the profane origin) of

---

32. In *Shahnameh* (lines 3309-3402), after the division of the father's kingdom, the elder sons, dissatisfied with the father's decision, kill the younger brother. In C. Valerius Flaccus' *Argonautica* (VI.621-64), Colaxes (Kolaksay) fights with Apres (Arpoksay). *Cf.* Raevskij 2006: 38-43, 91, 144-147.
33. Elizarenkova, Toporov 1973: 65-70.
34. Gamkrelidze, Ivanov 1995: 749; West 2007: 345-347; Shaw 2012: 57-76.
35. Leńczyk 1964: 5-61; Rybakov 1981: 248, 265, 277, 300-303; Komar, Xamajko 2011: 166-217.

the earthly ruler determined his defective status in comparison with the older brothers (holders of divine sacredness). In folklore, their statuses are reversed – the older brothers are ordinary men, while the third brother is outstanding. In fairy tales of mythological origin, the younger brother often appears at the first stages of the action as retarded, stupid, or 'underdeveloped' (Latin *Brutus*, Russian *Ivan the Fool*), but in the end he becomes the main hero of the narrative[36].

From the point of view of the cosmological myth, the younger brother played the role of a hero, who associated with both supernatural worlds as an intermediary or ferryman (king-priest)[37]. This mythological concept, combining the 'inferiority' and 'heroism' of the younger brother, may have influenced the poetics of fairy tales[38]. Over time, the relative positions of the brotherly rulers of the three worlds begin to change under the influence of the military function of the terrestrial 'brother', who amasses a large number of people and material assets under his control. The military powers as an alternative to the former religious authority of Slavic princes developed in close long-term contact with the western, Byzantine and Islamic civilizations. In the public life of Slavic society and hence the consciousness of its people, the princes became more and more significant, while their former divine 'brethren' received the role of assistants. Fairy tales have retained a memory of the former seniority of the two brothers, but the folkloric motif developed the mythological idea of the priority of their younger brother. This distinctive position of the younger brother in the triad of the rulers of the universe was the possible basis for the custom of the ultimogeniture in the princely succession of the pre-Christian era (before the adoption of princely primogeniture from Byzantium).

Magical fairy tales about the three kingdoms show that the mythological consciousness structured into three parts not only time, but also space. The oldest territorial organization of archaic societies also went back to a tripartite structure. Ancient Greek Sparta consisted of three *phylai*, archaic Attica of *trittyes*, Rome of three tribes (Varro *de lingua Latina* V, 55). The early medieval Saxons were divided into three tribes (Eastphalen, Angarii and Westphalen) and were ruled by three kings[39]. The *regnum Saxonum* was divided into three provinces – Westphalia, Eastphalia and Angria. In the same way, the Moravian prince

---

36. Bettini 1987: 71-120.
37. V. Misjugin stresses the magical character of the peculiar properties of the third brother. See Al'bedil, Misjugin 1984: 102-111.
38. For another idea of the 'younger brother', see Meletinskij 1958: 64-160.
39. Widukind, *Res gestae saxonica* I, 14.

Svyatopolk (870-894) divided the state among his three sons so that the elder was proclaimed 'Grand Duke', and two his younger brothers were subordinate to him ('under his hand')[40]. Similarly, Boleslav III the Red (*Ryšavý*) (992-1003) ruled the Czech country conjointly with the brothers Jaromir and Oldřich[41]. Cnut the Great, who died in 1035, left his power to three sons: Harold Harefoot in England, Sveyn in Norway, and Harthacnut in Denmark[42]. Scandinavian sagas distinguish three major cities of Rus' - Novgorod, Kiev and Polotsk, although they know many other cities, and Smolensk is included in the quarter of the most famous[43]. Kiev, Novgorod and Polotsk especially clearly function as the three main cities of Rus' in the 'Eymundar saga'. Icelandic sagas also often divide Rus', called Gardariki, into three parts, Holmgard (Novgorod), Kenugard (Kiev) and Etunheim (the land of giants)[44]. Despite Novgorod's subordination to Kiev, Holmgard-Novgorod was considered by Scandinavians as the capital of Rus', where the 'main throne of the king of Garda' is located[45]. In the *Saga of Didrik of Bern* (ch. 22-26), compiled in the mid-12th century but reflecting earlier times, the Russian state is the land with its capital in Holmgard and the main cities are Smolensk and Polotsk[46].

*

The *Primary Chronicle* models the Novgorod land in three parts with midpoints at Novgorod, Izborsk and Beloozero, although the Varangians were invited by four tribes – the Chud, the Slovene, the Krivichians and the Ves'[47]. The Krivichians had their own land around Polotsk and Smolensk and the Ves around Beloozero. The addition of these two tribes to those which invite the Varangians is probably indicative of the claims of Novgorod to these cities at the beginning of the 12th century. The city of Novgorod consisted of three separate settlements (*konzy* 'ends') - Nerevsky, Lyudin and Slovensky[48]. The tripartite structure is associated with 3000 'warriors' (*voi*) of the Novgorod army, the council of 300 notable

---

40. Const. Porphyr. *De administer. Imp.*, cap. 41.
41. Thietmar. *Chron.* V.23.
42. Adam. Bremen, *Gesta Hammaburg. eccl. pontif.* II, 74.
43. See Jackson 2000: 130-131.
44. Petruxin 1995: 53.
45. See Jackson 2000: 59.
46. See Veselovskij 1906: 134-136, 169. Cf. Janin, Aleškovskij 1971: 48-49 n. 55.
47. A. Kuza argues the three-tribe federation of Novgorod, the Slovene, the Krivichians, and the Chud/Ves'. See Kuza 1975: 146-152.
48. Janin, Aleškovskij 1971: 40.

persons ('golden belts')[49], 300 *grivny* of the tribute to the Varangians at the time of Prince Oleg, 3000 *grivny* of tribute collected by Novgorod at the time of Yaroslav the Wise, and 300 children of the 'priests and seniors' taken to be trained by Yaroslav in 1036[50]. In later Novgorod there were three churches of St. Peter and St. Paul, which expressed the idea of triumph over paganism and, apparently, consecrated local temples in each of the three urban settlements. Judging by the names of the habitations, the Slovensky 'end' looks like a residence of the Slavs, the Nerevsky (Merevsky) 'end' like that of the Mereans (*Merya*), and the Lyudin 'end' was named after the Chud' (Chud < Thyud > Lyud).

In the Arabic geographical literature, three groups (*asnaf, synf*) of Ruses are mentioned, living at a distance of approximately 150 km from each other (four days' journey). One of them, the nearest to Bulgar, was 18-20 daily passages from this city, and the ruler of these Ruses lived in the city of Kuyabá (*Kukiyana, Ku.a.na, Kuya.a*), which exceeded Bulgar in size. The second group of Ruses (or their country) were called Art(h)aniya (*Authani*), and their ruler lived in the city of Art(h)a (*Artab*). The most remote (from Bulgar) group of Ruses was called Salaviya (*as-Slaviyya, Jalaba*), and their ruler lived in the city of Salav (*Sla.a*). Ibn Haukal calls these Ruses the best (or highest, most important) of all. All three cities are fortified. Merchants exported from their countries skins of 'black leopards' (*anmar*) and black foxes (*as-sa'alib*) and lead (or tin); the Ruses also produced valuable blades for swords and swords themselves. Arta is noted as a city dangerous to outsiders, who avoid visiting it.

Arabian and Persian authors referred to the three Rus(sian) kingdoms or three groups of Ruses in the 10th century. One of the first to mention them was Ahmed ibn Sahl Balkhi in his treatise *Figures of the Climates* (*Suwar al-aqalim*), ca. 920. The unsaved work of al-Balkhi was twice extended by the Iranian geographer al-Istakhri in his *Book of Ways and Countries* (*Kitab al-Masalik wa-l-mamalik*, I, 6, 1, 7-8), in the 930s and 950s. The second edition of al-Istakhri was used by Muḥammad Ibn Ḥawqal in *The face of the Earth* (*Ṣūrat al-'Arḍ*, or *Kitāb Ṣūratu l-Arḍ*) ca. 950-980. The same material is mentioned in the Persian anonymous treatise *Hudud al-'Alam* (*The Limits of the World from East to West*). Al-Idrisi, an Arab geographer at the court of the Sicilian king Roger II, also included the information in his work *A Diversion for the Man Longing to Travel to Far-Off*

---

49. Janin 1970: 50.
50. *PSRL*, t. 3, p. 175: "and they gathered warriors 4000: the Varangians were 1000 and the Novgorodeans were 3000".

Places (*Kitab nuzhat al-mushtaq*), ca. 1154. In modern studies of these accounts, Kuyabá is usually identified with Kiev and Slavia (Salaviya) - with Novgorod, but Artaniya remains a mystery[51]. However, the identification of Kuyaba with Kiev is based only on the similar-sounding names, and Slavia is identified with Novgorod because the latter was inhabited by the Slovenes.

The *Hudud al-Alam* places all three groups of Ruses in the basin of the 'Rus River', which is considered to be the tributary of the Atil, that is, the Volga. All authors correlate the Rus' country with the neighbouring city Bulgar. The Arab scholar Mas'udi in his *Meadows of Gold and Mines of Gems* localizes the region of the Rus in the east of the Slavic world and refers to the campaigns of the Ruses along the 'Khazar river' which flowed to the Azov Sea[52]. According to Idrisi, the Rus' (*ar-Rusiyya*) were of two kinds. Some of them lived in the east and were divided into three groups from Kuyaba, Artania, and Slavia. In this case, the three cities of the Ruses in the 10th century could be those which later became known as Murom, Suzdal and Rostov. The distances between them were just four days journey, Murom being closest to Bulgar on the Oka River. Rostov was reachable from Bulgar along the Volga with an additional day's passage. Suzdal was the furthest of the three from Bulgar. Rostov (Artab) was situated in the area inhabited by the Merians (Artania), Murom (Kuyaba) was in the country of the Muroma tribes, and Suzdal (Salav), occupying the central position, apparently had a mainly Slavic-speaking population (Salaviya).

The other group of Ruses lived in the neighbourhood of Hungary and Danube Bulgaria (*Unkariya* and *Jiasuliyya*). By the time of Idrisi (the first half of the 12th century), these Ruses had already defeated the Burtases, Bulgars and Khazars and subdued their lands. Obviously this group of Ruses, who subdued all the surrounding lands, is Kievan Rus'. Information about the 'Russian country' contemporaneous with the references of Arabic authors to the eastern Ruses, is known from the treatise of the Byzantine emperor Constantine Porphyrogenitus *On the management of the empire* (compiled in 948-952). The capital of these Ruses (Ρῶς) was Kiev (Κιοάβα, Κίοβα), from which their princes (*archons*) annually went from November to April to collect tribute (*polyudie*). During this period, they visited some tribes of the Slavs – the Drevlyans (Βερβιάνοι), the Dregovichi

---

51. Hrbek 1957: 628-652; Thulin 1979: 99-139; Dubov 1982: 104-123; Petruxin 1982: 143-158; Mačinskij 1985: 3-23; Karsanov 1992: 5-13; Konovalova 1995: 139-148; Gorskij 1999: 43-52.
52. See Jackson, Kalinina, Konovalova, Podosinov 2007: 135-157, 222.

(Δρουγουβιτοι), the Krivichians (Κριβιτζοι / Κριβηταιηνοὶ), the Severians (Σεβερίοι) and others (οἱ Λενζανῆνοι καὶ αἱ λοιπαὶ Σκλαβηνίαι). On their return in the spring, Kiev assembled boats (μονόξυλοι) to sail that carried the tribute and goods for sale from the Slavic lands along the tributaries of the Dnieper. All goods collected in this way were transported by the Kiev princes for sale to Byzantium along the Dnieper and across the Black Sea. Emperor Constantine names several cities that which were subject to the Ruses and sent boats -μονόξυλοι - to Kiev – Νεμογαρδάς, τὸ κάστρον τὴν Μιλινίσκαν, Τελιούτζα, Τζερνιγῶγα and Βουσεγραδέ. Modern scholars identify them as Novgorod, Smolensk, Lyubech, Chernigov and Vyshgorod. Novgorod on the Volkhov was outside the Dnieper basin, and Emperor Constantine does not mention the population of the Novgorodian land among the tributaries of Kiev. Smolensk, the city of the Krivichians, seems a more likely northern outpost of the original 'Russian land' with its capital in Kiev.

Novgorod ('new town') is a typical designation for any new settlement. There are two possible identifications for Νεμογαρδάς-Novgorod, where, according to Emperor Constantine, Prince Svyatoslav, a son of Igor, ruled for a short period. (1) Constantine writes that all towns which sent their boats to Kiev were located on the tributaries of the Dnieper (Ταῦτα οὖν ἅπαντα διὰ τοῦ ποταμοῦ κατέρχονται Δανάπρεως, καὶ ἐπισυνάγονται εἰς τὸ κάστρον τὸ Κιοάβα). Judging by the 'itinerary' (τὰ πολύδια, ὃ λέγεται γύρα) of the tribute collectors, this city, named first in the list of tributary cities, could be not very far from Kiev[53]. One can suggest that the new town replaced the burnt Iskorosten as a new urban centre of the Drevlyan land. This city, which was later the princely city of Oleg Svyatoslavich and Svyatoslav Vladimirovich, was named Ovruch. Therefore, Ovruch (or any other town on a western tributary of the Dnieper) could be the 'new town' in which Svyatoslav Igorevich may also have ruled. Three of the Russian cities mentioned by Emperor Constantine - Lyubech, Chernigov and Vyshgorod (as Τελιούτζα, Τζερνιγῶγα and Βουσεγραδέ) - were situated about 200 km from Kiev. Smolensk is more distant, ca. 450 km from Lybech, and Novgorod on the Volkhov is more than 500 km from Smolensk. Νεμογαρδάς and Μιλινίσκα could well have made up a triad of cities with Kiev, being located on the right tributaries of the Dnieper, the Teterev and the Pripyat'. If this is the case Μιλινίσκα can be identified with Malin rather than Smolensk. L. Voytovich has recently identified Νεμογαρδάς-Novgorod with the settlement in Gnezdovo, 12 km from Smolensk[54].

---

53. On the *polyudie*, see Rybakov 1993: 316-329.
54. Vojtovič 2015: 37-55.

(2) If Emperor Constantine listed the cities from north to south, the remotest city from Kiev could be Novgorod on the Volkhov. Under the year 947 the *Primary Chronicle* refers to the voyage of Princess Olga to Novgorod on the Volkhov river, during which she established trading-posts and collected tribute along the rivers Msta and Luga. Although the Chronicle under 882 states that it was Prince Oleg who "commanded that Novgorod should pay the Varangians tribute to the amount of 300 *grivny* a year for the preservation of peace", it seems more probably that the tribute was established during the expedition of Olga in 947. Kiev searched for a new way to the Baltic Sea on the rivers Lovat', Luga and Msta, bypassing the traditional routes on the rivers Pripyat' and Dvina, which were occupied by the Varangians. Princess Olga most likely acquired Novgorod, an insignificant town on the Volkhov in 947, obliging to pay 300 *grivny* per year to the Varangians who possessed this country[55].

Emperor Constantine did not mention any triad in the structure of the Rus' settlements on the Dnieper, unlike the Rus' on the Middle Volga. However, the chronicles present a different picture, suggesting that triads of princes may have represented the succession in Kievan Rus' until the end of the 11th century. Although the *Primary Chronicle*, created early in the 12th century, does not mention the ternary structure of the Rostov-Suzdal land, the very idea of triadism was expressed in the reign of Rurik with his brothers in Novgorod, Beloozero and Izborsk. After the deaths of Sineus and Truvor, Rurik was not the sole ruler, but was accompanied by Askold and Dir. This way of thinking, which goes back to the mythological archetype of the trinity, is manifested in the chronicler's desire to organize the newly formed unity of Novgorod and Kiev under the rule of three rulers. Askold and Dir were sent by Rurik from Novgorod to Kiev, and after their deaths, the unified lands were in the hands of the triad Rurik, Oleg and Igor. The idea of the triple managing of the Russian land was still alive in the consciousness of the chronicler in the late 11th and early 12th centuries[56]. Mentioning the division of the earth among Shem, Ham, and Japheth, the *Primary Chronicle* stresses the parallelism between the myth of creation and the foundation of the Russian state[57]. Noah's sons, after casting lots so that none might encroach upon his brother's share, lived each in his appointed portion of the divided earth, and were considered an example to the Russian princes, who swore not to lay claim to a brother's princedom in Lyubech in 1097.

---

55. *Cf.* Žix 2010: 320-326.
56. See Misjugin 1980: 38-48.
57. *Cf.* Petruxin 1995: 61.

***

The legend of Rurik belongs to the undated introduction of the *Primary Chronicle*, which was compiled in its final version in 1110-1118. The early version of the Kievan dynasty in the *Sermon on Law and Grace*, created by Metropolitan Hilarion between 1036 and 1054, did not mention Rurik and his brothers. Among the ancestors of Prince Vladimir (baptised as Basil), Hilarion lists his father Svyatoslav and grandfather Igor. In fact, the Rurikid dynasty (*Rurikovichi*) began after Yaroslav the Wise. The descendants of his brother Izyaslav, who was allocated Polotsk by their father, held the name *Rogvolodovichi*, after Rogvolod, their maternal grandfather. The name *Rurikovichi* was probably initially adopted by a branch of Prince Vladimir's descendants in Novgorod, who competed with both the *Rogvolodovichi* of Polotsk and the *Yaroslavichi* of Kiev.

Indeed, modern studies show a certain regularity in the choice of princely names[58]. It was customary to give children the names of outstanding ancestors, which makes it surprising that no prince was named Rurik until the second half of the 11th century. The first holder of this name was Rurik Rostislavovich (? -1092), the eldest of the great-grandchildren of Yaroslav the Wise. The eldest son of Yaroslav and Ingegerd - Vladimir (1020-1052) - was installed in Novgorod after his father moved to Kiev in 1036. In the previous generation, Vladimir Svyatoslavovich assigned Novgorod to his elder son Vysheslav and Polotsk to the second son, Izyaslav. Izyaslav's descendants formed the dynasty of *Rogvolodovichi* in Polotsk. In Novgorod, however, this principle did not take root, since Vysheslav died before his father and the rule of Novgorod was (without his father's permission) seized by his brother Yaroslav. Prince Vladimir apparently intended to punish Yaroslav and restore the rightful order, but he died while preparing the campaign. The internecine strife between Vladimir's sons, which began after his death, led to the strengthening of Yaroslav's position in Novgorod, as he received the support of Scandinavian mercenaries after he married the Swedish princess, Ingegerd Olofsdotter. Having seized power in Kiev, Yaroslav left his eldest son Vladimir in Novgorod, apparently hoping to make him the founder of a new dynasty. However, Vladimir Yaroslavich died before his father. According to the chronicles, his successor Rostislav ruled either in Rostov or in Galich in the Volhyn district. However, the *Primary Chronicle* reports under 1064 that "Rostislav, son of Vladimir, the grandson of Yaroslav, fled to Tmutorokan, and Porey and Vyshata, the son of Ostromir, the chieftain (*voevoda*) of Novgorod,

---

58. Sverdlov 2003: 576-578; Litvina, Uspenskij 2006: 11-15.

fled with him". This means that Rostislav Vladimirovich held Novgorod until 1064 and was expelled from his city by his uncles, the triumvirate of Yaroslav's sons, who ruled the 'Russian country' with its capital in Kiev. Expelling his second cousin Gleb Svyatoslavich, Rostislav occupied Tmutorokan, but two years later he was poisoned by Crimean Greeks. Rostislav had three sons - Rurik and his brothers Volodar and Vasilko (both died in 1124). Rostislav spent his childhood in Novgorod: his mother was (according to one account) Oda, daughter of Count Leopold of Staden, and his grandmother Ingegerd, daughter of Swedish king Olaf. As the above-cited fragment of the *Chronicle* shows, Rostislav had a close relationship with the Novgorod nobility, who had claimed the independence of Novgorod from Kiev since the early 11th century.

The purpose of the legend of the invitation to the Varangians was to justify the primacy of Novgorod as the 'Russian country', from where this concept was allegedly transferred to Kiev[59]. This fictitious superiority was necessary to the Novgorod nobility to substantiate their independence from Kiev, which they enjoyed under Yaroslav. Perhaps that is why Rostislav chose the name Rurik, unknown earlier in Rus', for his eldest son. The name *Rurik*, possibly meaning 'ruler of Rus" (*Rus'* + *rex*, *rex Rugorum*), was shaped with the help of the royal root '*rik*' cognate with Latin *rex*, like the Ostrogothic *Hermanarik*. Rurik sounds similar to the Latin *Roricus*, the Scandinavian *Hrörekr* and the West-Slavic *Rerek/Rereg* and partly had the same meaning. The legend about the invitation of the Varangians in its original version was born in the family of the descendants of Vladimir Yaroslavich in order to justify their rights to rule Novgorod in 1052-1064. Discussing the historical prototypes of the legend (from the Baltic Slavs, the Scandinavians or the Baltic-speaking people) is beyond the limits of this article. After Rostislav's death, Prince Vseslav of Polotsk captured Novgorod, but the Yaroslavichi brothers organized a campaign against him and made Novgorod subordinate to Kiev in 1068. Henceforth the separatism of the Novgorod nobility was expressed by playing on the contradictions between the claims of the members of the ruling house of the Yaroslavichi. The death of Rostislav turned his sons Rurik, Volodar and Vasilko into outcasts, but their legend was used by the compiler who composed the *Chronicle* in the 1110s, on the instructions of Prince Mstislav (Harald) the Great, who ruled in Novgorod from 1096 to 1117 and succeeded his father Vladimir Monomakh to the Kievan princedom in 1125-1132.

---

59. *Cf.* Šaxmatov 2001: 210-239.

The order of princely succession is unclear before Yaroslav's 'Testament' of 1054[60]. Chronicles certainly refer to the brotherly triads of Svyatoslav's sons –Yaropolk, Oleg, Vladimir, and Yaroslav's sons - Izyaslav, Svyatoslav, Vsevolod, who ruled the indivisible 'Russian country' (*Russkaya zemlya*)[61]. One can suggest that the *Primary Chronicle* extended the triadism of Yaroslav's descendants back into the past, calling into existence the triads of Ruric, Sineus, Truvor and Oleg, Askold, Dir. Oleg was a relative of Rurik and went from Novgorod to the south, capturing first Smolensk and then Kiev, making the latter his capital. Shortly before Oleg arrived in Kiev, the city was taken by Askold and Dir, who were then killed by Oleg, who argued that they were not of a princely family (*boyare*, not *knyazya*). This murder resembles the sudden death of Sineus and Truvor. These heroes simply had no function in the *Chronicle*, as the Christian compiler focused on the sole rule of every prince and did not understand ancient pagan customs. In fact, the legendary Rurik, Sineus and Truvor were replaced by the triad of Oleg, Dir and Askold. Scholars sometimes consider only Askold as coming from the north, attaching Dir to the local dynasty in Kiev, because Mas'udi mentions a Slavic king with a similar name (*ad-dajr*)[62]. Modern scholarship that adopts this approach develops the mythological model invented by the chronicler.

Oleg, who declared Kiev 'the mother of Russian cities', functioned as the hero of the original foundation myth of Kiev. He and Princess Olga were not mentioned by Metropolitan Hilarion among the Kievan rulers preceding his patron Yaroslav the Wise – the princes Vladimir, Svyatoslav and Igor. The *Primary Chronicle* represents Oleg the Seer (*Veschy*) as the young prince Igor's tutor, not a prince, but until Igor's maturity he ruled Kiev as prince and concluded a treaty with Byzantium in 911. Oleg, Askold and Dir seem to be three legendary founders of the 'Russian land' around Kiev. In the *Primary Chronicle*, their history was combined with the history of Rurik's triad, and Askold, Dir and Oleg became aliens in Kiev. The Kievan myth began to acquire pseudo-historical features when it was combined in the annalistic tradition with another myth of foundation – the story of Rurik and his brothers. Oleg's campaign from Novgorod to capture Kiev is described by the chronicler on the model of Vladimir Svyatoslavich's conquest of the city in the late 970s. In turn, the stories of Oleg and Vladimir

---

60. For the problem, see Dimnik 1996: 87-117; Ostrowski 2012: 29-31.
61. For the narrow meaning of the 'Russian country' (i.e., Kiev, Chernigov, and Pereyaslavl), see Nasonov, 1951: 216-220; Halperin 1975: 29–38; Ostrowski 2012: 42 with bibl. in n. 61. *Cf.* a criticism of Lind 1982: 66-81.
62. Kotljar 1986: 54.

were modelled on a real historical example, namely the capture of Kiev by Prince Yaroslav in 1036[63].

Kiev was deprived of its own foundation myth after Oleg was made a 'relative' of Rurik and a stranger from the north. Because the chronicler needed to explain the origins of Kiev, taken by Askold and Dir and Oleg, he constructed a new foundation myth on the basis of a simple etymologization. From the name of Kiev, the name of its founder, Kiy, was produced, and the names of his brothers Shchek and Khoriv from the notable Kievan 'mountains' - *Shchekovitsa* and *Khorivitsa*. In this way, Kiev came to be founded by three brothers - Kiy, Shchek and Khoriv – in accordance with the mythological archetype, which required two additional brothers as founders[64].

One might attribute the mythological idea to the peculiar thinking of the Russian chronicler rather than to the real order of inheritance of princely power in early Rus'. In scholarship the 'three brothers' motif is usually considered as the heritage of mythology, folklore and, at best, religious practice[65]. However, A. Nazarenko draws attention to the trinity as the systemic principle of princely succession in the Rurikovichi clan, which alone ruled the Russian country (clannish sovereignty)[66]. The power in Rus' was in the hands of a group of brothers (*corpus fratrum*), who were sons of one father (the previous prince), just as it was in the Frankish kingdom and some other early medieval societies. Initially, none of the brothers had an advantage over the others, although Kiev was owned by a senior in age, and this did not contribute to stability in their relations. Despite their seniority, the Kievan princes were not sovereign rulers if their brothers were alive. This prompted the princes of Kiev (Yaropolk, Svyatopolk) to plot the death of their brothers. An attempt to prevent violence was the designation of a favourite son (Prince Vladimir > Boris), and then the eldest son supervising the order among his brothers (Prince Yaroslav > Izyaslav). The latter principle produced the institution of seniority, according to which the eldest of the brothers had the preemptive right to the Kiev throne (the oldest among the living Rurikids).

V. Misyugin tried to explain the succession in Rus' by triads of brothers on the basis

---

63. Mel'nikova 2002/1: 143-150, notes the series of motifs in the texts of the first Russian princes. Early historical narrative was designed under the influence of mythological cyclicity.
64. Modern scholarly trend is to emphasize the origins of the Kievan brothers-founders in early oral tradition. See Mel'nikova 2002/2: 9-16; Ščavelev 2007: 105-126.
65. Petruxin 2000: 13-412.
66. Nazarenko 1986: 149-157; 1995: 83-96; 2000: 500-519.

of the '*ndugu* rule', known from the East African chronicle *History of the Galla* (late 16th century)[67]. This rule was formed during the transition from the social (group) relationship to an individual kinship and implied the transfer of inherited value not to all sons of the father, but only to three of them (in fact, there was an inheritance from one triad to another). If there were fewer than three sons, they were supplemented by nephews (cousins). Initially, the title of ruler was given to its holder for a limited time, after which he conceded it to his next brother. In historical times, when the inheritance became lifelong, the preeminent right usually had the youngest of three brothers, while two his older '*ndugu*' played the role of his attendants.

The role of third brother in folklore and mythological tradition has repeatedly attracted scholarly attention. Many nations have tales of three brothers, of which the two oldest are ordinary, while the third is singled out for a special status short of intelligence, dexterity, property, etc. But finally, the third brother turns into a wonderful hero and embarrasses his brothers. Anthropologists explained this phenomenon of the fabulous Ivan the Fool as the memory of the ultimogeniture (minorate), according to which the younger son was the main heir of family property. During the transition from the large family to an individual family, hereditary law was accompanied with the replacement of the ancient order of ultimogeniture by primogeniture. This change was reflected in the fairy-tale rivalry between elder brothers and a younger one and the idealization of the latter as socially obedient under the new social order[68]. We need to take a closer look at the connection between the princely succession and the mythological thinking of the Slavs regarding the structure of the universe.

***

According to Hilarion, the first known prince of Kiev was 'old' Igor. The *Primary Chronicle* refers to his campaigns against Byzantium in 941 and 944 and an unsuccessful attempt to collect tribute in the Drevlyan country, which led to his death in 945. The campaign of 944 was described by Liutprand, bishop of Cremona, and Igor's death was known to the Byzantine historian Leo the Deacon. According to the *Primary Chronicle*, Prince Igor ruled alone, but M. Priselkov writes that the Treaty of 944 portrayed him (Igor) as the head of a large princely family and one of three brothers. Igor's eldest brother had left a son (Igor too), who already had two children - Volodislav and Predslava, while Igor's other dead brother Uleb had left a widow Sfandra and a son Akun who had three children

---

67. Misjugin, Černecov 1978: 151-192; Misjugin 1980: 38-48; 1983: 85-134.
68. See Meletinskij 1958.

(Turd, Fast, Sfirka)[69]. According to another version of the family relationships, Uleb and Volodislav were brothers of Prince Igor. Judging by the composition of ambassadors 'from the Rus' clan' to the Byzantine emperors, Rus' was headed by three related nuclear families. Alongside Prince Igor and his brothers, Uleb and Volodislav, their wives Olga, Predslava and Sfandra played an important role. Their children, one from each family - cousins Svyatoslav, Igor and Prasten Akun - were probably regarded as heirs[70].

Svyatoslav was still a child when his father Igor died. Other sons of Igor and Olga are not mentioned by the chronicle. But Leo the Deacon, describing the Rus" war with Byzantium, says that Svyatoslav (Σφενδοσθλάβος) did not command the army of Rus' alone: there were two outstanding chieftains alongside him, Ikmor (Ἴκμορ) and Sfenckel (Σφέγκελος). Their names can be associated with the names of Svyatoslav's cousins - Igor and Akun (Yakun, Hakon)[71]. In ritual terms, it does not matter whether they were brothers or cousins, because in archaic times kinship had the meaning of belonging to a social network linked by either blood, age or ritual ties rather than having an individual familial relationship to someone else[72].

After Svyatoslav, the *Chronicle* more clearly names triads of brothers of each succeeding generation, who received the highest authority and control over the lands of the Rus'. When he departed to campaign in the Byzantine Empire to seek a princedom on the Danube, Prince Svyatoslav left his three sons - Yaropolk, Oleg and Vladimir - to reign in Rus'. Possibly he had other children, but the chronicle mentions only three. Moreover, these three acts as heirs following a certain rule of succession to the throne. Svyatoslav's sons appear in the *Chronicle* as real persons, unlike their legendary predecessors. However, in terms of inheritance, they form a triad just as Kyi, Shchek and Khoriv had, or Rurik, Sineus and Truvor. In comparison with the previous triad - Svyatoslav, Igor and Akun – Svyatoslav's sons were siblings, not cousins. As it is known, the brothers fought amongst themselves and the younger Vladimir gained the Kievan throne, ruling alone from 980 to 1015.

The story of Vladimir Svyatoslavich is similar to the story of his son Yaroslav. Rogneda did not want to marry Vladimir, just as Ingegerd did not want to be

---

69. Priselkov 1941: 241.
70. Also see Beleckij 2001: 25-29.
71. For Ikmor and Sfenkel from Ingimarr and Sveinketill, see Rydzevskaja 1978: 206.
72. Kolesov 1986: 55-57.

Yaroslav's wife. Vladimir is called a servant's son (*robichich*), and the mother of Yaroslav - Rogneda was a captive (actually a slave) of Vladimir. Both Vladimir and Yaroslav reigned in Novgorod at a very young age under the leadership of the Novgorodean chieftains Dobrynya and Constantine Dobrynich respectively. Both conquered Kiev with the help of mercenary groups of Varangians. Both the *Sermon of Law and Grace* and the *Primary Chronicle* were intended to present Yaroslav as a worthier son of Vladimir Svyatoslavich than his brothers (especially Mstislav). Therefore, in the biography of Vladimir there is a tendency to liken him to Yaroslav, and in fact his origin and early years are written on the same model as the life of Yaroslav[73]. The common features in both biographies are: (1) the prince is younger than his rival-brothers, (2) the lowered status of origin, (3) the arrival at Kiev from Novgorod, (4) the connection with the Varangians, (5) Dobrynya relates to Constantine Dobrynich as Vladimir does to Yaroslav, and lastly, (6) the usurpation of the rule of Kiev by both of them.

According to the *Primary Chronicle*, under the year 980, Prince Vladimir had ten sons and two daughters, and twelve sons in 988. I. Danilevsky pointed out that both lists of Vladimir's sons are designed on the number 12. Danilevsky emphasizes the influence of the biblical tradition, but apparently 'twelve' also had a significance in the Slavic world, connected with the calendar cycle of 12 months. According to Fredegar (*Chron.* 48), the founder of the first known Slav state, Samo, had 12 Wendish wives, who gave birth to 22 sons and 15 daughters. By the time of Prince Vladimir's death in 1015, according to the *Primary Chronicle*, nine of his sons were alive: Yaroslav, Svyatopolk, Svyatoslav, Mstislav, Boris, Gleb, Stanislav, Pozvizd, and Sudislav. In the course of the internecine strife, three of them were killed: Boris, Gleb and Svyatoslav. The chronicle, created in the reign of Yaroslav and his descendants, depicts the events of this time as the struggle between *accursed* Svyatopolk and *wise* Yaroslav. The six surviving sons of Vladimir - Yaroslav, Svyatopolk, Mstislav, Stanislav, Pozvizd, Sudislav - are organized in two triads in the *Chronicle*. About the last three brothers almost nothing is known, and it seems that they were inserted into the list with the sole purpose of making the number up to 12. The triad of Yaroslav, Svyatopolk and Mstislav are the main actors between 1015 and 1036. Thus, according to

---

73. In the 'Memorial and Panegyric of Jacob the Monk and Life of Prince Vladimir' (*Pamjat' i pohvala Jakova mniha i zitie knjazja Vladimira*), the beginning of a new 'Christian era' is dated from the baptism of Prince Vladimir, when he was 28. The *Primary Chronicle* under the year 1016 states that Yaroslav became the Kievan prince (that means the beginning of a new 'Yaroslav's era') in his 28. See Priselkov 1996: 57.

the *Primary Chronicle*, three sons of Prince Vladimir died during the life of their father, three were killed, three disappeared from the *Chronicle*, and three remained. This suggests that the struggle was conducted between the triads of brothers.

According to Thietmar of Merseburg (*Chron.* VII.72, VIII.73), only three sons of Vladimir waged a struggle after his death. Vladimir's direct successors were two sons, between whom Rus' was divided, and the third - Svyatopolk – was imprisoned together with his Polish wife. Having escaped from prison, he found support from his father-in-law, King Boleslaw I. The general outline of the plot is clearly similar to the fairy tales of two older 'normal' sons, who received the most significant part of the inheritance, and a third 'deprived' son, who ultimately acquired a much greater status than his brothers. Apparently the motif originated in the description of the archaic ritual that in the period of state formation turned into a 'paradigm of the throne succession' in Rus'[74].

To summarize the chronicle account, three 'brothers' are also singled out in the initial period after the death of Prince Vladimir: Svyatopolk in Kiev, Yaroslav in Novgorod and their nephew Bryachislav Izyaslavich in Polotsk. In 1019, with the support of the Varangians, Yaroslav defeated Svyatopolk, who henceforth disappeared from history. However, he was soon replaced by another 'third brother' - Mstislav. Mstislav, who was previously in distant Tmutorokan, appeared at Kiev in alliance with the Kasogians and Khazars in 1023. Yaroslav fled from Kiev back to Novgorod, but, according to the chronicler, Kiev did not accept Mstislav and he took the throne of Chernigov. In 1024, Yaroslav employed a certain Yakun (Hákon, mod. Håkon, but also identified by some as Anund Jakob, later king of the Svear) with a force of Varangians to attack Mstislav but they were defeated at the Battle of the Lystven River. After the victory of Mstislav, the brothers divided the Russian land between Kiev and Chernigov, using the Dnieper as a border. However, the chronicler says that Yaroslav was afraid of Mstislav, and therefore avoided Kiev, ruling the city with the help of his men but remaining in Novgorod himself (under the protection of the Varangians). Judging by the chronicle, all Yaroslav's activity between 1024 and 1036 was conducted from Novgorod. The sporadic struggle with the Poles for the Cherven cities was carried on jointly by both princes. Only in 1036, when Mstislav died and was buried in the church of St. Savior in Chernigov, do we read that "Yaroslav assumed the entire sovereignty and became the sole

---

74. See Petruxin 1995: 59-60.

ruler in the land of Rus". Only now did Yaroslav captured Kiev, leaving his son Vladimir in Novgorod. The chronicler depicts the battle of Setoml in 1036 as a conflict with the Pechenegs, but his mentioning of the destiny of Sudislav, who was imprisoned by Yaroslav, implies a different reading of the events.

Sudislav appears as if from nowhere in the chronicle: is it not possible, even likely, that between 1024 and 1036, the Rus' country was ruled not by two brothers, but three - Sudislav, Mstislav and Yaroslav. Mstislav was in Chernigov, Yaroslav in Novgorod, and Sudislav - where? If he was one of the suggested ruling triad, the answer must be Kiev. His subsequent unprecedented persecution for totally incomprehensible reasons suggests that he had a more legitimate right to the Kievan throne than Yaroslav. The triumvirate of Yaroslav's sons freed their uncle Sudislav from prison only five years after the death of Yaroslav, in 1059. By this time Sudislav had become a decrepit old man and apparently ceased to represent the danger that had forced Yaroslav and his successors to keep him in confinement. Nevertheless, the triumvirs still tried to protect themselves from any possible claim by their uncle. Sudislav was forced to swear an oath, and one can assume that it was a renunciation of any claim to power. After this, Sudislav was tonsured as a monk and thus removed from secular life and deprived of his former rights: extra insurance for the new ruling triad, in case the oath was broken. Prince Sudislav was not just deprived of power in his lifetime – as a legitimate prince he was removed from history, that is, the chronicle. Obviously, this was done under the influence of Yaroslav, who initiated the writing of the chronicle immediately after the death of Mstislav. Reading between the lines of the chronicle, its narrative shows that Yaroslav and his descendants feared Sudislav, although in modern scholarship he is often considered an insignificant prince of Pskov. The basis for this is that his prison was in this town, it made sense not to imprison Sudislav in Kiev if he had previously been prince there: better for Yaroslav to move him far away[75]. The removal and imprisonment of Sudislav indicates that he had priority to the title of Prince of Kiev. Even the sons of Yaroslav knew that their succession to their father could be challenged by Sudislav: only his death in 1063 ended the threat.

Consequently, it is permissible to hypothesize that after the death of Prince Vladimir and the internecine struggle between his sons, power in the Rus'

---

75. According to Kuza 1975: 176 n. 145, Sudislav's imprisonment in Pskov means rather that he has never been a prince there. Sudislav as a prince in Pskov is referred to only in later chronicles. See *PSRL* t. 5, p. 120; t. 15, p. 114; t. 28, p. 215, 314; Šaxmatov 2001: 89-90, n. 2.

country passed to the triad of brothers - Sudislav, Mstislav, and Yaroslav. At first, other brothers took part in the struggle and they are also organized as triads in the *Chronicle*. The most famous of the losers are Svyatopolk, Boris and Gleb. Expelling Sudislav from Russian history, the chronicler nevertheless focuses on the concept of brotherly triadism, substituting in his place Bryachislav of Polotsk as a 'brother' of Mstislav and Yaroslav (actually, he was their nephew).

A similar version is found in *Eymund's Saga*, according to which, after the death of Prince Vladimir, three brothers were established in the main cities of Rus': Borislav (*Burizlafr*) in Kiev, Yaroslav (*Jarizleifr*) in Novgorod and Bryachislav (*Uartilafr*) in Polotsk[76]. To Yaroslav comes a Norwegian king Eymund, one of three sons of King Ring, two of whom (Rerek and Dag) perished, along with their father, in the struggle with King (St) Olaf Haraldsson. Arriving to Novgorod, the Scandinavians served as mercenaries of Yaroslav in his struggle with his brother and after accomplishing many military feats, they kill Borislav on the third attempt. Yaroslav gets the kingdom of his brother. Subsequent events led to the clash between Yaroslav and Bryachislav, which ended in a peace treaty and redistribution of kingdoms - Yaroslav remained in Novgorod, Bryachislav moved to Kiev, and Polotsk was given to Eymund. Three years later, Bryachislav died and Yaroslav received Kiev, while Eymund allegedly ruled Polotsk until the end of his days and, dying, gave the city to his friend and relative Ragnvar.

V. Petrukhin points out that the three cities, Kiev, Novgorod and Polotsk, each built its own church of St. Sophia[77]. Each of them claimed to 'model' the centre of the world, Constantinople (*Tsargrad*) with a church of St. Sophia[78]. The three cities symbolized the tripartite structure of the Russian country.

In general, the events described by Eymund's Saga are reminiscent of the chronicle version. Yaroslav really ruled in Novgorod, was related to the Swedish king Olof Skötkonung, and used Scandinavians as mercenaries in his battle with his brothers. He temporarily seized Kiev in 1016-1019, but a clash with Mstislav forced him to stay in Novgorod. The death of Mstislav enabled Yaroslav to capture Kiev. Polotsk became entirely independent after the death of Vladimir the Great, and Bryachislav, ruling the city, did not obey the Kievan prince. In other respects, the version of the saga subordinates the course of events to the requirements of its epic story, in which the main character was Eymund, and

---

76. See Rydzevskaja 1978: 89-104; Jackson 2000: 305-322.
77. Janin, Aleškovskij 1971: 47-48.
78. See Petruxin 1995: 52-61, esp. 58.

the historical characters and events provide a background for his activities. N. Ilyin came to the conclusion that in Eymund's Saga, Yaroslav fought with his brother Boris (whose name the saga interpreted as *Burizlafr / Borislav*) rather, than with Svyatopolk[79]. V. Yanin suggested that the murderers of Boris were sent by Yaroslav, not Svyatopolk[80]. According to I. Danilevsky's reconstruction, after the death of Vladimir Svyatoslavich, the throne of Kiev was occupied by Boris, whom his father loved, according to the chronicler, more than other sons[81]. Yaroslav defeated the new Kievan prince in the battle of the Dnieper, with the help of Scandinavian mercenaries. The reign of Eymund in Polotsk belongs to pure fantasy[82]. Neither the *Chronicle* nor *Eymund's Saga* refer to the enigmatic role of Sudislav in the princely succession in Rus'.

***

The sole rule of Yaroslav the Wise in Kiev from 1036 to 1054 ended with the transfer of the Russian lands to his sons, with the instructions to the younger ones to honour their older brother[83]. According to the *Chronicle*, Yaroslav had six sons - Vladimir (1020-1052), Izyaslav (1024-1078), Svyatoslav (1027-1076), Vsevolod (1030-1093), Vyacheslav (1036-1057) and Igor (?-1060). At the moment of Yaroslav's death, the eldest son Vladimir was already dead, Izyaslav was in Turov, Svyatoslav in Vladimir, Vyacheslav in Smolensk, and Vsevolod was 'with his father' in Kiev, but of Igor nothing is known. A. Nasonov argues that Yaroslav's 'Testament' was constructed in the 1070s as a manifestation of the chroniclers' criticism of the contemporary princely rivalry[84]. The 'Testament' reflected the situation when three sons of Yaroslav - Vladimir, Vyacheslav and Igor - were already dead, and political life was determined by the relations of his other three sons with their cousins and nephews[85].

The six known sons of Yaroslav formed two triads. In the *Tale of Boris and Gleb*,

---

79. Il'in 1957: 156-169. For the identity between *Boris* and *Burizlafr*, see Mixeev 2009: 200-211.
80. For the discussion of the problem, see Mixeev 2009: 152-264.
81. See Danilevsky 2001: 336-354.
82. See Jackson 2000: 128-129.
83. *PSRL* 1, 161-162; 2, 149-150; 3, 160, 181-182.
84. Nasonov 1969: 48.
85. Martin Dimnik 1987: 369-386, argues that Yaroslav designated his three eldest sons and their descendants as the only legitimate heirs to Kiev, who were to follow a lateral system of succession.

the monk Jacob reports that Yaroslav designated as his heirs and successors of his throne not all of his sons, but only the three elder ones. The Scandinavian sagas also know of only three sons of Ingegerd: Valdamar, Vissivald and Holty (Hjalti - ?) the Bold[86]. Valdamar is identified with Vladimir and Vissivald with Vsevolod, while Holty remains a controversial figure. The other three sons of Yaroslav could have been from another wife or wives. T. Vikul points the unusual attention of the chronicler to the dates of birth of Yaroslav's sons. She suggests that the chronicler intended to present Izyaslav, Svyatoslav and Vsevolod, who divided the Rus' country among themselves, as the older sons, which in fact did not correspond to reality[87]. Yaroslav was largely dependent on the relatives of his wife Ingegerd and his 'Varangian retinue', recruited from the Swedes and Norwegians. His eldest son Vladimir was allocated Novgorod, whose nobility saw in Yaroslav a protector of their independence from Kiev. Another son of Ingegerd, Vsevolod, was with Yaroslav at the time of his death. The third son of Ingegerd (Holty the Bold) could be Vyacheslav, allocated Smolensk, a key city on the routes to both the Baltic and Volga regions. Izyaslav and Svyatoslav were sons (presumably) from other Yaroslav's wives and they were allocated the western cities, Turov and Vladimir. Igor, perhaps, was holding a neighbouring city (he received Vladimir after Svyatoslav left the city).

Having received news of Yaroslav's death, Izyaslav and Svyatoslav came from Turov and Vladimir to Kiev and seized power. Izyaslav took Kiev and Svyatoslav received Chernigov (if Mstislav had descendants who were still alive, they have been written out of history, it seems). Vsevolod received Pereyaslavl on the border of the steppe, which was hardly one of the major cities of Rus' at that time, although that the *Chronicle* (fictively) mentions Pereyaslavl in the treaties with Byzantium in the first half of the 10th century. It is probable that the third in the ruling triad was originally not Vsevolod, but Vyacheslav, who received the key city Smolensk. However, Vyacheslav died in 1057, and his brother Igor, having been moved to Smolensk, followed him in 1060, so that the brothers were forced to raise the status of Vsevolod[88]. This circumstance was hidden by Vsevolod's descendants, Monomakh and his son Mstislav, who edited the *Primary Chronicle*. In 1059, the triumvirs forced their uncle Sudislav, who was imprisoned in Pskov, to swear an oath, presumably one not to break the status

---

86. Jackson 1991: 159.
87. Vilkul 2003: 108-114.
88. After Igor's death, Smolensk was under the joint management of the Yaroslavichi triumvirate. See Sverdlov 2003: 441-442.

quo. However, after his death in 1063, Rus' was again racked by internecine strife. Rostislav Vladimirovich fled from Novgorod to Tmutorokan and after that the Prince of Polotsk, Vseslav, "began a war". The *Primary Chronicle* does not clarify against whom or why this war was waged. At the beginning of 1067, Vseslav took Novgorod, apparently, having learned of Rostislav's death. The Yaroslavichi triumvirate attacked Vseslav and defeated him in the battle of Nemiga. A few months later, he was tricked into captivity near Smolensk and put in prison in Kiev, along with two his sons. But after the triumvirs were defeated by the Cumans (*Polovtsi*) on the River Alta in 1068, the people of Kiev liberated Vseslav and proclaimed him as their prince. The Cumans seem to have attacked Kiev in support of Vseslav and against the Yaroslavichi brothers. The assault was not against the Russian people, because at the same time the people of Kiev also opposed Yaroslav's sons. Presumably there was something in the policies of Izyaslav and Vsevolod that did not suit the Cumans, the people, and the prince of Polotsk. These Cumans, who besieged Kiev, broke off the siege as soon as Vseslav became the prince. Given Vseslav's fame as a prince close to paganism, one can assume that it was the Polish relations of Izyaslav and Byzantine ties of Vsevolod, which caused the resistance to them.

After the Battle of Alta, Svyatoslav retired to Chernigov and did nothing to help his brothers during the uprising of the people in Kiev. Izyaslav led the troops of the Polish king Boleslaw to Kiev and Vseslav fled to Polotsk, after seven months of rule. Izyaslav allocated Polotsk to his son Mstislav and then another son, Svyatopolk, but the latter was expelled by Vseslav in 1071. At the same time, the pagan magicians (*volkhvy*) raised a revolt in Rostov and Beloozero. The rebellion was suppressed by Yan Vyshatich, the son of the Novgorodian chieftain, who fled with Rostislav in 1064. In Novgorod, Prince Gleb Svyatoslavich personally killed a magician with an axe. This attempt of pagan restoration is associated with the increase of Christian influence in Rus'. The triumvirs supported different Christian churches - Izyaslav was close to Catholic Poland, Svyatoslav inclined to Catholic Germany, and Vsevolod was married to a Byzantine princess. After the death of Rostislav Vladimirovich, Svyatoslav's son Gleb reigned in Novgorod. Prince Svyatoslav Yaroslavich established his control over huge territories - the Novgorodean and the Rostov lands, and all the left bank of the Dnieper from Chernigov to Tmutorokan. His elevation among the brothers led to 'discontent among the Yaroslavichi' in 1073. However, Svyatoslav unexpectedly died from an unsuccessful operation in 1076, and Izyaslav was killed during the Battle of Nezhatina Niva in 1078 by a spear launched into his back from his own positions. Vsevolod became the prince of Kiev and obtained the opportunity to manage princedoms for his sons and nephews. Archaic triadism lost its practical importance in the princely succession, but it was traditionally kept until the princes' congress in Lyubech in 1097. For the last four years of his life Vsevolod ruled in a triumvirate with his sons, Vladimir, who occupied Chernigov, and Rostislav, sitting in Pereyaslavl. The situation which, according to the chronicles, was determined by Yaroslav's 'Testament' in 1054, was restored in a new form in 1089 1093. Three central cities, Kiev, Chernigov, and Pereyaslavl, were placed in the hands of the Yaroslavichi brothers. On the periphery, Svyatopolk Izyaslavich ruled in Turov, Davyd Svyatoslavich in Novgorod, and Oleg Svyatoslavich in Tmutorokan. After the death of Vsevolod Yaroslavich in 1093, Rus' was under the control of a new triumvirate - Svyatopolk Izyaslavich in Kiev, Vladimir Vsevolodovich Monomakh in Chernigov and his brother Rostislav Vsevolodovich in Pereyaslavl. Rostislav soon died, and Monomakh moved to Pereyaslavl, being forced to cede Chernigov to Oleg Svyatoslavich[89].

In 1097, Svyatopolk Izyaslavich, Vladimir Monomakh, Davyd Igorevich, Vasilko Rostislavich, and the Svyatoslavichi Davyd and Oleg met in Lyubech to make peace and decided: "Why do we ruin the land of Rus' by our continued strife against one another? The Polovtsians harass our country in diverse fashions, and rejoice that war is waged among us. Let us rather hereafter be united in spirit and watch over the land of Rus', and let each of us guard his own domain; with Svyatopolk retaining Kiev, the heritage of Izyaslav, while Vladimir holds the domain of Vsevolod, and David, Oleg, and Yaroslav between them possess that of Svyatoslav. Let the domains apportioned by Vsevolod stand, leaving the city of Vladimir in the hands of David, while the city Peremyshl belongs to Volodar son of Rostislav, and Vasilko son of Rostislav holds Terebovl"[90]. Presnyakov pointed out that patrimonial law concerned only the three main cities of the Russian land - Kiev, Chernigov, Pereyaslavl[91]. These cities turned into independent principalities. The organization of the land by triads was preserved among the Cherven cities - Vladimir, Peremyshl and Terebovl, which were given to Davyd Igorevich, Volodar Rostislavich and Vasilko Rostislavich. In the Chernigov land, the inheritance of Svyatoslav Yaroslavich went to his three sons Davyd, Oleg and

---

89. Lind 1982: 73-74 noted the custom of rule by triumvirates. He writes on p. 80: "there is more emphasis on joint tripartite rule in this period [after the death of Svyatopolk in 1113] than on seniority".
90. *Primary Chronicle* 1953: 187-188.
91. Presnjakov 1993: 37.

Yaroslav. The Lyubech Congress distributed the lands along the Oka and the upper Volga. In the *Novgorodean First Chronicle*, their status was determined by the 'will' of Yaroslav in 1054: "Yaroslav died and left three sons, the oldest Izyaslav, the middle Svyatoslav, and the youngest Vsevolod. They divided the country, and the oldest Izyaslav took Kiev and Novgorod and many other cities around Kiev, while Svyatoslav took Chernigov and the whole eastern country as far as Murom, and Vsevolod took Pereyaslavl, Rostov, Suzdal, Beloozero, and the Upper Volga region"[92]. In reality, this distribution of lands belongs to 1096, when Monomakh and his sons forced Oleg Svyatoslavich and his brothers from the north-eastern Rus'. At the Lyubech Congress it was stressed that the grandsons of Vladimir Yaroslavich – the Rostislavichi - should not aspire to rule Novgorod but be content with the cities that Vsevolod distributed to them. Novgorod was intended to be under the control of the heir to the throne of Kiev.

✷✷✷

The order of managing the 'Russian country' by a triad of princes went back to the ritual designation of the settled territory on the basis of mythology. It was based on the idea of a universe consisting of three worlds. In each generation, the third son (the youngest) received a new town (Novgorod), which was built on the newly settled (occupied) lands. He was the principal successor (minorate) and probably had a sacred status, like the 'King of Ruses' portrayed by Ibn Fadlan in 921. Pre-state society did not have tools to organize large territories, and therefore, in every compact region the same ternary structure was reproduced. For example, the Drevlyan triad of cities was Iskorosten, Ovruch and Kiev, captured by the Rus' prince Oleg, whose previous capital was Vyshgorod. The burning of Korosten after the death of Igor suggests that it could be a ritual accompanying the change of generations of rulers, accompanied by a corresponding foundation of a new town for the youngest son of the deceased prince.

The situation began to change when the increased density of the population reduced the amount of vacant land by the 10th century. The original triad of towns of the Rus', who arrived from the north or the west and settled on the Dnieper, is unknown: they might have been either (1) Lyubech, Chernigov and Vyshgorod, or (2) Lyubech, Vyshgorod and Kiev, captured from the Drevlyans. The changing of the traditional order showed itself in the declaration of Kiev as 'the mother of Rus' cities'. According to the chronicle version, Svyatoslav was a child at the time of his father's death, and probably the youngest son

---

92. *PSRL* t. 3, 160.

of Igor and Olga. Together with his mother, he participated in the funeral rituals of the deceased prince Igor and the burning of Iskorosten. Constantine Porphyrogenitus indicates that Svyatoslav received a certain Novgorod, while Kiev was left in the hands of Princess Olga.

Wars with neighbouring tribes and occupation of new lands led to the expansion of the Russian land, which demanded a new organization for it. Apparently, Kiev captured Smolensk, while some Varangians established themselves in Turov and Polotsk. After the death of Prince Igor, the Kievan government began reforming the rules of succession. The *Primary Chronicle* refers to Princess Olga's trip to the basin of the rivers Luga and Msta in the late 940s. The purpose of the voyage could be the search for a new route to the Baltic Sea, bypassing Polotsk on the Dvina, occupied by Rogvolod. Olga got a place for a new town for 300 *grivny* annual payment to the Varangians, which was paid up to the reign of Yaroslav[93]. A new city on the Volkhov was founded for her son Svyatoslav, but Kiev remained the capital of the Russian land. The de facto ruler of Kiev was the princely widow Olga, who originated from Vyshgorod[94]. We have no evidence for the distribution of other sons and nephews of Prince Igor in the Russian land. Olga's baptism had the purpose of giving religious sanctification to new principles of succession. One of them was the legitimation of her widow status, impossible in paganism (as Prince Mal's matchmaking shows). Another principle was primogeniture in the succession of princedom, which was accepted in the next generation of Svyatoslav's son.

In the transitional period of Olga's reign, her youngest son Svyatoslav acted abroad exclusively as a military chieftain. This situation allowed Rus' society to break with the idea that the main role of the ruler would be communication with the gods, as the 'king of Rus'', described by Ibn Fadlan. In his own country, such a sacred ruler was a ritual figure, while abroad, he was considered to have passed into the 'other world', where he was completely free from any restriction on his behaviour. Having attained this freedom to act, Svyatoslav showed himself to be an outstanding warrior, defeating the Khazar Khaganate, overrunning Bulgaria and entering into war with Byzantium (unsuccessfully). His successes created the conditions for expanding the influence of the Russian country. His

---

93. It seems to be the Polotsk princes who conceded to Kiev the territory for a new town on the Volkhov in the 940s, and when Yaroslav stopped paying this money in 1015, Prince Bryachislav of Polotsk had the right to demand Novgorod back.

94. *Primary Chronicle* 1953: 81 "She imposed upon them a heavy tribute, two parts of which went to Kiev, and the third to Olga in Vyshgorod; for Vyshgorod was Olga's city".

short-term rule in Novgorod (on the Volkhov, or was the new town Smolensk?) gave impetus to the annexation of the north-western territories to the Kievan Rus'. His campaign against the Khazars was in the interests of the Ruses who colonized the upper Volga and the Oka river rather than Kiev's interest. Before his campaign in Bulgaria, Svyatoslav distributed cities to his sons, which looks like his final abandonment of Kiev, where he never showed himself as a ruler.

Being abroad, free of the control of the Kievan elite, Svyatoslav maintained his adherence to paganism. Probably, therefore, when the question of the succession arose, the triad of cities again became the organizing structure of the Russian land. Svyatoslav's sons received reigns in Kiev, Ovruch and Novgorod (which was formerly governed by Svyatoslav himself). After the 'reign' of Olga, it was the return to the triad management system. But the distribution of brothers according to their seniority indicates the introduction of the principle of primogeniture, according to which the main successor (the eldest, not youngest, brother in the triad) was nominated to govern not a new city, but Kiev, which became the permanent capital of the Russian land ('the mother of Rus' cities').

Yaropolk, Oleg and Vladimir were full brothers, and they inherited from their father. Kiev was distributed to the senior Yaropolk, but the traditional rule gave priority to the younger Vladimir. The struggle between the brothers was programmed by this collision. The victorious Vladimir adopted Christianity and tried to reconcile the ancient norms of succession with the principle of primogeniture borrowed from Byzantium. As is known, Vladimir was called by Hilarion (*Sermon on Law and Grace*) by the title 'kagan'[95], and there is a suggestion that he accepted the Byzantine title 'Caesar' (*Tzar*)[96].

Simultaneously, the military successes of Svyatoslav and Vladimir led to the expansion of Kiev's control beyond the Russian country on the upper Dnieper - the subordination of Polotsk, Novgorod, Rostov, Murom and Tmutorokan. Vladimir therefore faced a new problem, one his predecessors had not had. Kiev had expanded its control over very widespread territories and needed a new organisation to hold them together under its leadership. Vladimir tried to solve this problem by placing his sons in the main cities of the neighbouring lands and making them his vassals. However, the attempt of Vladimir, and later Yaroslav, to create vassal principalities with more or less autonomous sub-dynasties of their

---

95. Vysockij 1966: 49-52, № 13.
96. There is a suggestion that the title 'Tzar' was taken by Yaroslav the Wise in 1037. See Toločko 1992: 94, cf. 137-138.

sons were unsuccessful. Only the Polotsk princedom achieved independence for a certain period. Economic interest, especially the control of trade routes, was the catalyst for the formation of the megastructure that included Kiev, Smolensk, Novgorod, with the addition of the Volyn country, the Oka-Volga country, and Tmutorokan. Kievan Rus', the Novgorod land, Rostov-Suzdal and Vladimir-Volyn retained triple structuring. Novgorod, Rostov and Murom were included in the Russian land in a broad sense. Novgorod was attached to Kiev, Rostov to Pereyaslavl and Murom to Chernigov.

Prince Vladimir the Great apparently hoped that Kievan Rus' would be managed by the triad of his younger sons Boris, Svyatoslav and Gleb[97]. But his eldest son Sviatopolk rebelled against this, insisting to primogeniture. In the ensuing internecine struggle, this principle was established, although Yaroslav, who supported it once he had achieved control of Kiev, was not Vladimir's eldest son. The Russian land, which occupied a central position in the East-Slavic complex chiefdom, had three main cities. Under Vladimir the Great, they were Kiev, Ovruch and Chernigov, under Yaroslav the Wise, Kiev, Chernigov and Smolensk, and under the Yaroslavichi brothers Kiev, Chernigov and Pereyaslavl[98]. The separation of each of these cities into independent principalities under the descendants of the Yaroslavichi formed new triads: (1) Kiev, Novgorod and Vladimir Volynsky, (2) Chernigov, Murom, and Tmutorokan, and (3) Pereyaslavl, Rostov, and Beloozero. The fragmentation of the former 'Russian country' into the Kievan, Chernigov and Pereyaslavlean princedoms and the Drevlyan country also stimulated the formation of independent princedoms in Novgorod, Rostov, Smolensk, and so on. All this demanded a new system of succession on the basis of primogeniture, which could replace the ancient triads. The ladder system was approved at the Congress of Princes in Lyubech in 1097. Chroniclers of the late 11th and early 12th centuries described the princely succession of early Rus' on the model of the new ladder system[99]. In other words, the early history of princely succession in Kiev was described anachronistically.

---

97. Before the adoption of Christianity, Vladimir Svyatoslavich tried to reform paganism on the model of the structures that existed among the Baltic Slavs. The *Primary Chronicle* mentions the pantheon created by him, headed by Perun.

98. *Primary Chronicle* 1953: 94: "He (Prince Vladimir) had three hundred concubines at Vyshgorod, three hundred at Belgorod, and two hundred at Berestovo in a village still called Berestovoe". Vyshdorod, Belgorod and Berestovo modelled the tripartite structure of Rus'.

99. For the latter system of succession, see Stokes 1970: 268-285; Kollmann 1990: 377-387; Toločko 1992: 77-102; Martin 2006: 267-282. Cf. Sverdlov 2003: 434-514.

References

Abaev, V. I., 1949: *Osetinskij jazyk I fol'klor*, Moscow.
Abaev, V. I., 1965: *Skifo-evropejskie izoglossy*, Moscow.
Afanasiev, A. N., 1957: *Narodnye russkie skazki v trex tomax*, Moscow.
Al'bedil, M. F., Misjugin, V. M., 1984: "Etnoistoričeskaja osnova sjužeta o trex brat'jax (po marerialam drevneindijskogo eposa", in *Fol'klor i etnografija. U etnografičeskix istokov fol'klornyx sjužetov i obrazov*, Leningrad, p. 102-111.
Alföldi, A., 1974: *Die Struktur des voretruskischen Römerstaates*, Heidelberg.
Beleckij, S. V., 2001: "Neskol'ko zamečanij o genealogii pervyx pokolenij roda Rjurikovičej", *Vostočnaja Evropa v drevnosti i srednevekov'e: genealogija kak forma istoričeskoj pamjati*, Moscow, p. 25-29.
Bettini, M., 1987: "Bruto lo sciocco", *Il protagonismo nella storiografia classica*, Geneva, p. 71-120.
Casebook 1987: *Xrestomatija po istorii južnyx i zapadnyx Slavjan*, Moscow.
Colarusso, J., 2002: *Nart Sagas from the Caucasus: Myths and Legends from the Circassians, Abazas, Abkhaz, and Ubykhs*, Princeton.
Dimnik, M., 1987: "The "Testament" of Iaroslav "The Wise": A Re-examination", *Canadian Slavonic Papers*, 29, p. 369-386.
Dimnik, M, 1996: "Succession and inheritance un Rus' before 1054", *Mediaeval Studies*, 58, p. 87-117.
Dubov, I. V., 1982: *Severo-Vostočnaja Rus' v epoxu rannego srednevekov'ja (istoriko-arxeologičeskie očerki)*, Leningrad.
Dumézil, G. 2001: *Osetinskij epos i mifologija*, Владикавказ.
Elizarenkova, T. Ja, Toporov, V. N., 1973: "Trita v kolodce: vedijskij variant arxaičeskoj sxemy", *Sbornik po vtoričnym modelirujuščim sistemam*, Тарту, p. 65-70.
Fomin, V. V., 2005: *Varjagi i varjažskaja Rus'*, Moscow.
Gamkrelidze, Th. V., Ivanov, V. V., 1995: *Indo-European and the Indo-Europeans: a reconstruction and historical analysis of a proto-language and a proto-culture*, 1, ed. by Werner Winter, Berlin.
Gilet, P., 1998: *Vladimir Propp and the universal folktale: recommissioning an old paradigm – story as initiation*, New York.
Gorskij, A. A., 1999: "Gosudarstvo ili konglomerat konungov? Rus' v pervoj polovine X veka", *Voprosy istorii*, 8, p. 43-52.
Grantovskij, E. A, 1960: Indo-iranskie kasty u Skifov. XXV MKV. Doklady delegacii SSSR, Moscow.
Halperin, C. J., 1975: "The Concept of the Russian Land from the Ninth to the Fourteenth Centuries", *Russian History*, 2, p. 29-38.
Hrbek, I., 1957: "Der dritte Stamm der Rus nach arabischen Quellen", *Archiv Orientalni*, 25, Praha, p. 628-652.
Il'in, N. N., 1957: *Letopisnaja stat'ja 6523 g. i ee istočnik*, Moscow.

Ilovajskij, D. I., 2002 (1890): *Načalo Rusi*, Moscow.
Jackson, T. N., 1991: "Islandskie korolevskie sagi kak istočnik po istorii Drevnej Rusi i ee sosedej X-XIII v.", *Drevnejšei gosudarstva na territorii SSSR: Materialy i issledovanija (1988-1989 g.)*, Moscow, p. 5-169.
Jackson, T. N., 2000: *Četyre skandinavskix konunka na Rusi*, Moscow.
Jackson, T. H., Kalinina, T. M., Konovalova, I. G., Podosinov, A. V., 2007: "*Russkaja reka*": *Rečnye puti Vostočnoj Evropy v antičnoj i srednevekovoj geografii*, Moscow.
Janin, V. L., 1970: "Problemy social'noj organizacii Novgorodskoj respubliki", *Istorija SSSR*, 1, p. 44-54.
Janin, V. L., Aleškovskij, M. X., 1971: "Proisxoždernie Novgoroda (k postanovke problemy)", *Istorija SSSR*, 2, p. 32-61.
Karsanov, A. N., 1992: "K. voprosu o trex gruppax rusov", *Germenevtika drevnerusskoj literatury X-XVI vv.*, 3, Moscow, p. 5-13.
Kmietowicz, F., 1976: "Tituły wladców Slowian w tzw. "Relacji anonimowei", wschodnim źrodle z końca IX wieku", *Slavia Antiqua*, XXIII, p. 175-191.
Kolesov, V. V., 1986: *Mir čeloveka v slova Drevnej Rusi*, Leningrad.
Kollmann, N. S., 1990: "Collateral Succession in Kievan Rus'", *Harvard Ukrainian Studies*, 14, p. 377-387.
Komar, A., Xamajko, N., 2011: "Zbručskij idol: pamjatnik epoxi romantizma?", *Ruthenica*, X, Kiev, p. 166-217.
Konovalova, I. G., 1995: "Rasskaz o trex gruppax rusov v sočinenijax arabskix avtorov XII-XIV vv.", *Drevnejšie gosudarstva Vostočnoj Evropy 1992-1993*, Moscow, p. 139-148.
Kotljar N. F., 1986: *Drevnjaja Rus' I Kiev v letopisnyx predanijax i legendax*, Kiev.
Kuza, A. V., 1975: "Novgorodskaja zemlja", *Drenerusskie knjažestva X-XIII vv.*, Moscow, p. 144-201.
Leńczyk, G., 1964: "Światowid zbruczański w", *Materiały archeologiczne*, 5, p. 5-61.
Lincoln, B., 1976-77: "The Indo-European Cattle-raiding Myth", *History of religions*, 16, p. 42-65.
Lind, J., 1982: "The "Brotherhood" of Rus'. A Pseudo-Problem Concerning the Origin of "Rus'", *Slavica Othiniensia*, 5, p. 66-81.
Litvina, A. F., Uspenskij, F. B., 2006: *Vybor imeni u russkix knjazej v X-XVI vv. Dinastičeskaja istorija skvoz' prizmu antroponimiki*, Moscow.
Lowmianski, X., 1985: *Rus' I normanny*, Moscow.
Mačinskij, D. A., 1985: "Rostovo-Suzdal'skaja Rus' v X v. i "tri gruppy rusi" vostočnyx avtorov", *Materialy k etničeskoj istorii Evropejskogo Severo-Vostoka*, Syktyvkar, p. 3-23.
Majer, M., 2017: "A Note on the Balto-Slavic and Indo-European Background of the Proto-Slavic Adjective *svętъ 'Holy'", *Studia Ceranea*, 7, p. 139–149.

Martin, J., 2006: "Calculating Seniority and the Contests for succession in Kievan Rus'", *Russian history*, 33, p. 267-282.
Meletinskij, E. M., 1958: *Geroj volšebnoj skazki: proisxoždenie obraza*, Moscow.
Mel'nikova, E. A., 2000: "Rjurik, Sineus i Truvor v Drevnerusskoj istoriografičkoj tradicii", *Drevnejšie gosudarstva Vostočnoj Evropy 1998*, Moscow, p. 143-159.
Mel'nikova, E. A., 2002/1: "Pervye russkie knjaz'ja: o principax rekonstrukcii rannej istorii Rusi, Vostočnaja Evropa v drenosti i srednevekov'e", *Mnimye real'nosti v antičnoj i srednevekovoj istoriografii*, Moscow, p. 143-150.
Mel'nikova, E. A., 2002/2: "Legenda o Kie: o strukture i xaraktere letopisnogo teksta", *A se ego srebro. Zbirnik prac' na pošanu M. F. Kotljara z nagorodi jogo 70 riččja*, Kiev, p. 9-16.
Mixeev, S. M., 2009: *"Svjatopolk sede v Kieve po otzi": Usobiza 1015-1019 godov v drevnerusskich i skandinavskich istočnikach*, Moscow.
Mišin, D. E., 2002: *Sakaliba (slavjane) v islamskom mire v rannee srednevekov'e*, Moscow.
Misjugin, V. M., 1980: "«Pravilo ndutu» i sledy social'no-vozrastnogo delenija u nekotoryx evropejskix narodov rannego srednevekoj'ja", *Afrikanskij etnografičeskij sbornik. Trudy Instituta Etnografii AN SSSR*, 109, Leningrad, p. 38-48.
Misjugin, V. M., 1983: "Tri brata v sisteme arkaičeskix norm nasledovanija vlasti", *Afrikanskij Sbornik: Istorija, etnografija*, Moscow, p. 85-134.
Misjugin, V. M., Černecov, S. B., 1978: "«Xronika galla» kak etnoistoričeskij istočnik", *Afrikanskij etnografičeskij sbornik. Trudy Instituta Etnografii AN SSSR*, 105, Leningrad, p. 151-192.
Molé, M., 1952: "Le partage du monde dans la tradition iranienne", *Journal Asiatique* 240, p. 455-463.
Myths 1982: *Mify narodov mira*, t. 1-2, Moscow.
Nasonov, A. N., 1951: *'Russkaja zemlja' i obrazovanie territorii drevnerusskogo gosudarstva*, Moscow 1951.
Nasonov, A. N., 1969: *Istorija russkogo letopisanija XI – načala XVIII veka*, Moscow.
Nazarenko, A. V., 2000: "Porjadok predstolonasledija na Rusi X-XII", *Iz istorii russkoj kul'tury*, 1, *Drevnjaja Rus'*, Moscow, p. 500-519.
Nazarenko, A. V., 1995: "Porjadok predstolonasledija na Rusi X-XII vv.: Nasledstvennye razdely i popytki designacii", *Rimsko-Konstantinopol'skoe nasledie na Rusi: Ideja vlasti I političeskaja praktika. IX meždunarodnyj seminar istoričeskix issledovanij «Ot Rima k Tret'emu Rimu»*, Moskva 29-31 maja 1989 g., Moscow, p. 83-96.
Nazarenko, A. V., 1986: "Rodovoj sjuzerenitet Rjurikovičej nad Rus'ju (X-XI vv)", *Drevnejšie gosudarstva na territorii SSSR, 1985*, Moscow, p. 149-157.
Novikov, N. V., 1974: *Obrazy vostočnoslavjanskoj volšebnoj skazki*, Leningrad.

Novosel'cev, A. P., 1965: "Vostočnye istočniki o vostočnyx slavjanax i Rusi VI-IX vv.", *in* Novosel'cev, A. L., Pašuto, V. T., Čerepnin, L. V., Šušarija, V. P., Ščapov, Ja. N., *Drevnerusskoe gosudarstvo i ego meždunarodnoe značenie*, Moscow.

Ostrowski, D., 2012: "Systems of Succession in Rus' and Steppe Societies", *Ruthenica* XI, p. 29–58.

Pčelov, E. V., 2001: *Genealogija drevnerusskix knjazej*, Moscow.

Petruxin, V. Ja, 1982: "Tri centra Rusi: fol'klornye istoki i istoričeskaja tradicija", *Xudožestvennyj jazyk srednevekov'ja*, Moscow, p. 143-158.

Petruxin, V. Ja, 1995: *Načalo etnokul'turnoj istorii Rusi IX – XI vekov*, Smolensk.

Petruxin, V. Ja, 2000: "Drevnjaja Rus', Narod. Knjaz'ja. Religija", *Iz istorii russkoj kul'tury*, 1, *Drevnjaja Rus'*, Moscow, p. 13-412.

Presnjakov, A. E., 1993 (1909): *Knjažoe pravo v drevnej Rusi: Očerki po istorii X-XII stoletij*, Moscow.

Primary Chronicle 1953: *The Russian primary chronicle: Laurentian text* / S. Hazzard Cross and O.P. Sherbowitz-Wetzor trans. and ed., Cambridge, MA.

Priselkov, M. D., 1941: *Kievskoe gosudarstvo vtoroj poloviny X v. po vizantijskim istočnikam*, Učenye zapiski LGU. Serija istoričeskix nauk, Leningrad, 8, 73.

Priselkov, M. D., 1996 (2d ed.): *Istorija russkogo letopisanija 11-15 vv.*, Saint-Petersburg.

Raevskij, D. S., 2006: *Mir skifskoj kul'tury*, Moscow.

Rybakov, B. A., 1981: *Jazyčestvo drevnix slavjan*, Moscow.

Rybakov, B. A., 1993 (2d ed.): *Kievskaja Rus' i russkie knjažestva XII-XIII vv. Киевская Русь и русские княжества XII-XIII вв.*, Moscow.

Rydzevskaja, E. A., 1978: *Drevnjaja Rus' i Skandinavija v IX-XIV vv*, Moscow.

Šaxmatov, A. A., 2001 (1908): *Razyskanija o russkix letopisjax*, Moscow.

Ščavelev, A. S., 2007: *Slavjanskie legendy o pervyx knjaz'jax. Sravnitel'no-istoričeskoe issledovanie modelej vlasti u slavjan*, Moscow.

Shaw, J., 2012: "On Indo-European Cosmic Structure: Models, Comparisons, Contexts", *Cosmos*, 28, p. 57-76.

Serbian epos 1960: *Serbskij epos*, sostavitel' N. I. Kravcova, Moscow.

Sokolov, Ju. M., 1941: *Russkij fol'klor*, Moscow.

Sokolova, L. V., 1995: "Dažbog (Daždbog)", *Enciklopedija "Slova o polku Igoreve"*, 2, Saint-Peterburg, p. 79-82.

Stokes, A. D., 1970: "The System of Succession to the Thrones of Russia, 1054-1113", *Gorski Vijenac: A Garland of Essays offered to Professor E.M. Hill* / ed. R. Auty, L. R. Lewitter, A. P. Vlasto, Cambridge, p. 268-275.

Sverdlov, M. B., 2003: *Domongol'skaja Rus'. Knjaz' i knjažeskaja vlast' na Rusi VI – pervoj treti XIII vv.*, Saint-Petersburg.

Thulin, A., 1979: "The third tribe of the Rus'", *Slavia antiqua*, XXV, p. 99-139.

Toločko, A. P., 1992: *Knjaz' v Drevnej Rusi: vlast', sobstvennost', ideologija*, Kiev.

Toporov, V. N., 1977: "Avest. Θrita, Θraētaona, dr.-ind. Trita i dr. iix indoevropejskie istoki", *Annali di Ca'Foscari* 3, p. 41-65.

Toporov, V. N., 1987: "Ob odnom arxaičnom indoevropejskom elemente v drevnerusskoj duxovnoj kul'ture — *svet-*", *Jazyki kul'tury i problemy perevodimosti*, red. B. A. Uspenskij, Moscow, p. 184-252.

Ünal, A., 2001: "The Power of Narrative in Hittite Literature", *Across the Anatolian Plateau*, Boston, p. 99-121.

Vasil'ev, M. A., 1999: *Jazyčestvo vostočnyx slavjan nakanune kreščenija Rusi: Religiozno-mifologičeskoe vzaimodejstvie s iranskim mirom. Jazyčeskaja reforma knjazja Vladimira*, Moscow.

Veselovskij, A. V., 1906: *Russkie i vil'tiny v sage o Tidreke Bernskom*, IORJaS, XI, 3, Saint-Petersburg.

Vilkul, T. L., 2003: "Daty roždenija knjažičej: staršie I mladšie Jaroskaviči", *Ruthenica*, 2, p. 108-114.

Vojtovič, L. V., 2015: "Holmgard: de pravyly rus'ki knjazi Svjatoslav Ihorevič, Volodymyr Svjatoslavič ta Jaroslav Volodymyrovyč?", *Ukrajns'kyj istoryčnyj žurnal*, 3, p. 37-55.

Vysockij, S. A., 1966: *Drevnerusskie nadpisi Sofii Kievskoj*, I, Kiev.

West, M. L., 2007: *Indo-European Poetry and Myth*, Oxford.

Zaxoder, B. N., 1962/1967: *Kaspijskij svod svedenij o Vostočnoj Evrope*, 1, Moscow, 1962, 2, Moscow, 1967.

Žix, M. I., 2010: "K probleme vozniknovenija Novgoroda v kontekste centralizatorskoj politiki kievskix knjazej serediny X – XI načala vv.", *Rossijskij gorod v istoričeskoj petrospektive: materialy Vserossijskoj naučnoj konferencii, posvjaščennoj 250-letiju g. Iževska (Iževsk, 25-26 sentjabrja 2010 g.). Sb. statej*, Iževsk, p. 320-326.

Sovereigns and sovereignty among pagan Slavs

Patrice Lajoye

National Center for Scientific Research (CNRS)

patrice.lajoye@unicaen.fr

Abstract. The purpose of this article is to make an inventory of the Slavic terms used to designate a sovereign, to determine their origin and to show that there was probably no «military democracy» among the first Slavs. The question of sacred sovereignty is also addressed through the study of various foundational accounts known to the Slavs..

Keywords. King, prince, sovereign, sovereign, Indo-Europeans

AMONG ALL THE INDO-EUROPEANS, the king is not only the leader of the warriors, the one who governs. His status is often also religious, and his role can then take on a sacred character. Concerning the Slavs, some authors, especially Soviet ones, wanted to believe that the first Slavs didn't have notion of State, that they lived in small communities of free peasants, of clanic type. Thus, for Boris Grekov, the first Slavs lived in a sort of "military democracy"[1]. This point of view has long been shared, including by Western scholars, such as Francis Conte, for whom the first Slavs lived in a kind of democracy because the people could make or break the princes, depending on their behavior[2]. This assumption has since been widely criticized, particularly with regard to the Balkans, by Florin Curta[3]. On the other hand, another ressearcher, A. A. Prokhorov, has found traces of the concept of sacred kingship, but nevertheless on the basis of very recent documents that are the Russian *byliny*[4]. Moreover, Petr Sommer, Dušan Třeštík and Josef Žemlička saw clearly that the accession to the throne of the first Czech prince, Přemysl, was

---

1. Grekov 1947: 27.
2. Conte 1996: 184-185.
3. See Curta 2004: chap. 7.
4. Proxorov 2001.

possible only because he had been chosen by a figure of sovereignty, Libuše, which perfectly matches other similar Indo-European myths[5].

The purpose of this article is to propose a typology of the lexicon used to designate sovereigns in the ancient Slavic world, prior to Christianization, and to offer a brief overview of the different myths of royal lineage foundation, in order to identify the figure of sovereignty.

The names of pagan Slavic sovereigns

Greek and Latin terms

The Greeks, who were the first to speak about the Slavs in their writings, employ globally two different terms to designate the sovereigns of this people. The first is hegemon (ἡγεμον), « leader, chief », used in the sixth century by Menandre Protector, speaking of the mighties ruled by the Slav Dauritas[6]. It reappears later under the pen of Constantine VII Porphyrogenitus, to designate the archontissa Olga, widow of prince Igor[7].

Archon (ἄρχων), "magistrate" or "governor", with the feminine archontissa (ἀρκότισσα), is also a common term in Greek sources for Slavic rulers[8]. This term is used until the 13th century[9]. It is not used only for the Rus'. Porinos, the first and probably legendary prince of the Croats, is associated with this title in the work of Constantine Porphyrogenitus[10]. The same author indicates that the Serbs, settled in Dalmatia with the permission of the emperor, as well as their Bulgarian neighbors, had an archon ("ἄρχοντος τοῦ Σέρβλου"; "ἄρχων Βουλγαρίας")[11]. This title was worn by the Bulgarian khans before the reign of Boris, as evidenced by various inscriptions[12]. In Greek texts translated into Slavic languages, the word ἄρχων is almost always translated by *knjaz'* (see below)[13].

It should be noted that a Slavic officer in the service of Byzantium, Dargosklavos

---

5. Sommer, Třeštík and Žemlička 2007: 218.
6. Migne, *Patrologia Graeca*, 113, 1864, col. 908
7. Constantin VII Porphyrogenitus, *De cerimoniis aulae Byzantinae*, II.
8. Curta 2004: 326-327.
9. Korpela 2001: 9. A seal of Mstislav II (1167-1169) bears the legend μέγας ἄρχων Ῥωσίας : Soloviev 1966: 148.
10. Constantin VII Porphyrogenitus, *De Administrando imperio*, XXX.
11. Constantin VII Porphyrogenitus, *De Administrando imperio*, XXXII.
12. So a Greek inscription from Philippi: Pilhofer 2018.
13. Tchérémissinoff 2001: 158.

(modern Dragoslav), in the 8th century, gives himself the title of archon of Hellas[14].

The Latin sources are a little more varied. Bruno of Querfurt thus employs *senior* to qualify Vladimir of Kiev (*senior Ruzorum*), Bolesław of Poland[15] or the Germanic Emperor Henry II. The word seems here to have the broad meaning of "sovereign"[16]. The use of the word *princeps* is exceptional. It is found for example in the plural form in the *Annals of Magdeburg* to designate the leaders of the Liutici[17]. It is also found to designate Pribislav of Mecklenburg and the two sons of Vartislav, Duke of Pomerania, Boguslav and Casimir[18], or in the 12th century, to designate Kruto, ruler of the Wagri[19]. And sometimes it is used for "duke" or "prince"[20]

Dux ("duke") is, however, widely used in Latin sources, but this term most often refers to sovereigns subject to the Germanic emperor or kings, or their ancestors. Thus Cosmas of Prague call "duke" Přemysl, the mythical founder of the first Czech dynasty[21], just as Gallus Anonymus gives this title to Popiel, the first known ruler of Gniezno in Poland[22]. Boruth, the first ruler of Carinthia, is also called *dux*[23]. But dux is a term that applies only to sovereigns converted to Christianity or in any case subject to the Germanic emperor[24]. Only Bolesław I the Brave, duke of Poland, escapes this: at the end of his reign, he is crowned king, taking apparently advantage of the death of Henry II. However, his father, Mieszko, has already been called rex by Widukind[25]. In the same way, in the 9th century, the Croatian ruler

---

14. Oikonomidès 1998.
15. *Epistula St. Brunonis ad imperatorem Henricum II,* Meyer, 1931, p. 8.
16. Raffensperger 2017: chap. 5.
17. *Annales Magdeburgenses,* sub anno 1169 : *Liuticiorum principibus.*
18. *Diploma fundationis episcopatus Suerinensis* : Dynda 2017: 241.
19. Helmold, *Chronica slavorum,* XXV.
20. *Vita Prieflingensis* II,5 ; Ebbo II,7 and II,13 and III, 16.
21. Cosmas of Prague, *Chronica Boemorum,* I, VI.
22. Gallus Anonymus, *Cronicae et gesta ducum sive principum Polonorum,* I, 1.
23. *Vita S. Virgilii episcopi Saltzburgensis,* 7.
24. See Helmold, *Chronica slavorum,* I : « *Polonia [...] quondam habuit regem, nunc autem ducibus gubernatur; servit et ipsa sicut Boemia sub tributo imperatoriae maiestati.* » But, as we have seen, in the oldest Polish chronicle, the first sovereigns are called « dukes ».
25. Widukind, *Res gestae Saxonicae,* III, 66. On the variability of Polish titles at the time of Christianization : Urbańczyk and Rosik 2007: 263-264, 290-291. The ancient Polish writers have themselves been aware of the difficulty of translating the terms designating the sovereigns. Thus in the 13th century, the *Kronika Wielkopolska* explains: « *Et iuxta hoc*

Trpimir was designated as duke by epigraphy, but a contemporary text named him *rex Sclavorum*[26], a title still existing a century later (*Croatorum itaque rex*)[27]. Finally, it comes lately that the dukes of Bohemia take the title of king.

This title of king (*rex*) isn't use indifferently. The Latin sources mentioning Prince Igor all describe him as *rex Russorum*[28]. His widow, Olga, is called *regina Rusorum* by Reginon of Prüm[29]. Thietmar of Merseburg alsa designates Vladimir as *rex Ruscorum*[30].

The texts of the Carolingian or more recent epoch use the word *rex* only to designate sovereigns independent of the Roman German emperor. As a result, Helmold indicates that at his time, only the Rani, among the Slavs, have a king ("*Rani, qui et Rugiani, gens fortissima Slavorum, qui soli habent regem*")[31]. However, he also uses the term *regulus*, "little king", to designate certain rulers of the Abodrites, including the Wagri[32]. Similarly, Widukind of Corvey mentions two *subreguli*, reigning over the Wagri and the Abodrites[33]. He also uses this term to refer to an anonymous Bohemian prince attacked by Boleslaus the Cruel because he is suspected of being too close to the Saxons. Finally, Eginhard indicates that the Slavs follow "*primores ac reguli*", but that all are under the rule of a king[34].

However, the word *rex* has been used much earlier, concerning the Slavs. Thus, Jordanes designates the first known king of the Antes, Boz, with this term[35]. Similarly, the pseudo-Maurice, in his *Strategikon*, reports that the Sclaveni and the Antes have many kings[36]. We know the names of some, such as Ardagastos

---

dicitur Pan in Slavonico maior dominus, licet alio nomine iuxta diversitatem lingwarum Slavonicarum dicatur Gospodzyn, Xandz autem maior est quam Pan veluti princeps et superior Rex. Omnes autem domini Pan appellantur. Duces vero exercitus woyevody nominantur [...]. » : *Kronika Wielkopolska*, prolog.

26. Radovanović, 2009.
27. John the Deacon, *Chronicon Venetum*, VII, 31-33. On the hesitations between *dux* and *rex* among the Croats, see Budak 2008, especially p. 238-239.
28. Soloviev 1966: 148.
29. Reginon of Prüm, *Chronicon*, XIII, 374.
30. Thietmar of Mersebourg, *Chronicon*, III, 859-860.
31. Helmold, *Chronica Slavorum*, I, 2. Voir aussi I, 36.
32. Helmold, *Chronica Slavorum*, I, 84.
33. Widukind, *Res gestae Saxonicae*, III, 68.
34. Eginhard, *Annales*, s. a. 789.
35. Jordanes, *De origine actibusque Getarum*, XLVIII.
36. Pseudo-Maurice, *Strategikon*, XI, 4, 128.

or Musokios, mentioned by Theophilact Simocatta[37]. The term used by these two sources is ρεξ, a word given as "barbaric" by Theophilact[38]. In the Greek sources of Byzantine eras, this word is regularly used to refer to Germanic or Western rulers. When these texts are translated into Slavonic or Old Russian, ρεξ is replaced by *riksъ*[39].

Terms used by the Slavs but borrowed from other languages

Many of the words used by the Slavs to designate the sovereigns are borrowed, and one of these most surprising loans concerns the term meaning "king": Slavonic *kral'*, old Russian *korol'*, Ukrainian *korol'*, Belarusian *karol'*, Polish *król*, Slovak *král*, Slovene, Serbian and Croatian *kralj*, upper and lower Sorbian, Macedonian and Bulgarian *kral*. This word is simply taken from Charlemagne's name, *Carolus*[40].

The Turkish word *khagan* has also been used for a while in the sources concerning the Kievian Rus'. In the 11th century, Vladimir and his son Jaroslav were designated with this term, especially by the Metropolitan Hilarion, who even speaks of Vladimir as being *velikago kagana zemlja*: "great kagan of the earth"[41]. The term is slightly distorted in a Frankish Latin source, the *Annals of St. Bertin*, in the section due to Bishop Prudence († 861), at the year 839, where it is question of *Rhos vocari dicebant, quos rex illorum, Chacanus vocabulo*[42]. At the beginning of the 10th century, Perse ibn Rosteh also speaks of *khaqan Rus*[43]. These documents of the Carolingian period show that very early, from the time of paganism, the Russian rulers used this term, probably borrowed from the neighboring Khazar empire, to designate themselves.

Probably much older, dating perhaps back to the time when the ancient Slavs were near the Goths north of the Black Sea, is the common Slavic term **kъnędzъ*, from the ancient Germanic **kuningaz* (see English *king*, German *König*, Norse

---

37. Theophylact Simocatta, *Historiae*, VI, 9.1.
38. Whitby 1982; Curta 2004: 327-328.
39. Tchérémissinoff 2001: 161-162.
40. Vasmer, 1964-1973, sv. *Korol'*.
41. *Pamjatniki drevnerusskogo kanoničeskogo prava*, II, Petrograd, 1920: 102-103; Duczko 2004: 25.
42. *Annales Bertiniani, MGH, Scriptores* : 434. The word reappears in the form *chaganus* to designate the king of the "Normans" in the *Chronicon Salernitatum*, a text of the end of the 10th century : *MGH, Scriptores*, III, p. 523.
43. Duczko 2004: 25.

konungr) [44], which gave Russian and Ukrainian *knjaz'*, Serbian and Croatian *knez*, Slovak *knieža*, Czech *kníže* and Polish *książę*. It is employed in the *Life of Constantine* to designate Rastislav, prince of Moravia[45]. The text also indicates that Prince Rastislav is the suzerain of "his princes and Moravians" ("*c*" *knjazi svoimi i s Moravljany*"). The fact that the word is Pan-Slavic guarantees the antiquity of the loan, but where the Germanic words means "king", the Slavic words refer the lower rank of "prince". But in 944, the prince of Kiev Igor is designated as *velikij knjaz' Ruskij*: "great prince of the Rus'" [46].

A possible Slavic word?

The Merovingian chronicler known as Fredegar tells that the Slavs occupying the territory of what became Bohemia were subjects to the Avars, who regularly took their wives, and made men easily sacrificable soldiers. These Slavs revolted, and finally won. They would then have chosen to govern not one of them, but a Franc, Samo, who would have participated in the fighting and distinguished himself[47]. Samo becomes *rex Sclavinorum*.

Was Samo really a Frank? All sources after Fredegaire ignore this fact and make him a Slav[48]. His name itself is not specifically Germanic. Samo would it be then a Slavic name? It is remarkable to note that the name of the first ruler of Poland, son of the legendary Piast the plowman, is Semovit, a name that could be translated by the "Lord of the Land" or more surely the "Lord of the Family" [49], in other words, the source of the lineage. However, the chronicle of Gallus Anonymus bears in title the variant *Samovithay*[50], in other words the "Lord by himself". In Old Russian, the anthroponym *Semovit* can be written *Samovit*'[51]. *Samo* could then be a hypocorical form of *Samovit, a term which is

---

44. Vasmer 1964-1973: sv. *Knjaz'*.
45. *Žitije Konstantina*, 14.
46. *Russian Primary chronicle*: 33-34.
47. Fredegar, *Chronica*, IV, 48.
48. Geary 2008: 246. For Curta 1997: 151, this passage of Fredegar is an ethnogenesis myth.
49. The meaning of -*vit* has long been debated. The solution brought by Rozwadowski (1961: 159 seq.): "Pan, władca" ("lord") is by far the most convincing (the Slavonic *domovit'* serving for example to translate the Greek οἰκοδεσπότης, "Master of the House").
50. "*De duce Samouithay qui dicitur Semouith*": Gallus Anonymys, *Gesta principum polonum*, I, 3.
51. *Ipat'evskaja letopis'*, s. a. 1251.

close to the Sanskrit *samrāj*, "sovereign (higher to the king)" [52] or of the Gaulish anthroponym *Samorix* (same meaning) [53], and would simply designate the one that reigns by himself, the chief king, suzerain of all the other princes. It would then be the only Slavic term not borrowed from another language designating a king or a prince.

This hierarchy of sovereigns, understood by the term **Samovit*, is regularly shown in ancient sources. We have seen that the king of the Antes, Boz, had 70 *primatibus* below him[54]. The Slavs fought by Charlemagne have mighties and kings (*reguli*), placed under the authority of a king[55]. Rostislav, prince of Moravia, also has "his princes"[56]. Finally, Igor, in Kiev, is called *velikij knjaz' Ruskij*: "High Prince of the Rus'". This hierarchy is not specific to the Slavs: it is found elsewhere in the Indo-European world, for example in Ireland, where we find many *rí*, with above them the *Ard Rí Erenn*: "high king of Ireland". The Indians also have the *Mahārāja* ("Great King"), overlord of other kings. The Persians also had the "King of Kings" (*šāhanšāh*), an expression also found in Georgia. The pagan Lithuanians also had a *kunigaikštis didysis* ("great king", an expression that is most often translated as "grand duke").

The sovereignty of the Slavs

The ancient sources have preserved various stories of a clearly mythological character, showing the origin of a royal lineage.

The plowman king

The chronicler Gallus Anonymous informs us of the existence in Gniezno (Poland), of a legend showing how a plowman is at the origin of the first royal dynasty. There was at Gniezno a duke named Popiel, whose two sons were to be tonsured. A great feast was then prepared, but when two strangers appeared, they were driven out of the city. They took refuge in a suburb, where they arrived at the hut of a plowman who was also preparing a meal for his sons. The plowman gladly received them, even though he was poor. And while he had almost no beer for the festivities, the two travelers made it inexhaustible by a miracle. The duke

---

52. Macdonell and Keith 1912: 432.
53. Delamarre 2008: 82.
54. Jordanes, *De origine actibusque Getarum*, XLVIII.
55. Eginhard, *Annales*, s. a. 789.
56. *Žitije Konstantina*, 14.

and his guests were invited. One of the plowman's son was then tonsured and he received the name of Semovit. This boy grew up, and finally he was named Duke of Poland, ousting Popiel's family[57].

A similar legend existed in Bohemia. A judge (*iudex*) prince, Crocco, had three daughters, all more or less magicians, and one of them, Libuše (*Lubossa*), had to choose a husband, called to rule over the people. And the one she named was the plowman Přemysl (*Premizl*), founder of the Czech princely lineage[58].

This type of story is also associated with Saint Stephen and Matej Korvín in Hungarian legends[59]. In Ukrainian legends collected in the 19th century, the future King Solomon, rejected by his mother and wandering in the countryside, is recognized by his father who had made a golden plow before ordering that it is walked everywhere until someone guess its price[60]. Although well-known throughout Europe with many variations[61], the myth of the plowman king is thus firmly anchored in Slavic soil: it could therefore have been part of the oldest Slavic mythology.

The three foreign brothers

The *Russian Primary Chronicle* tells a surprising story about the founding of the city of Novgorod. The Slavic and non-Slavic peoples, who occupied the Baltic coast near the territory of the present city, were subject to the Scandinavians. But they rebelled and chased them away. Left to their own devices, however, they were unable to organize. Then they summoned three Scandinavians, three brothers, who could reign over them. The last survivor of the three, Rjurik, being called to found the first princely dynasty of the Rus'[62].

This story has long been believed, and many noble families in Russia have claimed to have come from Rjurik. However, the appeal to the Varangians finds an exact parallel in medieval Ireland, in a tale (*Audacht Morainn*) which relates how the Irish rebelled against their nobles, who overcharged them with taxes. They killed them all, except three who could cross the sea and take refuge in Scotland. Once

---

57. Gallus Anonymys, *Gesta principum polonum*, I, 1-3.
58. Cosmas, *Chronica bohemorum*, I, 6.
59. Golema 2007.
60. Dragomanov and Dragomanova 2015: 106-118.
61. Krappe 1923; Delpech 2015.
62. *Russian Primary Chronicle*, s. a. 862. On this legends, see Aleksandr Koptev's analysis in this volume.

free, the Irish, like the Slovenes in the Novgorod region, found themselves unable to govern themselves. So they called the three brothers, who returned from Scotland, after having been promised all the rich lands of the island[63].

According to the comparison made by Dmitry Nikolayev, one would have a population led by a class that does not belong to the same lineage as it. This population is rebelling and killing the ruling class or repeling it beyond the seas. It then tries to rule itself, without success. Three brothers of the ruling class are called, who return in exchange for the wealth of the people. This comparison with Ireland shows that we are dealing with a myth, which we could probably find elsewhere.

Three brothers and a sister

Another story implements three brothers, but adding a sister: that of the foundation of Kiev, as told by the *Russian Primary Chronicle*:

> While the Polyanians lived apart and governed their families (for before the time of these brothers there were already Polyanians, and each one lived with his gens on his own lands, ruling over his kinsfolk), there were three brothers, Kiy, Shchek, and Khoriv, and their sister was named Lybed'. Kiy lived upon the hill where the Borichev trail now is, and Shchek dwelt upon the hill now named Shchekovitsa, while on the third resided Khoriv, after whom this hill is named Khorevitsa. They built a town and named it Kiev after their oldest brother. Around the town lay a wood and a great pine-forest in which they used to catch wild beasts. These men were wise and prudent; they were called Polyanians, and there are Polyanians descended from them living in Kiev to this day. Some ignorant persons have claimed that Kiy was a ferryman, for near Kiev there was at that time a ferry from the other side of the river, in consequence of which people used to say, "To Kiy's ferry." Now if Kiy had been a mere ferryman, he would never have gone to Tsar'grad. He was then the chief of his kin, and it is related what great honor he received from the Emperor in whose reign he visited the imperial court. On his homeward journey, he arrived at the Danube. The place pleased him and he built a small town, wishing to dwell there with his kinsfolk. But those who lived near by would not grant him this privilege. Yet even now the dwellers by the Danube call this town Kievets. When Kiy returned to Kiev, his native city, he ended his life there; and his brothers Shchek and Khoriv, as well as their sister Lybed', died there also[64].

---

63. Nikolayev 2012.
64. *Russian Primary Chronicle*, english translation: Cross and Sherbowitz-Wetzor 1953: 54-55.

Les récits que Constantin VII Porphyrogénète nous a conservés de l'installation des Croates en Dalmatie montre certaines ressemblances avec celui de la fondation de Kiev, à ceci-près qu'il y est question de cinq frères et de deux sœurs :
The accounts that Constantin VII Porphyrogenitus kept of the settlement of the Croats in Dalmatia show some similarities to that of the founding of Kiev, except that there are five brothers and two sisters:

> But the Croats at that time were dwelling beyond Bavaria, where the Belocroats are now. From them split off a family of five brothers, Kloukas (Κλουκας) and Lobelos (Λόβελος) and Kosentzis (Κοσέντζης) and Mouchlo (Μουχλώ) and Chrobatos (Χρωβάτος), and two sisters, Touga (Τουγά) and Bouga (Βουγά), who came with their folk to Dalmatia and found the Avars in possession of that land. After they had fought one another for some years, the Croats prevailed and killed some of the Avars and the remainder they compelled to be subject to them. [...] From that time they remained independent and autonomous, and they requested the holy baptism from the bishop of Rome, and bishops were sent who baptized them in the time of Porinos (Πορίνου) their prince[65].

Porinos (or Porga) is presumably a name derived from Perun.

A 12th century Bulgarian text that has been called the *Bulgarian apocryphal chronicle* by Jordan Ivanov, but whose original title is *Tale on Isaiah the Prophet and how he was taken by the angels to seventh heaven*, gives us the legendary account of the ethnogenesis of the Bulgarians in the Balkans. This story begins in fact with an apocrypha well-known in the Slavic world, namely the *Vision of Isaiah*. Then it continues on a curious chronicle of the first Bulgarian kings, a chronicle which is in fact a compilation of legends, and which has almost no historical value. The history of the first king is also that of the installation of Bulgarians in Bulgaria:

> So he [Isaiah] heard another voice speaking to him: 'Isaiah, my beloved prophet, go west to the highest [most northern] land of Rome, separate a third of the Coumans, call them Bulgarians, and people the land of Karvona, which is liberated from the Romans and Hellenes.' Then I, brothers, on the orders of God, I came to the left of the country of Rome and I separated the third of the Coumans and showed them the way, I brought them to the Zatnousa river, and to another river called Ereousa. Then they will be great rivers. And the country of Karvona, which will be called Bulgaria, so that it is free of Hellenes for 130

---

65. Constantin VII Porphyrogenitus, *De Admnistrando imperio*, XXX, english translation Moravcsik and Jenkins 1967: 143-145. See also a variant of this story in chapter XXXI, which gives Porinos the name of Porga.

years. And it was populated by many people from the Danube to the sea. And a tsar was chosen from among them. And his name was Tsar Slav. And this tsar peopled towns and villages. Some of these people were pagans. And the tsar built a hundred mounds on Bulgarian soil, so he was called the the hundred mounds tsar. And during that time, everything was in abundance. And those hundred mounds were his kingdom. And this tsar was the first to reign over the Bulgarian lands, and his reign lasted a hundred and nineteen years until his[66].

In the three stories, we have a people settled on a land that was not their own, and has a leader of the same name (Kii in Kiev, Khrobatos among Croats, Slav among Bulgarians[67]). In the Central Middle Ages, this type of legend is common (we will remember for example Brutus for the Britons, Francus for the Franks). However, it should be noted that most of these legendary migrations, mostly literary, are due to a flight, especially after the Trojan War. This is not the case here: migration, as far as the Bulgarians are concerned, follows a dream, a vision.

Some motifs in the Bulgarian text are found elsewhere. For example, the three-fold division of the original people: the apocryphal says that one-third of the Coumans will be taken, and that this third part will name Slav as king. This is an information that is abundantly found in the Iranian world, as Éric Pirart finally showed: the first king of the Scythians, Targitaos is succeeded by Kolaxais (*(s)kuda-xšaya-: "He who has power over the Scythians"), the youngest of his three sons; Herakles is succeeded by Scythes, the youngest of his three sons; Feridun's successor is Iraj (Iran's namesake), the youngest of his three sons[68]. In any case, the master of the third is eponymous of the new main people. Knowing the closeness that existed between the Iranian peoples, the ancient Slavs and the proto-Bulgarians, does this mean that Slav was the youngest of three brothers? Not necessarily, because in some cases of founding of city (and no longer of people) we find three brothers, as we saw for the Kiev among the Polianes. Kii, eponymous of the new city, is here the eldest.

This type of story finds many parallels in various Indo-European mythologies, from Armenia to Ireland[69]. The Kievan version, however, finds its most exact

---

66. Ivanov 1976: 250-251, translation Viktoriya Lajoye.
67. But we can also find the eponymic hero *Boemus* who in chronicle of Cosmas of Prague (*Chronica Bohemorum* I, 2) leads his people to a new land where they can settle. Finally, they settle around the sacred Bohemian mountain called Řip and they name the surrounding land by his name. In later Dalimil's Old Czech chronicle he is rendered as *praotec Čech* (grandfather Czech).
68. Pirart 2003.
69. Lajoye 2010.

parallel in a 7th-century Armenian chronicle, the *History of Taron*, attributed to Zenob of Glak, which mentions characters with strangely assonant names with the Kievan names: the Armenian narrative being supposed to take place in the territory of Balounik, one can only be astonished by this triple coincidence that are the names Kii / Kouar, Xoriv / Horian and Poliani / Balounik. There is still debate among specialists as to which of the two legends originates from the other[70].

Sovereignty

The number three comes up very regularly in the mentioned legends: Crocco has three daughters[71], and Libuše is the youngest, the founders of Novgorod are three brothers, those of Kiev too, Tsar Slav took with him a third of Coumans. One could add to this list the three brothers Lech (eponymous of the Poles), Rus (eponymous of the Russians) and Czech (eponymous of the Czechs), sons of Pan prince of Pannonia, mentioned by the late medieval sources from Poland[72].

The accession to power of the new sovereign, however, is not done without a precise help. Piast, the Polish equivalent of the plowman king Přemysl, is discovered by "two strangers", whose visit to Duke Popiel is reminiscent of some biblical passages (notably Genesis 17 and 18). But the *Kronika Wielkopolska* makes it clear that they are the saints John and Paul[73]. Their supernatural character is therefore well marked. It is also found in the Bulgarian tale, which indicates that the order to migrate with a third of Coumans came in a celestial voice. Elsewhere, it's a woman who can intervene. Among the Croats, two sisters, Touga and Bouga, accompany their brothers. If they are two, their names are particularly assonant, an assonance that could betray a primitive uniqueness. In Bohemia, it is Libuše, daughter of Crocco, who chooses a husband, Přemysl (her subjects not wanting to be judged by a woman). In Poland, the counterpart of Crocco, Gracchus (Krakus), founder of Kraków, has two sons and a daughter, Wanda. His two sons being dead, it is Wanda who succeeds him. But Poland is then invaded by a German army. Wanda then takes the lead of the Polish troops, and on her approach, seeing her, the German soldiers give up fighting and

---

70. Ščavelev 2014: 240.
71. See de Lazero (1999: 145) which compares them to the Irish trio Mórrígan-Bodb-Macha.
72. For example the *Kronika Wielkopolska*.
73. Knoll and Schaer 2003: 17, fn. 7.

their leader commits suicide. Since Wanda gave its name to the Vistula, which becomes Vandalus, and to the people of the Vandals[74]. Wanda, like Libuše, is a rider and the two choose who they should (or not) marry and therefore make king.

In Kiev, there is no ancient legend associated with Lybed, sister of Kii, Ščekand Xoriv, but Lybed is still the name of a river flowing in the city and is a tributary of the Dnieper, which recalls the case of Wanda and Vistula in Krakow. It was regularly thought that his name related to modern Russian *lebed'* (Ukrainian *lebid'*): "swan". This woman would then obviously belong to the other world, like all Russian and European women-swans[75]. However, this name could also be etymologically similar to that of Libuše.

Conclusion

It is clear in the end that the pagan Slavs have known a royal institution firmly implanted and similar to that of other Indo-European peoples, with a great king whose vassals are smaller kings. These kings are not chosen as part of a military democracy and are not elected only in the context of a war: we can see the existence of dynasties very early. These dynasties are themselves founded thanks to the benevolence of a female personality who seems to be embodied sovereignty, similar, for example, to the mythical Irish queen Medb[76].

Sources

Annales Magdeburgenses, ed. Pertz, *MGH, Scriptores* 16, 1859, 107-196.

Constantin VII Porphyrogenitus, *De Admnistrando império*, ed. Migne, *Patrologia Graeca*, Paris, 1864, 113.

Constantin VII Porphyrogenitus, *De Cerimoniis aulae Byzantinae*, ed. Reisk, Bonn, 1830.

Cosmas of Prague, *Chronica Boemorum*, ed. Holder-Egger, *MGH, Scriptores*, 30/1, 1896, 37-43

Einhard, *Annales regni Francorum*, ed Kurze, *MGH, Scriptores rerum Germanicum* 6, 1895, 1-178.

---

74. « *Unde fluvius Wisla a Wąda regina Wandalus nomen accepit. A quo Poloni et caeterae slavonicae gentes eorundem ditioni adhaerentes, non Lechitae sed Wandalitae sunt appellati* » : Wincenty Kadłubek, *Chronica seu originale regum et principum Poloniae*, 2.

75. The regular presence of an ornithomorphic character in the legends of foundation or ethnogenesis has been noted: Ščavelev 2010.

76. On the warlike sovereignty of Ireland, see Le Roux and Guyonvarc'h 1983.

Fredegar, *Chronica*, ed. Krusch, *MGH, Scriptores rerum Merovingicarum* 2, 1888, 18-193.
Gallus Anonymus, *Cronicae et gesta ducum sive principum Polonorum*, ed. Knoll and Schaer, *The Deeds of the Princes of the Poles*, 2003, Budapest.
Helmold, *Chronica slavorum*, ed. Holder-Egger, *MGH, Scriptores*, 30/1, 1896, 35-37.
Ipat'evskaja letopis', Polnoe sobranie russkix letopisej 2, Saint-Petersburg, 1908.
John the Deacon, *Chronicon Venetum*, ed. Pertz, *MGH, Scriptores* 7, 1846, 4-38.
Jordanes, *De origine actibusque Getarum*, ed. Mommsen, *MGH, Auctores antiquissimi* 5/1.
Kronika Wielkopolska, ed. Kürbis, *Monumenta poloniae historica* ns VIII, *Chronica poloniae maioris*, 1970, Warsaw.
Pseudo-Maurice, *Strategikon*, ed. Dennis, *Corpus Fontium Historiae Byzantinae* 17, 1981, Vienne.
Menander Protector, *De legationibus barbarorum ad Romanos*, ed. Migne, *Patrologia Graeca*, Paris, 1864, 113.
Reginon of Prüm, *Chronicon*, ed. Kurze, *MGH, Scriptores rerum Germanicum* 50, 1890.
Russian Primary chronicle, Povest' vremennykh let, ed. Likhačev, 1950, Moscow.
Theophylact Simocatta, *Historiae*, ed. Bekker, *Corpus scriptorum historiae byzantinae*, 1834, Bonn.
Thietmar of Mersebourg, *Chronicon*, ed. Lappenberg, *MGH, Scriptores* 3, 1839, 733-871.
Vita S. Virgilii episcopi Saltzburgensis, ed. Wattenbach, MGH, Scriptores 11, 1854, 86-95.
Wincenty Kadłubek, *Chronica seu originale regum et principum Poloniae*, ed. Bielowski, *Monumenta poloniae historica* II, 1872, 249-447.
Widukind, *Res gestae Saxonicae*, ed. Waitz, *MGH, Scriptores* 3, 1839, 416-467.
Žitije Konstantina, ed. Vaillant, *Textes vieux slaves*, 1, 1968, Paris.

Bibliographie

Budak, Nevan, 2008: "Identities in Early Medieval Dalmatia (Seventh-Eleventh Centuries)", in Ildar H. Garipzanov, Patrick J. Geary et Przemysław Urbańczyk (éd.), *Franks, Northmen, and Slavs : Identities and States Formation in Early Medieval Europe*. Turnhout, Brepols. 223-242.
Conte, Francis, 1996: *Les Slaves. Aux origines des civilisations d'Europe centrale et orientale (VIe-XIIIe siècles)*. Paris, Albin Michel.
Cross, Samuel Hazzard, and Sherbowitz-Wetzor, Olgerd P., 1953: *The Russian Primary Chronicle, Laurentian Text*. Cambridge, The Mediæval Academy of America.

Curta, Florin, 1997: "Slavs in Fredegar and Paul the Deacon : medieval *gens* or 'scourge of God' ?", *Early Medieval Europe*, 6, 2: 141-167.

Curta, Florin, 2004: *The Making of the Slavs. History and Archaelogy of the Lower Danube Region, c. 500-700.* Cambridge, Cambridge University Press.

Delamarre, Xavier, 2008: "Indo-Gallici Reges", *Études celtiques*, XXXVI: 79-84.

de Lazero, Octav-Eugen, 1999: "The dynastic myth of the Přemyslids in the *Chronica Bohemorum* by Cosmas of Prague", *Ollodagos*, XII: 123-175.

Delpech, François, 2015: *Trésors et talismans : le cycle de la Charrue d'Or.* Bruxelles, Mémoires de la Société belge d'Études celtiques.

Dragomanov, Mikhaïl, and Dragomanova, Lydia, 2015: *Travaux sur le folklore slave, suivi de Légendes chrétiennes de l'Ukraine.* Lisieux, Lingva.

Duczko, Wladyslaw, 2004: *Viking Rus. Studies on the Presence of Scandinavians in Eastern Europe.* Leiden, Brill.

Dynda, Jiří, 2017: *Slovanské pohanství ve středověkých pramenech.* Prague, Scriptorium.

Geary, Patrick J., 2008: 'Slovenian Gentile Identity : From Samo to the Fürstenstein', *in* Ildar H. Garipzanov, Patrick J. Geary et Przemysław Urbańczyk (éd.), *Franks, Northmen, and Slavs : Identities and States Formation in Early Medieval Europe.* Turnhout, Brepols. 243-257.

Golema, Martin, 2007: 'Medieval Saint Ploughman and Pagan Slavic Mythology', *Studia Mythologica Slavica*, X: 155-177.

Grekov, Boris, 1947: *La Culture de la Russie de Kiev.* Moscou, Éditions en Langues étrangères.

Ivanov, Jordan, 1976: *Livres & légendes bogomiles (aux sources du catharisme).* Paris, Maisonneuve et Larose.

Knoll, Paul W., and Schaer, Frank (trans.), 2003: *Gesta principum Polonorum. The Deeds of the Princes of the Poles.* Budapest, Central European University Press.

Koder, Johannes, 1983: 'Zu den Archontes der Slaven in De Administrando Imperio 29, 106-115', *Wiener Slavistisches Jahrbuch*, 29: 128-131.

Korpela, Jukka, 2001: *Prince, Saint, and Apostle: Prince Vladimir Svjatoslavič of Kiev, His Posthumous Life, and the Religious Legitimization of the Russian Great Power.* Wiesbaden, Otto Harrassowitz Verlag.

Krappe, Alexander Haggerty, 1923: 'La légende de Libuše et de Přemysl', *Revue des études slaves*, III, 1-2: 86-89.

Lajoye, Patrice, 2010: 'À propos de la *Chronique apocryphe bulgare* et du *Livre des Conquêtes de l'Irlande.* Le troisième fils et le tiers du peuple', *in* Joël Hascoët, Gaël Hily, Patrice Lajoye, Guillaume Oudaer et Christian Rose (dir.), *Deuogdonion. Mélanges en l'honneur de Claude Sterckx.* Rennes, Éditions T.I.R. 373-384.

Le Roux, Françoise, and Guyonvarc'h, Christian J., 1983: *Mórrígan – Bodb – Macha. La souveraineté guerrière de l'Irlande.* Rennes, Ogam – Celticum.

Macdonell, Arthur Anthony, and Keith, Arthur Berriedale, 1912: *Vedic Index of Names and Subjects*, vol. II. Londres, Murray.

Meyer, Carl Henri, 1931: *Fontes historiae religionis Slavicae*. Berlin, Walter de Gruyter.

Moravcsik, GY., and Jenkins, R. J. H., 1967: *Constantine Porphyrogenitus De Administrando Imperio*. Washington, Dumbarton Oaks.

Nikolayev, Dmitry, 2012: 'Fír Flathemon in the *Russian Primary Chronicle*? The Legend of the Summoning of the Varangians and the Prefatory Matter to Audacht Morainn', *in* Maxim Fomin, Václav Blažek et Piotr Stalmaszczyk (éd.), *Transforming Traditions : Studies in Archaeology, Comparative Linguistics and Narrative. Proceedings of the Fifth International Colloquium of Societas Celto-Slavica held at Příbram, 26-29 July 2010*. Łódz, Wydawnictwo Uniwersytetu Łódzkiego. 113-126.

Oikonomidès, N., 1998: 'L'archonte slave de l'Hellade au VIIIe siècle', *Vizantijskij vremennik*, 55: 111-118.

Pilhofer, Peter, 2018: 'Neue Inschriften für die 2. Auflage. Eine protobulgarische Inschrift', *Die Inschriften von Philippi im Bild*, 2018, http://www.bilddb.philippoi.de/368.pdf

Pirart, Éric, 2003: 'Vive le cadet ! Remarques sur une succession mythique indo-iranienne ancienne', *Ollodagos*, XVII, 2: 177-197.

Proxorov, A. A., 2001: 'K postanovke problemy stadial'nogo predstavlenij o sakral'nosti knjažeskoj vlasti v slavjanskom jazyčestve', *Vybranyja navukovyja pracy Belaruskaga dzjaržaunaga universiteta*, 2: 42-51.

Radovanović, Bojana, 2009: 'Titre de Trpimir selon les dires de Gottschalk', *Istorijski Časopis*, LVIII: 33-42.

Raffensperger, Christian, 2017: *The Kingdom of Rus'*. Kalamazoo and Bradford, Arc Humanities Press.

Rozwadowski, Jan Michał, 1961: *Wybór pism: Językoznawstwo indoeuropejskie*. Warsaw, Państwowe Wydawn. Naukowe.

Ščavelev, A. S., 2010: 'Tri motivno-semantičeskie paralleli v slavjanskix legendax o pervyx knjaz'jax', in *Čelovek i drevnosti. Pamjati Aleksandra Aleksandroviča Formozova (1928-2009)*. Moscow. 814-818.

Ščavelev, A. S., 2014: 'K voprosu o sledax drevneslavjanskix legenda v pis'mennyx tekstax drugix narodov', Πολυτροπος. *Sbornik naučnyx statej pamjati Arkadija Anatol'evič Molčanova (1947-2010)*. Moscow, Indrik. 237-242.

Soloviev, A. V., 1966: '"*Reges*' et '*regnum Russiae*' au Moyen Âge", *Byzantion*, 36, 1: 144-177.

Sommer, Petr, Třeštík, Dušan, and Žemlička, Josef, 2007: "Bohemia and Moravia", in Nora Berend (éd.), *Christianization and the Rise of Christian Monarchy. Scandinavia, Central Europe and Rus' c. 900-1200*. Cambridge, Cambridge University Press. 214-262.

Tchérémissinoff, Katia, 2001: *Recherches sur le lexique des chroniques slaves traduites du grec au Moyen Âge*. Paris, Association Pierre Belon.

Urbańczyk, Przemysław, and Rosik, Stanisław, 2007: "Poland", *in* Nora Berend (éd.), *Christianization and the Rise of Christian Monarchy. Scandinavia, Central Europe and Rus'* c. 900-1200. Cambridge, Cambridge University Press. 263-318.

Vasmer, Max, 1964: *Etimologičeskij slovar' russkogo jazyka*, 4 vol.. Moscow, Progress.

Whitby, L. M., 1982: "Theophylact's knowledge of languages", *Byzantion*, 52: 425-428.

Some aspects of pre-Christian Baltic religion

Roman Zaroff

Independent researcher, Australia

r_zaroff@yahoo.com.au

Abstract. This article provides an interpretation of certain, selected aspects of pre-Christian Baltic religion from the Middle Ages, prior to its official conversion to Christianity. The Balts were the last people on the European continent that became Christians, albeit many rites, customs and beliefs entered into Baltic folklore and many survived till today. In a post-Soviet era one observed a revival of scholarly interest in their ancient beliefs and many new interpretations. Moreover, it examines a revival of Neo-pagan movements in all the independent Baltic states. The paper attempts to interpret and reconcile some known Old Prussian deities with those of the Lithuanians and Latvians. It also explores the nature of Baltic beliefs addressing the question of its polydoxy, polytheism or henotheism..

Keywords. Balts, Baltic people, Baltic religion, Indo-European religions, pre-Christian beliefs, pagans, Old Prussians, Lithuanians, Latvians, gods and deities

THE PAPER EXPLORES the pre-Christian beliefs of Baltic speaking people, that is, the ancestors of modern Latvians and Lithuanians as well as those people who spoke the now extinct Prussian and related dialects. Any religion exists in its own social and historical context and is also not immune to external influences and pressures. Therefore, it changes and evolves. Recognising this, we will explore the religious beliefs of the Balts in a certain defined period of their history, namely the time around their conversion to Christianity. This equates roughly to the period between the 12th and 14th centuries.

It has to be acknowledged that the following short paper mainly addresses certain selected issues concerning the pre-Christian religion of the Baltic people. In particular, it concentrates on the question of the nature of this religion. There is no common agreement among scholars about the character of pre-Christian

Baltic religion. Some scholars, among them Polish historians Aleksander Brückner, Henryk Łowmiański, and in the 1990s Hungarian Endre Bojtár, argued that Baltic beliefs can be described as a polydoxy.[1] Briefly, polydoxy is a belief in the sacredness of all natural forces and phenomena. They are not personified but possess their own spirits and magical powers. Practically, in a polydoxy the world is inhabited by a limitless number of spirits and demons. There also exists a belief in the afterlife, the soul, and worship of ancestors characterised by specific cults and their associated rituals.[2] Some others, including Lithuanian scholar Gintaras Beresnevičius, argued for a well developed, sophisticated polytheism with a clearly defined pantheon of gods.[3]

This paper is divided into three sections. The first is a general overview of the Baltic peoples' political and social organisation, and their conversion to Christianity. It also addresses the issue of the sources and methodology used in research. The second explores selected deities and their functions, attributes, domains and distribution of cults, as well as the major locations of cults. Other topics such as regional deities, spirits, Baltic cosmology and survival of pagan traditions and beliefs are not discussed in detail. The third section focuses on certain expressions of religion such as places of worship, as well as evidence for priests and the priesthood.

Background

The smallest social unit in Baltic lands was the *lauks*, which were small family oriented settlements, households and the surrounding fields. They were ruled by a male head of the family. Larger political and territorial organisations called *terrula* in Latin (meaning a small land), existed in the early 13th century in Prussia, Latvia and Lithuania, and centred on strongholds or hill forts. Such a political territorial unit covered up to 300 square kilometres and could have up to 2,000 inhabitants.[4] They were known as *pulka*, comprising a dozen or so *laukses*.[5] Similar territorial organisations to *pulka* existed among the mediaeval Slavs and were called *vicinatus* in Latin or *opole* in Polish, *mir* or *obschina* among

---

1. Bojtár 1997: 278-279, 286-296; Łowmiański 1986: 50-53.
2. Bojtár 1997: 275.
3. Beresnevičius : 3-8.
4. Wojciechowski 1983: 62.
5. Białuński 1999: 138. Pulka-terrula territorial organization is also supported by archaeological evidence; Okulicz-Kozaryn 1997: 268-277.

the Eastern Slavs and *zadruga* or *župa* by the Southern Slavs.[6] The evidence from Prussia shows that *pulkas* were ruled by the tribal assembly *wayde* that regulated community matters. A larger assembly, usually comprising a dozen or so *pulkas*, was known as *kariowayde*. Such assemblies of a number of regional *pulkas* were attended by all free males who met in holy groves - where their decisions for treaties, raids, election of war leaders, targets of raids etc. were made.[7] The Prussian assembly *wayde* or rather *kariowayde* had a parallel in Scandinavian *thing* and Slavic *veche*. This was confirmed by the 9th century traveller Wulfstan who is recorded referring to Prussian lands where there were many "towns" each with its own "king".[8] No doubt he referred to numerous *pulka*-like territorial units and their leaders.

The issue of a larger tribal division, especially among the Prussians, is a bit confusing and may be misleading. This is so because some tribal names may more likely refer to regions rather than political entities. For example, according to Peter of Dusburg there were eleven major Prussian tribes, and the most prominent and strongest were the Sudovians (Yotvingians), Sambians, Nadrovians and Galindians.[9] There is some evident trend that, during confrontation with the Teutonic Knights, some war-leader tried to grab more power and control over a number of pulkas. Consequently during the 13th century some political and tribal consolidation was taking place in Bartia, Sudovia, Nadrovia and Galindia.[10] An example would be the larger tribal organisation of the Bartians (Barts) formed under pressure from the Teutonic Knights.[11] Still, it covered a relatively small territory of Bart on the middle and lower flows of the Łyna river (Alna in Lithuanian). There is however no evidence that these mentioned tribes ever formed any centralised political entity. It appears rather that a short term, one goal alliance was formed among the Prussians.

A similar situation existed among the Latvian tribes that included the Curonians, Semigalians, Selonians and Latgalians. In most cases they were organised into small territorial, social and political entities, usually no larger than a *pulka*, probably with the exception of the Coastal Curonians who were involved in Baltic trade, mainly with Scandinavia. According to Life of Anskar, in the 9th century

---

6. Zaroff 1999: 21-22.
7. Okulicz-Kozaryn 1997: 187; Długokęcki 2007: 34-36.
8. *The Old English Orosius*, pp. 16-17.
9. Peter of Dusburg, III.3-4, pp. 43- 45.
10. Okulicz-Kozaryn 1997: 278-280.
11. Okulicz-Kozaryn 1997: 276.

there was a Curonian "kingdom" comprising five towns.[12] This indicates that it must have been a small tribal political entity.

On the other hand it was a different story among the Lithuanian people. While the mediaeval Samogitians (Lith. Žemaičiai) might have subscribed to some regional affinities they were fully incorporated into the Lithuanian state by 1240. By the middle of the 13th century the Grand Duke, later king Mindaugas, brought all Lithuanian lands under his control, creating a fully fledged mediaeval state.[13]

The Balts were the last people in Europe that converted to Christianity. In the case of the Prussians, Christian missionaries reached their lands as early as the late 10th century,[14] however the real, albeit brutal and forceful Christianisation began with the arrival of the Teutonic Knights in the region in the 1230s.[15] The territory of modern Latvia at the turn of the 13th century was an area of struggle for political control between Denmark, the Hanseatic League and the Livonian Brothers of the Sword. The forceful Christianisation of Baltic people began there with a formal papal decree to create an Order by Pope Innocent III in 1204.[16] The case of the Lithuanians was different again. Their conversion was not enforced by any foreign power with an alien culture and language, but was instead a political decision by Lithuanian rulers. Mindaugas (reigned c. 1236-1263) accepted Christianity in 1250/51 for political reasons and after a short "flirt" with this new faith, Lithuania reverted to pagan beliefs in 1261.[17] The Lithuanian state consolidated and expanded further during the reign of pagan Grand Duke Gediminas (reigned 1315-1341).[18] Officially, Lithuania converted in 1387 when their ruler Jogaila married Polish princess Jadwiga and became a Polish king. Needless to say, the conversion of the Baltic people took many generations and an echo of pagan beliefs and rituals was well preserved in Baltic folklore till modern times.[19]

---

12. Rimbert, XXX.
13. Rowell 1997 : 60-67, 81.
14. Saint Adalbert mission of 997 in Canaparius, I, II.
15. Urban 1989: 50-51. Teutonic Knights were invited in 1228 by Polish duke Konrad I of Mazovia to assist him in conquest and Christianisation of the Prussians. Conrad gave them as tithe the Chełmno Land (Kulmerland).
16. Peter of Dusburg, I.1, p. 14, Scholia. The Livonian Brothers of the Sword merged with Teutonic Knights in 1236.
17. Rowell 1997: 20, 36.
18. Rowell 1997: 60-67.
19. Urban 1989: 186-187.

We also have to briefly address the modern, especially post Soviet, revival of so called Baltic pre-Christian religion in Lithuania and Latvia.[20] Broadly speaking these developments are modern intellectual constructs. An ideology or set of beliefs that attempts to interpret modern concepts and worldview by projecting this framework on people and societies that existed 800 years ago, mixed with some folklore and selective non critical drawing from historical sources, is of no concern to us here.

The major problem we are faced with in attempting a reconstruction of Baltic religion is the same as with any society and culture that left no sacred texts or any written records about their pre-Christian beliefs, deities, myths and cosmology. In the Baltic context we encounter the same obstacles as with the reconstruction of pre-Christian religion of their Slavic neighbours. Therefore, in our research we have to rely on written records by non-Baltic people and composed in most cases in Latin or German. Moreover, the available records were mainly written by Christian clergy, so the chroniclers we are concerned with had neither a knowledge of Baltic languages, nor a deep understanding of the societies and cultures they were writing about, or at best a limited understanding of the above. Also, as Christians they were not particularly concerned with pagan beliefs and regarded them as evil or at best as superstitions not worthy of mention. Therefore, we have to be aware that written sources might often have misunderstood Baltic religion, and above all they were heavily biased and sometimes even fictitious.

We also have a valuable source of information by way of rich ethnographic data from Lithuania and Latvia. Folklore and many traditions, customs and myths can provide insight into many aspects of pre-Christian Baltic religion. This however has to be approached with extreme caution and treated as supportive evidence only. First of all, ethnographic data was in most cases gathered many centuries after the conversion to Christianity and traditional beliefs and customs no doubt underwent changes over this time. Many could have mingled with Christianity, sometimes beyond recognition. Secondly, there is a certain trap in interpreting ethnographic data. Early Christianity was extremely intolerant toward pagan beliefs and aimed to destroy all traces of these, most often in a ruthless manner. Therefore, the upper layer of more pronounced and organised expressions of Baltic religion like major deities, cults and worship places were eradicated completely. In such a context the interpretation of extinct religious beliefs from ethnographic material mainly comprises an expression of its lower

---

20. Bojtár 1997: 282.

strata. This may prompt the conclusion that Baltic religion was a simple, rustic set of beliefs, more or less an animistic set of beliefs with elements of shamanism. Supportive information is provided by archaeological excavation of pre-Christian Baltic sites. This includes not only the territories of modern Lithuania and Latvia but also large sections of Belarus, North-Eastern Poland and Russian Kaliningrad Oblast. Additionally, data from excavations of the Fatyanovo culture may be used as supportive evidence. The Fatyanovo complex dates to the second half of the second millennium B.C.E. It emerged in the Eastern Baltic area and spread along the Volga and Oka rivers, in some areas reaching as far as the Ural mountains. The physical anthropology and a strong material cultural affiliation with Kurgan and later Baltic cultures indicates that it was ancestral to all later Balts or at least contributed to Baltic ethnogenesis.[21] It is worth noting that the Balts survived in some of the areas east of the modern Baltic linguistic frontier well into the Middle Ages. The people known as the Goliads who lived in the region of the Oka and Dnepr rivers were defeated in 1058 by Kievan prince Izaslav.[22] Their tribal name is cognate to that of the Prussian Galindians.

It is commonly accepted that Baltic languages retained many characteristics of original Indo-European speech or its earliest dialects. Unsurprisingly then, Baltic languages were intensively studied by linguists over the years. By analogy it can be postulated that Baltic religion must have retained many ancient, common Indo-European traits and beliefs. Therefore, wherever it will be applicable, the following work will employ a comparative approach to mythology, focusing especially on the Slavs as being linguistically and culturally closest to the Balts.

The sources dealing with Baltic religion are unfortunately limited. The main sources for Prussian history and religion are the *Chronicle of Prussian Lands* by Peter of Dusburg. His work covers the history of the Teutonic Knights of the 13th and early 14th centuries. He most likely wrote his chronicle in Königsberg (modern Kaliningrad) before 1326. Peter's knowledge and understanding of Prussian affairs has often been questioned and his heavy pro-Christian, pro-Teutonic Knights bias is apparent in his work. The other source is *The Prussian Chronicle* written by German priest Simon Grunau at Tolkmicko[23] in the 1520's. Most modern Western scholars however regard Grunau's work as unreliable. It seems that Simon Grunau recorded some local and regional deities and spirits,

---

21. On Fatyanovo culture: Gimbutas 1963: 34, 44-46, 91-93.
22. *Russian Primary Chronicle*, Year 1058; Okulicz-Kozaryn 1997: 27.
23. Tolkmicko - modern Poland in Elbląg (Elbing) County, German: Tolkemit.

mixed them with a few real but common Baltic deities, confused their names and created his own Baltic pantheon by frivolously linking them with Classical beliefs. Yet another source from the late 14th Century is the *New Prussian Chronicle* by Wigand of Marburg. He was a herald knight of the Teutonic Order and his chronicle covers the years 1293 to 1394. Wigand's work provides some, albeit limited, insight into Prussian pre-Christian beliefs and customs. Two other related sources are the anonymous documents *Constitutiones Synodales* and *Sudovian Book* from the early 16th century. Both describe the alleged Prussian pantheon. The data was supposedly collected from among the Sudovians who were forcefully resettled in Sambia after 1283. It is however apparent that the *Sudovian Book* is just a later redaction of *Constitutiones Synodales*,[24] with some minor differences in spelling and some added deities. Most later chronicles copied the list of names of deities from just those two documents, albeit with some variation in spelling and assigned attributes. It has to be acknowledged that those two sources are to a large extent the basis for modern neo-paganism and a revival of traditional, so called native religion in modern Baltic countries.

Although our main primary sources are often of dubious integrity, common sense dictates that not all information in *Constitutiones* and Simon Grunau's *The Prussian Chronicle* could have been invented and that there must be at least some genuine data. The question of how to sort fact from fiction in these works consequently arises. Short documents from the period are therefore generally the more reliable ones, though unfortunately only a few deal with the beliefs of Baltic people.

Most world religions evolved from simple worship of the forces of nature; however religion is not a static phenomenon. Here we can recall the argument by French sociologist and philosopher Emile Durkheim, concerning changes within religion being on par with social changes. This was taken further by American social scientist Guy Swanson. He postulated that more complex societies require more complex beliefs, rituals etc. In this context, all religions should be a reflection of the societies that practice them.[25] If we in fact observe different religions, not only in the context of pagan Central Europe, the above claim holds true.

As the data for Baltic pre-Christian religion is scarce and sketchy there is an ongoing discussion regarding whether it was a polydoxy or polytheism. A polydoxy is defined by the simple worship of natural phenomena, such as cults

---

24. Shiroukhov 2006: 19.
25. Religion mirrors society: Swanson 1964: 96; Wach 1973: 79; Bowker 1973: 26-28.

of celestial objects, natural elements and forces, plants, animals, fertility cults, ancestral worship and so on. In a polydoxy the clear personification of these forces and a defined pantheon are absent or at best vague.[26]

The gods and deities

Before continuing, it has to be remembered that just like among all the pre-Christian Indo-European beliefs, the Baltic pantheon was not a fixed and clearly defined assembly of gods and goddesses, nor was there a common liturgy, customs, etc.

From Peter of Dusburg's account we know that the Balts worshiped the Sun, Moon, stars and thunder, as well as various animals, birds, reptiles and amphibians. They also had holy groves, trees, fields, lakes, streams and wells.[27] As previously mentioned, later sources list and name some gods and deities but they often seem to be quite confusing, misunderstood and often invented. Nonetheless, it is worth looking into some slightly older documents, for example a certain document issued by bishop Michael of Sambia from around 1426 in which he lists eight points that are forbidden in the religious and ritual activities of Prussian people. Therein we do not find any names of gods or descriptions of their domains; however the entire document repeatedly uses the term "demons".[28] It deals with forbidden activities where offerings associated with important activities or celebrations, such as funerals or harvest festivals, are made. It appears from the text that the Prussians revoked and made offerings to their gods rather than merely natural forces in their important rituals. Not having them named should be no surprise, given that for a 15th century Christian bishop they would have all been considered identical, evil, demons, and simply not worthy of mention by name or having any attention paid to them. We can therefore conclude here that the Balts, and in this particular case the Prussians, had some defined and very likely personified deities whose names and domains were not recorded for posterity.

Written sources record well over 200 names of Baltic deities. In this short paper we will not investigate all of them, especially taking into consideration that many of them were mentioned only once or twice and were definitely lesser, minor deities or spirits. As it was already said the available sources are generally

---

26. Łowmiański 1986: 9, 50-51.
27. Peter of Dusburg, III.5.
28. Michael of Sambia, *Articuli per Prutenos tenendi et erronei contra fidem abiciiendi*.

dubious, but it has to be stressed again that it would be unwise to disregard them altogether.

In the *Constitutiones Synodales* we find the usual Christian condemnation of Prussians for practicing their old customs and continuously worshipping their old deities. This is followed by a list of deities in the following order: Occopirmus, Suaixtix, Ausschauts, Autrympus, Potrympus, Bardoayts, Piluutus, Parcuns, and Pecols together with Pocols. The writer then compares these Prussian deities with Classical Roman gods in the following order: Saturn, Sol (Sun), Asclepius, Neptune, Castor and Pollux, Ceres, Jupiter, Pluto and Furiae.[29] The so called Sudovian Book practically repeats the same names as those in *Constitutiones*. The exceptions are Ausschauts who is placed directly after the heavenly gods and Parkuns who is placed after the earth gods. The description of these gods closely corresponds to attributes of the deities listed in *Constitutiones*.[30]

When looking at the list from *Constitutiones,* even at first glance the Prussian "pantheon" appears to be too Classical. Nonetheless, far from regarding this entire list of gods and their attributes as pure fiction we can make some sense of it. The particular deities will now be discussed and analysed but not necessarily in the order in which they were listed in the sources.

Occopirmus - We begin with the "supreme god" (other spellings Ockopirmus, Occopirma, Occopirna) which was associated with Saturn, and therefore also with the Greek deity Cronus. This seems, however, not to be the name of a deity, but rather a description. In the Prussian language Occopirmus meant "The One who is First", from *aukti* - loosely translated as most, and *pirmas* - denoting the first.[31] The name Occopirmus however does not appear in any sources besides the related *Sudovian Book*. So, who was this mysterious Occopirmus? It can be assumed that this deity was a sky god, as there is no reason to believe that the Saturnian association was purely an invention of the mediaeval author. Therefore, if the people called their main deity Occopirmus - "The First One" - we can assume they referred to the sky, using a sobriquet or epithet instead of the god's real, proper name. This is also not a rare case in many other religions, with a prime example being Judaism. The sobriquet and use of the ordinal number "first" strongly implies a personification of the sky. It is worth recalling here that the term Dievas in Lithuanian denotes a Christian God, but in pre-Christian

---

29. Łowmiański 1986: 50-51.
30. *Schmalstieg 2003: 365.*
31. Labuda 1972: 334.

times it was a name for the sky. At the same time the name is cognate to a number of Indo-European sky deities such as the Vedic Dyaus, Greek Dzeus, Latin Dies pitar (Jupiter), and Germanic Tiwaz.[32] Furthermore, it is more than simply coincidence that all Balts concurrently associated the Latin term for the god "Deus" with their name for the sky. Hence, the only explanation is that the Christian God just replaced the old Baltic sky god Dievas. Otherwise why would all the Balts name the Christian God the Sky? After Christianisation the name survived in Baltic ethnographic sources, mainly denoting only ghosts and spirits. A Jesuit report from the year 1603 recorded instances of Samogidian peasants' *"plea to idol Dejwes"*.[33] Summarising, the name of the Prussian god Occopirmus - "The First One" was a euphemism or epithet used for the Sky God originally named Deivas in Prussian.

Due to a lack of historical records the reconstruction of Latvian mythology is primarily based on ethnographic data.[34] Therefore, it can only provide supportive evidence and be used in comparative analysis. Nonetheless, in one account the pagans in the area near Rezekne told the Jesuits in 1606 that they have a supreme Sky God, as well as an Earth deity and many minor ones.[35] Although the Sky God is not named in the document there is no reason to doubt that Latvian peasants were referring to Deyvis/ Dīvs.

We turn now to the Lithuanians. There are two prime sources that recorded Lithuanian deities. One is a Church Slavonic translation of the Greek *Chronicle* of John Malalas, written in the 13th century in Western Rus'. The other is the *Chronicle of Halich-Volhynia*, which was written by orthodox priests from the princely circles in the late 13th century, as the last entry for the year 1292 indicates. Let us firstly look at the *Malalas* translations which seem to be older. The Western Rus' version comes from the 13th century, but the earlier translation, also in Church Slavonic, was probably translated in Bulgaria in the 10th or 11th century.[36] In the

---

32. Bojtár 1997: 279. Dievs in Latvian, Dīvs in Latgalian, Deywis in Prussian and Deivas in Yotvingian.
33. *"We have', he said, 'a god with responsibility for the sky; we also have a god who governs the earth. Though this one is supreme on earth, he has under him various subordinate gods. We have a god who gives us fish; we have a god who gives us game; we have a god of corn, fields, gardens, herds - namely horses, cows and various animals"*. In *Annual Report of Society of Jesus 1603*, in Brückner 1904: 41-42.
34. Ivanov and Toporov 1980: 155.
35. *Annual Report of Society of Jesus 1606*, in Dowden 2000: 214.
36. Mierzyński 1892: Vol. 1, 126.

passage from the original Greek version we read: *"After the death of Hephaistos, his son Helios reigned over the Egyptians for 4477 days, that is, 12 years and 97 days….Helios the son of Hephaistos, was very generous"*.[37] While, in the earlier Slavic translation we read: *"After Svarog, reigned his son, named Sun who was also called Dazhbog, for he was a mighty lord"*.[38] The translator of the earlier Slavonic version, being most likely aware of the relation of Slavonic deities, substituted Svarog, the Sky God, for Hephaistos, and the Slavic Dazhbog, the Sun deity, for Helios. When we look into the later translation from the 13th century we find an additional passage concerning Lithuanian deities. It looks as though the translator knew both the Greek and earlier Slavonic versions and perhaps wanted to be inventive or intended to impress readers with his knowledge of Lithuanian religion. He therefore inserted the passage with the story of Sovij[39] and then recorded the Lithuanian deities Andaj (Андай), Perkūnas (Пєркоун), Žvoruna (Жвороуна) and heavenly smith Teljavel (Телявель).[40] The other source, the *Chronicle of Halich-Volhynia*, under the entry for the year 1252, referred to Grand Duke Mindaugas' alleged paganism. It recorded the duke's offerings to the Lithuanian deities Nenadiev (Нънадѣев), Teljavel (Телявель) and Divieriks (Диверикъз), as well as some others.[41] The same chronicle under the year 1257 recorded Lithuanian warriors calling and revoking their gods Andaj (Андай) and Divirks (Дивирикс).[42]

We will look now at the first deities from the above sources and in later parts at the others. The use of the two different names Nenadiev and Andaj, which are no doubt the same deity, suggests that the entries for 1252 and 1257 in the *Chronicle of Halich-Volhynia*, were made by different scribes. Whoever wrote the above entries in this chronicle most likely knew the earlier Slavonic translation

---

37. John Malalas, Book 2.1 and 2.2.
38. The Slavonic version of Malalas: John Malalas, *Chronicon*, in Istrin 1994: 69.
39. Mierzyński 1892: Vol. 1, 127-129, 133-134. The context of the passage suggests that Sovij instead of being a deity seems to be a substitute for a general term for the Balts, and Lithuanians in particular or perhaps is a figure from Lithuanian folk tales.
40. "*…приносити жрътвоу сквєрнымъ богам Андаєви и Пєркоунови, рєкшє громоу, Жвороунѣ, рєкшє соуцѣ, и Тєлѧвєли коузнєю, сковавшє єтоу слнцє…*". In Mierzyński 1892: Vol. 1, 129.
41. "*жрѧшє богамъ своимъ въ тайнѣ пєрвому, Нънадѣєви, и Телѧвели, и иверикъзу…*". In Mierzyński 1892: Vol. 1, 138.
42. "*Посвойски рєкущє 'янда', взывающє богы своя Андая и Дивирикса*". In Mierzyński 1892: Vol. 1, 139.

of Malalas. All three accounts, besides listing Nenadiev/Andaj as the first deity, differ in their spelling of the other deities and the order of these in the list. Each account also possesses some unique omissions and inclusions, as well as differences in some other details. Therefore, they seem to be reliable sources rather than dull copies.

The names Nenadiev/Andaj still sound corrupted, suggesting that the authors or scribes were not very familiar with Lithuanian language and beliefs, and that their information was second hand from some Slavic Rus' warriors. It seems that the various forms of both recorded names are a corruption of the Lithuanian *ant-dievis*, where *ant* means "on" in preposition form; and *dievis* means "the god". In such a case this would denote the highest, supreme deity. In all probability the name can be reconstructed as Antdievas, or shortened to Andievas. Again Andievas would not be the proper name of the deity, but rather its epithet or nickname, such as in the case of the Prussian Occopirmus. Henryk Łowmiański identified Andaj (Andievas) with a supreme Sky deity, whose cult among the Balts supposedly merged, fused or intermingled with the thunder god.[43] Moreover, Latvian scholar Haralds Biezais argued that in Latvia the deity Dievs (Deves), although mentioned by name as late as 1604 in some Christian correspondence, was a primeval Latvian Sky deity. He based his claims on rich ethnographic data and a comparative analysis of common Indo-European cosmology and mythology.[44] Verses from Latvian folklore like "*Devas has magnificent horse. By it, the Sun, Moon and Morning Star come out*" or "*the sons of God ride horses*",[45] support this claim.

In light of this cumulative evidence it can safely be postulated that in pre-Christian Baltic religion there was a supreme, personified Sky deity known as Dievas (Lithuanian spelling), and that in some cases Dievas was referred to as Occopirmus (Auktprimas or similar) among some Prussian tribes, or as Andaj (Andievas) by the Lithuanians. The reason why the term Dievas was not in common use is unclear. However, there is a strong possibility that the real name of the deity might have been a taboo. Hence, it might have been called or revoked by its sobriquet/epithet names instead. This apparent absence of Dievas in sources can possibly be attributed to a certain hypothetical characteristic.

---

43. Łowmiański 1986: 221n.
44. Biezais 1975: 884-885.
45. Mierzyński 1892: Vol. 1, 105.

In Indian mythology Dyaus the creator turned into a passive, inactive god.[46] Similarly, in Slavic religion the Sky god Svarog, the father of some other deities, lost interest in worldly affairs.[47] Perhaps, therefore, the Baltic Dievas also turned into an otiose deity.

Sun and Fire - A god named **Suaixtix** (other spellings: Swayxtix; Svayjkstis) in *Constitutiones Synodales* was associated with Sol, that is the Sun. The author of the *Sudovian Book*, on his own initiative, added that this was a god of light. This was also copied and repeated by Simon Grunau. In Lithuanian language *šviesa* means light, shine; and *šviesus* - the bright. The proper name of the deity was probably Svaikstikas. There is no reason to doubt Svaikstikas solar association or it in fact being the Sun God. There is however a certain problem, namely that the name Svaikstikas has not been reported in any other sources. We can conclude that here again the Baltic manner of use of euphemisms or epithets might apply. This is so because the solar cult is well attested in modern ethnographic data among both Lithuanians and Latvians. No doubt it is an echo of an earlier solar cult, so strong that despite vigorous and ruthless persecution by the Church it survived till modern times.

A solar cult, as mentioned, is well attested in ethnography. To cite a few examples: Many Lithuanian folk songs refer to the Sun. One goes as follows: *"The Sun rode, into apple orchard, on nine wheels, having one hundred horses"*.[48] Another one says: *"Under the maple tree where spring resurge, where sons of god dance in moonlight with the daughters of the Sun"*.[49] Sometime around 1392, Czech missionary Hieronymus of Prague[50] reported that sun worship was widely practiced in Lithuania.[51] Similarly in Latvian folklore we encounter frequent references to the Sun and also common association of the Sun with horses. To cite a few, we find phrases like: *"the Sun with two golden horses"*, *"the Sun drove by two golden horses through the gate"*, *"the Sun on the mountain holds the reins of the horses"*, *"the Sun saddles a hundred black horses"* or *"the Sun daughters ride horses"*.[52] So, as we can see, we have clear evidence of personification of the Sun

---

46. Dumézil 1966: Vol. 1, 178.
47. Zaroff 1999: 53.
48. Mierzyński 1892: Vol. 1, 67.
49. Mierzyński 1892: Vol. 1, 73.
50. This was a lesser known Czech missionary named Hieronymus, but not Hieronymus of Prague - the Hussite burnt at the stake at Constance in 1416.
51. Narbutt 1835: Vol. 8, 472.
52. Mierzyński 1892: Vol. 1, 105.

and worship of a solar deity. As mentioned earlier, there are countless examples of such personification in Baltic folklore. Therefore, it is very unlikely that such personification would have taken place after conversion to Christianity, and it definitely has to be an echo of pre-Christian traditions. Therefore, the Prussian god Svaikstikas was in all probability a solar deity. Its unusual name can be attributed to two factors. Firstly, Prussian societies were deeply fragmented and many different traditions, including naming, could develop. Secondly, as it was rightly pointed out by Lithuanian scholar Gintaras Beresnevičius, the Balts had a custom of using euphemisms in naming their gods.[53]

An interesting issue is that the Sun is called *Saule* in modern Lithuanian and *Saulė* in Latvian, so both are of a feminine gender. On the other hand, in practically all ancient Indo-European beliefs the Sun deity was of the male gender. Hence, the open question exists of whether the pre-Christian Sun deity was a male acquiring female characteristics after conversion, or perhaps it was female in the first place. Whatever the case, this issue which goes beyond the scope of this work, requires further investigation.

Teljavel - (Телѣвелъ) is a Lithuanian deity mentioned in the Old Church Slavonic translation of Malalas' *Chronicle* which also differed from the original source by way of some additions referring to Lithuanian beliefs. In this source Teljavel appears as a deity who smithed the Sun and threw it onto the sky.[54] We also find Teljavel in the *Chronicle of Halich-Volhynia* of the 13th century, in the entry for 1252. It was listed second, after Nenadievs/Andaj which we already identified as a euphemism for Dievas. The name Telavel or Teljavelis does not correspond to any Baltic word that could be associated with religious beliefs or mythology. However, at the same time we have the Lithuanian term *kalvis*, a blacksmith. This strongly indicates that the author of Malalas' translation might have misspelled the name. Therefore, the name should appear in the form of Kelavelis (Kalvis) or similar.[55] It is worth noting that Rus' sources referred to the Lithuanians as fire worshippers on a number of occasions, and on at least one occasion called Grand Duke Algirdas so.[56] The previously mentioned Hieronymus of Prague reported that Lithuanians worshipped a holy fire. At some unspecified location an eternal fire was kept and maintained by the priests,

---

53. Beresnevičius: 3-4.
54. Mierzyński 1892: Vol. 1, 127-129.
55. Bojtár 1997: 311.
56. Mierzyński 1892: Vol. 2, 28; Urban 1989: 121.

and local people came to the site to perform offerings and ask the priests for divination.[57] Canon priest Mikalojus Daukša in his 1599 Lithuanian translation of the collection of sermons entitled *"Postilla catholica"* advised the Samogitians on what is against the 1st Commandment. The advice is a long list but it includes the worship of Fire, Žemina, Perkūnas and the forest deity or spirit Modejna.[58] According to Jan Długosz the Samogitians were also fire worshippers. A holy, worshiped and much venerated eternal fire was kept and maintained, apparently placed on some tower like structure on a hill located by the river Nevėžis. In 1413 King Jogaila visited the site, ordering that the fire be extinguished and the structure demolished.[59] In 16th century Prussia people would still address fires inside homes with the saying *"Ocho moy myte szwante panicke!"* meaning "Oh! my little sacred Fire".[60]

An important clue is found in the translation of Malalas' *Chronicle*. In it, Teljavel is described as a heavenly smith who forged and placed the Sun in the sky.[61] This myth resembles a common Indo-European tradition found in Greece. Hephaistos, the Greek god of Fire mentioned in the original Greek version of Malalas, was a divine blacksmith who forged a chariot for Helios, the Sun God. The association of Kelavelis (Teljavelis) with blacksmithing and forging conceptually links him with fire. Hence, it is reasonable to postulate that Kelavelis was a Lithuanian euphemism or epithet for the Baltic God of Fire. Regretfully, at this stage of research, we are not able to reconstruct the common Baltic name for the fire deity. Here again the context of historical accounts leaves no doubt about the personification of this deity.

Perkūnas - Most attested in all sources and tradition was no doubt Perkūnas (in Lithuanian) - an atmospheric deity - the god of thunder, lightning and rain. He was recorded as Pērkons in Latvian, Perkūns in Old Prussian and Parkuns in Sudovian. There is also no doubt about the antiquity of the deity and his Indo-European origins. The name Perkūnas derives from the Indo-European root *perk*, *perg* or *per*, meaning to strike, and is directly associated with a striking thunderbolt.[62] In Indian mythology there was a weather god, Parjanya, whose domain was thunderstorms and monsoons. Besides the Vedic Parjanya in most

---

57. Narbutt 1835: Vol. 8, 471-472.
58. Brückner 1904: 42.
59. Jan Długosz, Year 1413, pp. 477-488.
60. Brückner 1904: 19.
61. Mierzyński 1892: Vol. 1, 127-129.
62. Gimbutas 1971: 165-166; and Gieysztor 1982: 45-48.

Indo-European mythologies we find conceptually similar deities among the Celtic, Greek, Germanic, Slavic and Hittite people.[63] Perkūnas also made things grow, and like the Slavic god Perun, is associated with an oak tree and cattle. So, there is no surprise that across the Baltic lands there are numerous accounts clearly indicating a post pagan veneration of an oak tree and associated rituals, including practices of food and drink offerings under or in the vicinity of those trees. It is also worth noting that in Baltic mythology oak trees were associated with masculinity, while lime trees were associated with femininity.[64]

The importance and antiquity of Perkūnas in Baltic mythology is also supported by the fact that his name spread to the Finno-Ugric people. In the Finnish language the term *Perkele* denotes evil and the root "*perk-*" is definitely of Indo-European origin, hence in its geographical context a clear borrowing from the Baltic or proto-Baltic language. Moreover, the pre-Christian Mordvins of the middle Volga basin once worshiped a thunder god called Purginepas.[65] A reasonable interpretation would be that the Mordvins might have borrowed the name of this deity, if not the whole concept, from the previously mentioned Indo-European speakers of Fatyanovo culture of the second half of the second millennium B.C.E.[66] or from mediaeval Slavs or Balts of the region. Whatever the case, a Perkūnas-like deity must have been common among the Old European population of Eastern Europe in the middle of the second millennium B.C.E. This in turn clearly indicates a continuity of this common Indo-European religious concept. The name is well attested in Baltic toponomy. To cite some examples, there is a village called Perkūniškės in Žemaitija, north-west of Kaunas. Also, ethnographic data reported by Johannes Voight in the 19th century mentions a place called Perkunlauken, literally meaning "Perkuns Fields" near modern Gusev, in Kaliningrad district.[67]

The historical and ethnographic sources across the Baltic lands recorded Perkūnas frequently. Worship of Perkūnas among the Prussians is attested by *Constitutiones Synodales* where he was called Parcuns, and this is repeated in

---

63. Zaroff 1999: 56-60.
64. *Annual Report of Society of Jesus 1606*, in Dowden 2000: 73. For Years, 1583, 1603, 1605, 1614, 1618 in Brückner 1904: 40-41.
65. Łowmiański 1986: 221.
66. Fatyanovo culture: Gimbutas 1963: 34, 44-46, 91-93.
67. Mierzyński 1892: Vol. 1, 80. Modern Russian: Gusev; Lithuanian: Gumbinė; German: Gumbinnen; Polish: Gąbin.

the *Sudovian Book* as *Parkuns*.[68] It has been commonly accepted by scholars that *Pergrubrius* listed in the *Sudovian Book*, and associated there with nourishment of leaves and grasses,[69] is in fact is a corrupted recording of Perkūnas.

As for Latvian lands, *Statuta Provincialia Concilii Rigensis* issued by Henning of Scharfenberg, an archbishop of Riga, in entries for 1428 stated that Latvians still practice pagan rites and worship the god of thunder - "*...scilicet a tonitruo, quod deum suum appellant..*" - meaning "namely thunder, that god they revoke".[70] This of course must have been referring to the Latvian Pērkons. Many Latvian folk songs leave no doubt about the clear position of Perkūnas in the Baltic pantheon, such as one with the lyrics: "*Perkons struck at the oak, with nine flashes, three flashes cleaved the trunk, six cleaved the top*".[71]

The god Perkūnas appears most often in Lithuanian sources. Here again we will cite only a few examples. The so called *Livonian Rhyme Chronicle*, written around 1290, mentions Perkūnas in relation to a certain Lithuanian campaign in 1219.[72] The Hungarian source known as *Chronicon Dubnicense* also records the sacrifice of a bull to a deity whose name is unknown, under entries for the year 1351, to confirm the agreement between Grand Duke Kęstutis and Polish and Hungarian kings.[73] Also, during the 1365 campaign against the Teutonic Knights near Ragainė, in Prussia, Kęstutis performs a similar bull and human sacrifice which included the killing and burning of victims.[74] At this point it is worth recalling the 6th century Greek historian Procopius of Ceasarea who wrote about a Slavic deity, identified as Perun, to whom cattle and people were sacrificed.[75] Based on Balto-Slavic cultural and linguistic closeness it can be assumed that the Lithuanian sacrifices of bulls[76] were also devoted to Perkūnas, despite him not being mentioned by name. We find Perkūnas (Перкоун) associated with

---

68. Łowmiański 1986: 50-51 and *Schmalstieg 2003: 365. See Appendix.*
69. *Schmalstieg 2003: 365.*
70. Mierzyński 1892: Vol. 2, 147, 149.
71. Dowden 2000: 221.
72. Mierzyński 1892: Vol. 1, 115-116.
73. *Chronicon Dubnicense.* In Mierzyński 1892: Vol. 2, 76.
74. Wigand, XIII, p. 155., Lith. *Ragainė*, Ger, *Ragnit*, Rus. *Nieman.*
75. "*For they (Slavs) believe that one god, the maker of the lighting, is alone lord of all things, and they sacrifice to him cattle and all other victims*". Procopius of Ceasarea, *History of the Wars,* Book VII.XIV.23.
76. Okulicz-Kozaryn 1993: 237.

thunder in the 13th century Slavonic translation of Malalas *Chronicle*.[77] In 1547 priest Martynas Mažvydas wrote *The Simple Words of Catechism* in Lithuanian languages. In the Preface he complained about peasants still revoking and making oaths on *Perkūn* or *Żemėpata*.[78] In his sermon translation, the previously mentioned Mikalojus Daukša also mentions worship of Perkūnas.[79] Another account from the 16th century by Hieronymus Maletius mentions a local tradition, stating that a perpetual fire was kept on a hillside along the Nemunas River in Lithuania, which apparently was also dedicated to Perkūnas.[80] Worship of Perkūnas is also attested in Samogitia as late as the early 17th century, and associated with lightning, oaks or sorb trees. A Jesuit mission conducted there reported numerous cases of the destruction of holy oaks and stated their association with the worship of Perkūnas.[81]

One more issue concerning Perkūnas has to be addressed. In the *Galich-Volhyn Chronicle* a god named Diviriks (Диверикъз/Диверикс) was listed, third after Andaj and Telavelis on one occasion and second after Andaj on another occasion.[82] Hence, it appears this is an important deity. The name is, however, clearly a corrupted form of the Lithuanian *Dievų rikis*, "Lord of the Gods",[83] so although the high standing of Diviriks is beyond doubt, his identification poses a problem. Therefore, if Diviriks was not a deity on its own, the interpretation of Lithuanian scholar Gintaras Beresnevičius and Pole Aleksander Brückner seems to be most plausible. They identified Diviriks as being the Lithuanian euphemism for Perkūnas.[84]

We have to look more closely at Perkūnas' role and significance in the Lithuanian case. Both the Prussians and the Latvian tribes never formed any larger, long lasting political entities. On the other hand we had a different development in Lithuania. It is well attested that by the mid-13th century Lithuania was a well organised state, which was the result of a process that must have begun much earlier. In a sense we can say they were lucky as they had more time to internally organise themselves than their other Baltic brethren. Briefly, the

---

77. Mierzyński 1892: Vol. 1, 128.
78. Rowell 1997: 119; Brückner 1904: 19.
79. Brückner 1904: 42.
80. Dowden 2000: 79.
81. *Annual Report of Society of Jesus 1606* in Dowden 2000: 214.
82. Mierzyński 1892: Vol. 1, 138-139.
83. Beresnevičius: 3; Mierzyński 1892: Vol. 1, 138.
84. Beresnevičius: 3; Brückner 1904: 25.

Prussians and Latvians were a buffer zone protecting the Lithuanians against the Teutonic Knights approaching from the East and West and the Poles from the south. As mentioned at the beginning of this work, religion mirrors the society that practices it, but religion also transforms and unifies society as well as being instrumental in ethnic emergence and consolidation. Simply, they are in a mutual, reciprocal relationship. Here we have a case where a part of state-building was also an attempt at creating a state cult. It is clear that the Lithuanian rulers were doing so, especially "fathers of Lithuania" Grand Dukes Mindaugas and Gediminas. As part of this long process Perkūnas became a major state god.[85] Although initially being a god of thunder, lightning, storms and rain, it turned into a dominant deity. Put simply, Perkūnas fit this role the best. As he reigned over the violent elements he evolved into a war god of a people who were practically in constant military conflict with encroaching neighbours. The Lithuanians practiced not only animal but also human sacrifice. As cruel as they are, elaborate human sacrifices are unlikely to be made for non-personal forces of nature. For example, in 1320 they burnt a Teutonic Knight - Gerhard - in full armour and on a horse as a sacrifice to their gods.[86] In 1388 they sacrificed another knight, Nicholas Kassof - a commander of Klaipėda. He was also burned in a pit, on horseback in full armour.[87] There is no doubt these two, and other similar human sacrifices, were definitely of a military character and performed as part of war. There is also no doubt that it was for Perkūnas.

Pikulas or Vēlinas ? - Pikulas-like names appear in sources and ethnographic data with various spellings such as *Pecols, Peckols, Picullus, Pikuolis, Pykullas and Pocols*. The name derives from the already cited Prussian word for hell - *pykuls*, or it is cognate to the Lithuanian equivalent *pictas*, meaning "angry (evil)", or to the Latvian *pikals* denoting "evil demon".[88] Pikulas was listed in *Constitutiones Synodales*, however it appears that its author wrote down everything he heard from the Prussians and/or other informants without any understanding of, or care about, what he was recording. As a result two deities are listed there as *Pecols atque Pocols*, meaning "Pecols and Pocols". This is obviously a mistake where the Latin *atque* - "and" - was used instead of *uel* - "or". As there were two deities instead of one it was not a huge leap to "Romanise" them and to link

---

85. Gimbutas 1963: 202; Puhvel 1974: 78, 83.
86. Peter of Dusburg, III.338.
87. Wigand, XXVII, p. 323.
88. Bojtár 1997: 308-309. See *Constitutiones Synodales* and *Sudovian Book* in Appendix.

them with the chthonic Pluto and Furiae.[89] In view of their associaton with hell, darkness, the devil or an evil spirit, as well as other attributes and characteristics of Pikulas, they comply with the etymology of the name and indeed the Prussian Pikulas which must have represented the dark forces of the World. The available ethnographic evidence equals him with an evil demon or spirit, a being conceptually cognate to the Slavonic term *čert*.[90] However, there was a similar mythical deity or spirit among the Lithuanians and Latvians called Vēlinas. Both Lithuanian and Latvian ethnographic data provides rich and frequently noted evidence for this mythological figure. Various spellings found in Baltic languages and dialects recorded this mythological figure as Vēlinas, Vélnias, Vēlenas, Velas, Vēlés, Velionis or Vēls.[91] In later, and even in modern times the name was applied to a devil or devilish creature, but rich ethnographic evidence across Baltic lands leaves no doubt that in pagan times this deity was a common Baltic deity. Reconstruction based on ethnography allow us to link Vēlinas with death, the dead, the underworld, and generally with dark forces of the world. However its domain also included pasture and live flock, and especially cattle.[92] At he same time this deity was strongly associated with clairvoyance and prophecies.[93] A strong and undisputed conceptual similarity between Prussian Pikulas and Vēlinas seems to be certain as they share practically all attributes, function and domains. So, both Pikulas and Vēlinas appear to be the same mythological figures, albeit differently named. The claim may be supported by passage in 1629 work *Dictionarium trium linguarum* by C. Szyrwid where he writes: *Velnias yra Piktis* - "Velnias is Piktis (Pecols)."[94] A different naming may as well be a result of taboo, common among the Baltic deities, and avoiding to invoke the Vēlinas name, especially because of his nature.[95] The extend to which Vēlinas was pronounced and complex in pagan times it is hard to determine. Still, there is no doubt that in pre-Christian it was a major deity, and not a minor spirit or demon. A comparative mythology may be useful here. Among the pre-Christian Slavs, their god Veles appears in number of written Eastern Slavic sources on number of occasions, as well as in Southern Slavic folklore. Without

---

89. See *Constitutiones Synodales* and *Sudovian Book* in Appendix.
90. Boryś 2006: 91.
91. Shiroukhov 2006: 43-44.
92. Gimbutas 1974: 87-88.
93. Winn 1995: 96-97; *Beresnevičius: 7-8;* Gimbuta 1974: 89.
94. Puhvel 1974: 84.
95. Gimbutas 1974: 90.

going into much of details Veles' characteristics, attributes and domains closely match those of Baltic Vēlinas. Conceptual similarities prompt us to accept that both Baltic Vēlinas and Slavic Veles are cognate deities and are from an ancient common Balto-Slavic tradition.[96] Moreover, by association, both may be conceptually related to a common Indo-European deity, represented by Indian Varuna. This association would require a further investigation, but unfortunately it goes beyond the scope of this paper. It is very likely that ethnographic data is merely an "echo" of pre-Christian Vēlinas we intend investigate. That is merely a suppressed residue of his much more elaborated position in Baltic mythology and cults. We can assume that, as a result of Christian pressure and persecution Vēlinas was reduced, together with his Prussian synonymous Pikulas, to a mere demon and evil spirit. Only by the comparison with Slavic Veles, we can accept he was a personified and an important deity in Baltic mythology. As a consequence of his dark, his morbid ideation, death associated and sinister nature it is unlikely that he was worshipped in the same manner like the other gods. However, it is most likely sacrifices and offering were made to Vēlinas to appease and placate him.[97] For these reasons it is legitimate to postulate So, we can postulate that Pikulas-like figures in *Constitutiones Synodales* were in fact Vēlinas disguise in a taboo like name.

Mother Earth, Žemyna - All the Balts were farmers and agriculture played a vital part in their lives. Practically all such societies and cultures have had some form of Mother Earth deity. Such a cult was widespread and of utmost importance to the Balts.[98] Žemyna, the Mother Earth, nurtured all life forms, people, animals and plants. Tacitus in the 2nd century described people who he called Aesti (Esti) on the south-eastern Baltic coast practicing a cult of "mother of gods".[99] It is commonly accepted that the name Esti was applied here not to ancestors of the Estonians but to the Balts.[100] Tacitus relied on second hand sources and of course "mother of gods" denoted Mother Earth. It is worth noting that in Latvian the Earth Goddess was called *Zemes Māte*, the Earth Mother.[101] In the preface to

---

96. Zaroff 1999: 14-17.
97. Gimbutas 1974: 90.
98. Okulicz-Kozaryn 1997: 117-118.
99. Tacitus, *Germania*, XLV.
100. Without going into further details, in the same account Tacitus wrote that this Esti collect and trade with amber which is very rare on the Estonian coast but common alongside shores inhabited by the Balts.
101. Gimbutas 1963: 191.

the already cited Lithuanian Catechism of Mažvydas we have a fragment about peasants making oaths on *Žemėpata*.[102] Also, the previously cited translation of *Postilla catholica* by Mikalojus Daukša noted worship of Žemina.[103]

We have to recall here the document known as the *Treaty of Christburg*. It was an agreement between the Teutonic Knights and Prussians of Pomezania in 1249. It stated that the latter will cease to worship *Curche*, the goddess of harvest and grain, and stop making offerings to her, and other gods, and will also stop maintaining pagan priests (Tulissones vel Ligaschones), who performed certain rituals at funerals. The treaty also stated that they will stop cremation of the dead with horses, persons, arms, or any other property, *"as they are not the creators of the Sky and Earth"*.[104] As the Christburg document indicates, *Curche* was a female deity who received offerings from harvested cultivated plants, presumably mainly of various grains. Her agrarian affiliation is supported by etymology as the Latvian word *kurke* means a small or dry seed.[105] The name spelled in sources as *Curche* or *Kurche* must be a corruption of Kurka/e. The toponomy of the area formerly inhabited by Prussians (Former German East Prussia) bears a large number of place names, localities or settlements which derive or include the root *kurke-*. For example, we have Kurki near Olsztynek, which was called Kurke in German. Also, the place and locality names containing the same root *kurk-* exist not only in Prussian but also in Lithuanian taxonomy.[106] The common agricultural domains of Žemyna and Kurka prompt us to claim that they were the same, and as was common among the Balts, Kurka was simply another local Pomezanian name for Žemyna.

Žemyna was a rustic deity; therefore, her cult was local, confined to small communities and lacked the character of other more elaborate ones. She was of even less interest to mediaeval chroniclers than the "devilish" gods of the warriors. Therefore, we have no accounts describing what form it took in the period before the Christianisation of the Balts. The only information accessible to us is later ethnographic records, from the time when her cult was forbidden and suppressed, hence it is hard to estimate to what degree Žemyna was personified and to what degree she was perceived as a force and a part of nature. Nonetheless, as we know she had an individual, personal name with which the Balts addressed her and made offerings.

---

102. Brückner 1904: 19.
103. Brückner 1904: 42.
104. *Treaty of Christburg*, 13.
105. Labuda 1972: 334n.
106. Białuński 1993: 7-9; Długokęcki 2007: 24; Mierzyński 1892: Vol. 1, 95.

Natrimpe - Natrimpe and deities with related names are scattered across the various sources. This includes names like Autrimp, Autrimpo, Patrimpas, Potrympus and Potrimpus. Natrimpe is first mentioned in a 1418 memorandum - *Collatio Espiscopi Varmiensis* - sent by John III, Bishop of Warmia, to Pope Martin V.[107] *Constitutiones Synodales* listed *Autrympus* and *Potrympus*, and by the order of their listing linked them to Neptune. Although deriving from *Constitutiones Synodales*, the *Sudovian Book* was more inventive and added particular attributes to the two deities - *Autrimpus*, the god of oceans and seas; and *Potrimpus*, the god of running waters. Later, Simon Grunau reported the deities *Pattolo, Patrimpo* and *Perkūnas*; and claimed they formed the main trinity of the Prussian pantheon.[108] In terms of the concept of being a part of the Prussian trinity, this does fit the common tri-partite cosmologic division of the world of the Indo-Europeans, however no other evidence supports this idea. Comparing the three deities with the Christian Holy Trinity is very likely Simon Grunau's invention (*pattolu*-Patollo will be discussed later). In all probability all of them were the same deity with different prefixes, such as *pa-* for under and *ant-* for onto. In such a case the name can be reconstructed as Trimpe or more likely Trimpas. Some etymological explanations proposed that the deity's name may derive from the Lithuanian root *trimp-*, meaning to trample, to tread, to stomp. It was also postulated that it may derive from the Latvian *tirum-pus*, loosely translated as "half of the field", which would associate it with arable land and agriculture.[109] Ethnographic evidence also provides some information. It has been recorded that Latvian peasants cast a spell invoking the wrath of Trimpe upon the fields and possessions of their enemies or adversaries. Also, 19th century Lithuanian writer, historian and ethnographer Simonas Daukantas knew of a saying recorded as „*ek sau po trimpo*",[110] perhaps with the meaning "be damned!, go to hell!" and conceptually related to the Polish saying *"niech cię diabli wezmą!"* meaning "let the devils take you!" As can be seen, Trimpas/Natrimpe escapes a clear explanation, although such a deity or spirit was definitely known to the Baltic people. Various functions, associations and domains have been proposed for the abovementioned deity irrespective of

---

107. "*colentes patollu, Natrimpe et alia ignominiosa fantasmata*" - "worship patollu, Natrimpe and other ignomious spirits". In Mierzyński 1892: Vol. 2, 144-146.
108. „*Der götthin woren 3, Pattolo, Patrimpo, Perkuno, die stunden in einer eichen, dy 6 elen dicke war.*" Simon Grunau, 3, Vol. 1, 62.
109. Bojtár 1997: 304 and n31
110. Brückner 1904: 52.

its various recorded names. These included fertility, agriculture, chthonic, lunar, magic and wisdom.[111] Lack of hard historical written evidence prevents us from claiming that Trimpas/Natrimpe was either a personified deity or simply an evil demon or spirit,

Patollo, included in Simon Grunau's Baltic "trinity",[112] appears to be a product of his invention. He must have copied it from *Collatio* and misinterpreted it as a deity. It is worth noting that in the 1418 document *patollu* is written before Natrimpe, but it was in lower case while Natrimpe in the upper.[113] It appears that *patollu* was not the name of a deity, but rather an adjective for Natrimpe, related to the Prussian term *pukuls* meaning hell.[114] It is apparent that without the most likely accidentally inserted comma, *patollu Natrimpe* would just mean "hellish, evil Natrimpe",[115] which is no doubt a description in line with the author's perception of Baltic religion as evil in its totality.

The other deities from both *Constitutiones Synodales,* and its expanded version, the *Sudovian Book,* were not mentioned in any other reliable source. Therefore, they cannot be considered anything more than just factious beings or minor deities, spirits or demons confined to small regional localities. This seems to be the case of Ausschauts, Bardoayts, Barstucke, Markopole, Piluuytus/Pilnitis and Puschkayts.[116] (For their alleged attributes see the Appendix). In the Latvian case we lack sufficient reliable sources to conduct a reasonable evaluation of the issue we are concerned with. From the trio of Dievs, Māra and Laima, being supposedly the main Latvian deities, only Dievs (already discussed as the common Baltic Sky God) is relatively reasonably attested in ethnography. As for Māra and Laima, we cannot determine whether they were ever personified, or how widespread their cults were.

To conclude this section, in the period we are concerned with, the Balts worshipped a number of well defined and personified deities. This included a Sky God - Dievas, who was known under various epithet-like names within the highly fragmented political and social environment. Further, the Sun and Fire were personified too, and worshiped across the Baltic lands, and again those

---

111. Możdżeń 2011: 226-227.
112. Simon Grunau, 3, Vol. 1, 62.
113. Mierzyński 1892: Vol. 2, 144-146.
114. Bojtár 1997: 309n39.
115. Bojtár 1997: 308-309, 309n39.
116. Schmalstieg 2003: 365.

gods were known under epithet-like names. Perkūnas, initially an atmospheric god, was also a common Baltic deity, although his characteristics, expression and importance varied regionally, and in the Lithuanian case he was elevated to the position of a state deity with a pronounced military function. Pikulas and cognates were taboo names of Vėlinas, a personified, common Baltic chthonic deity. Whose domain were also a domestic animal herds and flock. Žemyna, the Earth Goddess, was a common Baltic deity, most likely personified, but because of her rustic nature she lacked clear defined characteristics. In the case of Trimpas it cannot be established for certain whether it was personified deity or just demon or spirit with undefined identity and domains. The others were in all probability minor, regional spirits or demons and some are suspected of being fictitious.

Places of worship, priest and idols

The evidence for Baltic places of worship, their character, expression and the existence of some form of pagan priesthood is sketchy. According to Peter of Dusburg there was a certain outstanding sacred place in the Prussian lands that he called *Romowė* (Romuva), located in the Nadrovia region where a priest-like person called *Kriwe* (Krive) was regarded as a pope-like figure in pagan Prussian religion. He also stated that Krive exercised religious power and authority over all Prussian tribes and people, as well as the Lithuanians and the Latvian tribes, and there was a holy fire kept burning all the time.[117] Peter of Dusburg's account cannot however be taken seriously at face value. First of all, with the tribal political and social structure of the Balts in the 11th-13th centuries, with the exception of the Lithuanians, in no way would they have a single, common, unified and highly centralised religious cult. Secondly, no other independent sources or documents ever mention Romuva or Krive, despite them supposedly being such an influential religious centre and such a pope-like pagan priest respectively. So what can this account by Peter of Dusburg tell us? Surely not everything he has written on Romuva and Krive is an invention, but rather an exaggeration. The most plausible explanation is that Peter of Dusburg based his story on someone's spoken account describing a central cult location of the Nadrovia tribe, likely an open site where there was a sacred grove, and very likely with a central holy oak tree. It would have been run by a priest who exercised religious authority and was very likely influential in local political matters.

---

117. Peter of Dusburg, III.5, p. 45-46.

Around the 12th-13th centuries such major religious centres did exist among the Prussian, Lithuanian and Latvian tribes.[118] Such open sanctuaries and worship centres were also common among the pagan Germanic, Celtic and Slavic people. It is worth mentioning here the open cult centre established by prince Vladimir of Kiev around 980, near the city on the banks of the Dnepr River.[119]

No doubt the name Romuva has nothing to do with Rome. It may derive from the Prussian word *ruomot*, meaning "to grow"[120] or from the Proto Baltic verb *rim-/rima-*, meaning "quiet, serene".[121] As for Krive, to link the name with the word *krive*, meaning "crooked", and to then associate it with a bent priests' staff is not convincing.[122] The term most likely derives from the Lithuanian *krivūlė*, meaning a pulkas or tribal assembly.[123] It looks as though Peter of Dusburg confused the decision making powers of an assembly and attributed them to one person. Undoubtedly the holy sites were presided over by a priest, or sometimes by a number of priests. Besides attending to the eternal sacred fire, they would have provided some other "services" such as performing sacrifices and providing oracles and divination sought by people from pulkas in the vicinity. The sanctuaries would have also received one third of the war booty supposedly for offerings and sacrifices to the gods.[124] In reality, even if some part of the booty was utilised for these purposes, the rest was kept by the priest and used for keeping the holy site functioning, as well as for supporting himself, other priests, and the associated "housekeeping" personnel.

As a matter of interest it is worth mentioning here a sacred, ancient oak, apparently still standing in 1595, which was mentioned by German geographer Hennenberger at Veluve in the Eastern Prussian region of Nadrovia.[125] We are far from identifying Veluve as the site of the mysterious Romuva, but in all probability there must have been Prussian sacred sites located there. In 1294 the Teutonic Knights destroyed *Romene*, a village and pagan sanctuary in the

---

118. Okulicz-Kozaryn 1997: 328-330.
119. *Russian Primary Chronicle,* Year 980; Rowell 1997: 134.
120. Okulicz-Kozaryn 1997: 328.
121. *The Tower of Babel, an Etymological Database Project.*
122. Rowell 1997: 126.
123. Mierzyński 1892: Vol. 2, 37-42.
124. Peter of Dusburg, III.5, p. 45-46.
125. Sulimirski, Chlebowski, Wawelski 1882: 264. Lithuanian - Veluve, German -Welau, Polish -Welawa, modern Znamensk.

Lithuanian region of Aukštaitija.[126] A similar locality named *Romain* on the Nemunas river was recorded by Wigand of Marburg and some evidence indicates that a sacred grove was located there.[127] The root *romo/e-* or similar occurs in many place names throughout Prussia and Lithuania.[128] Therefore, we can postulate that they may be an echo of ancient cult centres, but not to the level of significance postulated by Peter of Dusburg. Also, in the year 1249, papal legate Jacob (James) of Pope Innocent IV reported that the Prussians worshipped their gods in holy groves.[129] Such a grove as a place of worship was also mentioned around Rezekne in eastern Latvia as late as the turn of the 17th century.[130]

Wigand mentions a Lithuanian sacred site, in Wandeiagel district in 1384, where the Teutonic Knights, allied with Grand Duke Vyatautas, captured a couple of hundred people. The use of the wording *domos sacras* "sacred houses" indicates some buildings or structures at the locality, and being in the plural form indicates there were at least two structures. One was therefore most likely a sanctuary, and the other possibly the priest's or priests' dwelling.[131] This is the first of the two cases from Baltic lands for pagan temples.

Fifteenth century Polish chronicler Jan Długosz (Ioannes Dlugossius) noted that there was a "holy" eternal fire kept at a pagan shrine at Vilnius in the 14th century. The fire was attended to by a priest named *žynys* (*žynčius*) – "the wise one". After the official conversion of Lithuania, king Jogaila ordered that the holy fire be extinguished and the shrine be demolished.[132] *Bychowiec Chronicle* of the 16th century referred to a semi-legendary figure named Lizdeika, an advisor to Lithuanian Grand Duke Gediminas. Lizdeika was called a "soothsayer and a highest pagan priest".[133] Whether Lizdeika and the legend of the "Iron Wolf" associated with him are true is beside the point. The important thing is that in

---

126. Peter of Dusburg, III.259, p. 186.
127. Wigand, VI, p. 53, and n. 10. Also spelled Romin. North-East of Kaunas, in vicinity of Seredžius where the Dubysa River flows into Nemunas. Wigand of Marburg chronicle stops in 1394.
128. Okulicz-Kozaryn 1993: 235; Mierzyński 1892: Vol. 2, 101-104.
129. Brückner 1904: 16.
130. *Annual Report of Society of Jesus 1606*, in Dowden 2000: 214.
131. Mierzyński 1892: Vol. 2, 117; Wigand, XXV, p. 297. Unclear where was the area called Wandeiagel. Possibly around Švenčionys in Lithuania. In Hirsh version *domos* was changed to *edes* – a tell (a mound).
132. Jan Długosz, Year 1387, pp. 183-184, Mierzyński 1892: Vol. 2, 31.
133. *Bychowiec Chronicle*, pp. 137-138.

Lithuanian tradition a high standing pagan priest was in the closest circle of the ruler of the Lithuanian state in the early 14th century, and has furthermore had an important advisory role. This sacred site in Vilnius was probably located where the St. Stanislaus cathedral now stands. Building churches on the sites of pagan sacred places and temples was common practice in mediaeval times across Europe. It is plausible that after the demolition of Mindaugas' church in Vilnius in the second half of the 13th century, that pagan sanctuary was re-established on the site during Gediminas' reign in the early 14th century.[134] In all probability the Vilnius' shrine was devoted to Perkūnas.[135]

The account about the mission of Saint Adalbert, who was martyred in 997 by the Prussians in Pomezania, gives us insight into the issue of the Baltic priesthood. Adalbert was most likely beheaded for some sacrilege at a holy place. Firstly, he was not killed immediately after crossing into Prussian territory. Secondly, in the Baltic as well as the Slavic context, beheading was a typical form of execution. Thirdly, it is worth noting that three companions of Adalbert, including his half brother Gaudenty (Radzim), were released.[136] So, he was executed as the result of a decision by a local assembly where usually, and no doubt in this case, a local priest participated and was influential. In *Vita sancti Adalberti* Canaparius wrote about the executioner being a certain *Sicco, sacerdos idolorum* - "Sicco, the priest of idols".[137] However, Sicco was not a personal name but rather a corruption of the Prussian term *zigo*, denoting a priest-healer.[138] Moreover, his title is an indication for the existence of idols in at least some Prussian sacred sites. Another evidence for the existence of idols is an account about Saint Bruno's martyrdom in 1009, who was executed either by the Sudovians or Lithuanians.[139] According to the eyewitness account of Wipert, a companion and survivor of Bruno's mission, Saint Bruno burnt some pagan idols. Wipert used the Latin term *simulacra*, a plural for *simulacrum* - an image. Therefore, Wipert's first hand account cannot be ignored. Bruno, like Adalbert, was beheaded for some sacrilege and this was no doubt sanctioned by the tribal assembly and priest.[140] The *Chronicle of*

---

134. Rowell 1997: 132; 134-136.
135. Rowell 1997: 136-137.
136. Bruno, II.34. In Mierzyński 1892: 43.
137. Canaparius, I.30, Bojtar 1997: 318.
138. Canaparius, I.30, Okulicz-Kozaryn 1997: 236.
139. Białuński 1999: 138-139. Prussians and Lithuanians were often confused by the Mediaeval authors so the exact location of St. Bruno's martyrdom is unclear.
140. Thietmar, VI.95; Białuński 1999: 141-142.

Greater Poland, in describing the Polish crusade against the Prussian pagans in 1166, led by Bolesław IV the Curly, suggests that the Prussians had idols of their deities.[141] A Baltic hilltop site excavated at Tushemlya in Belarus and dated to the 6th-8th centuries was not a dwelling place, yet there were a number of post holes uncovered. Russian archaeologist Piotr Tretyakov interpreted it as being a sacred, holy site of the early Balts.[142] Unusual post holes might have been places where idols could have once stood.

Divination and fortune telling was widespread among the Balts on all levels of social and political life. Here we can discuss some examples of divination for issues of utmost importance. For example, bones or other lots were often cast to predict the outcome of battles.[143] The *Livonian Rhyme Chronicle* records for 1259 that in Samogitia a holy man called the "sacrificer" cast lots before a military expedition against Curland, in an attempt to predict the outcome. The Samogitians then vowed to offer a third of their spoil to the gods.[144] Also, on a certain occasion around 1290 a Lithuanian host was returning from a raid. Peter of Dusburg describes this event as follows: *"A Lithuanian in a first rank of host cast the lots and predicted disaster falling upon them"*.[145] According to Henry of Livonia the Latvians performed a divination involving a horse going over a spear laid down on the ground. This divination took place around 1186 somewhere alongside the Gauja River, in Vidzeme region and was conducted by a person called *ariolus* in Latin, meaning soothsayer. The purpose was to decide on the fate of a Cistercian missionary monk named Theodoric, who was to either be sacrificed to the gods or be freed.[146] Taking into consideration that the life of a missionary was at stake it seems that this so called *ariolus* was a person of some standing, most likely a tribal priest. Also, according to Peter of Dusburg, a female priestess or oracle at a certain sanctuary, apparently widely renowned and respected for her divination, regularly advised all the Galindians on many issues including tribal matters of significant importance, such as decisions concerning

---

141. *Chronicle of Greater Poland*, Year 1166, p. 150.
142. Gimbutas 1963: 180.
143. Peter of Duisburg, III.5: Urban 1989: 20.
144. Mierzyński 1892: Vol. 1, 118. *Livonian Rhymed Chronicle* is sometime attributed to a knight Dietlebs von Alnpeke, composed around 1296.
145. Peter of Dusburg, III.241.
146. Mierzyński 1892: Vol. 1, 103. Similar custom is also known from the temple of Slavonic god Sventovit, in Arkona, at Rügen Island, in the 12th century.

wars and planned booty raids.[147] While again Peter of Dusburg might have exaggerated her influence as being all over Galindia, she must have nonetheless been a "full time" priestess rather than simply a wandering fortune teller.

Summarising this section, the Balts, like the early Germanic and Slavic people, worshipped their gods mainly in open sanctuaries. They were usually well defined holy groves and called *alkas* in Lithuanian.[148] This shows a clear separation of the sacred and profane. Although open sites dominated the landscape, there is some evidence for special structures or shrines as places of worship. This was most profound in Lithuania, which comes as no surprise, as an organised cult was a part of the state building process there. The more important cult centres often maintained sacred fires, conducted sacrifices to the gods and provided divination.[149] Such places must have required constant maintenance. So, while the smaller or less significant sites might have been attended to by numerous healers, wisemen and women, and other "wanderers", major shrines had "full time" priests along with their attendants. The idols of gods in sanctuaries were not common, but evidence indicates their presence in some places. As idols were uncommon and definitely made of wood, they had little chance of surviving the climate in the Baltic region, which may explain the lack of archaeological evidence in this respect.

Conclusion

It has to be remembered that historical records, especially from Prussia, mainly provided information for the lower strata of complex Baltic beliefs. When more elaborate and visible cults and gods disappeared from public life after Christianisation, they only survived in the folklore, customs and traditions of the people.

We can say that Henryk Łowmiański and Endre Bojtár were correct only in stating that most, if not the majority of the numerous Baltic "gods" listed and mentioned in historical sources or surviving in ethnographic records were in fact demons, spirits and purely defined minor functional deities. It is also the case that historical accounts are often erroneous, distorted or biased, or sometimes there are deities and stories invented by the chroniclers. All of this prompted them and many other scholars to claim that Baltic religion was in

---

147. Peter of Dusburg, III.4.
148. Mierzyński 1892: Vol. 1, 70.
149. Rowell 1997: 124.

principle a polydoxy that was a relatively simple cult of forces of nature.[150] The big number and multiplicity of "gods" in records, especially from Prussia, can be easily explained. As we know, Baltic societies, with the exception of Lithuanians, were small, tribal, clan oriented groups. With social and political fragmentation it should not come as a surprise that throughout the course of time their beliefs underwent further, different and separate developments in their own different cultural, social, political and geographical context. Their beliefs, gods and rituals and other forms of religious expression therefore substantially diversified from common Baltic traditions. Baltic pre-Christian religion had many facets and expressed itself in many simple as well as complex forms and ways.

Nonetheless, we are able to reconstruct a higher stratum of pre-Christian religion. There existed a personified sky deity known as Dievas, which etymologically is cognate to the name of the Vedic Dyaus and other Indo-European deities of celestial domain. In many instances the Sky God Dievas was called by euphemistic names, which was common practice among the Balts. Hence we have names like Occopirmus and Andievas. The personified Sun god of at least one section of Prussian people was called Svaikstikas. It was again probably an epithet for the more common name Saule. The fire deity was most pronounced among the Lithuanians who called it Kelavelis. The most attested, and a major god of late Lithuanian paganism, was Perkūnas. The concept of this deity was deeply rooted in common Indo-European tradition and beliefs. He was initially an atmospheric deity, but definitely in Lithuania and most likely in many other Baltic lands evolved into a war god. This finds parallels in the transformation of the Germanic Thor and Perun in Kievan Rus' into war deities. The cult of Žemyna, the Earth Goddess, was practiced universally but no doubt in different forms in different regions and areas. The goddess, while not as visible in the sources, is ever present in Baltic ethnographic data. She was also most likely personified by the Balts. In the case of minor deities Trimpas and Pikulas, the currently available evidence prevents us from clearly establishing if they were personified or not. Many others who were discussed or omitted in the above paper were either spirits, demons or simply inventions.

Also, it is worth noting that relatively simple cults of nature and natural forces could have sacred places, but not well defined sanctuaries like in the Baltic case. These would not have places where eternal fires were kept, complex rituals, offerings and elaborate sacrifices were performed, divination made, and where

---

150. Łowmiański 1986: 53n.

sometimes idols of gods stood, either in the open or in built structures. Such simple cults would also not have places of worship requiring the presence of full time priests and their attendants for their maintenance. They would also not have priests who often collected a third of the war booty. We have to acknowledge that the complexity of any religion is not defined by the size of its temples and we have to remember that not long ago even in Christianity, for many people the world was inhabited by demons and spirits. In the real world, religion exists on different levels and with different complexity, and expresses itself in many ways. After all we have monumental cathedrals existing at the same time as small roadside shrines with merely a single figure of a saint.

The cumulative evidence presented above allows us to state that Baltic pre-Christian religion was without a doubt polytheistic. It was an evolving polytheism as shown especially by the Lithuanian developments, and it was a continuous process, which is nothing unusual in respect to all religious beliefs.

Appendix

Constitutiones Synodales (fragment) - In Łowmiański, pp. 50-51.

"Referemus etiam rem miram: est adhuc in Bruthenis nostris Sambiensibus Sudorum quidam manipulus, ut reliquam abominationum superstitionum, reliquias gentilitatum taceamus, hirco et non furtim nonnumquam faciens, ad instar olim Samaritanorum, una cum vero Deo vana prisci erroris nomina tremens; sunt autem pro lingua barbara barbarissimi hi: Occopirmus, Suaixtix, Ausschauts, Autrympus, Potrympus, Bardoayts, Piluutus, Parcuns, Pecols atque Pocols, qui Dei, si eorum numina secundum illorum opinionem pensites, erunt: Saturnus, Sol, Aesculapius, Neptunes, Castor et Pollux, Ceres, Juppiter, Pluto, Furiae".

Sudovian Book (fragment) – An English translation from Schmalstieg, p. 365.

"Ockopirmus - - the first god of heaven and the stars; Swayxtix - the god of light; uschauts - the god of the lame, sick and healthy; Autrimpus - the god of oceans and seas; Potrimpus - the god of running water; Bardoayts - the god of boats; Pergrubrius - who nourishes leaves and grass; Pilnitis - this god enriches and fills barns; Parkuns - the god of thunder, lightning and rain; Peckols - the god of hell and darkness; Pockols – the flying souls or devils; Puschkayts - the earth god under the elder tree; Barstucke - the little people; Markopole - the people of the earth."

Acknowledgement

I would like to express my sincere gratitude and thanks to Mr. Robert Ryniuk, (B.A., Slavic Studies & Criminology, Monash University, Melbourne, Australia) for substantial linguistic advice and assistance in editing of the above work.

Maps

Map 1. Baltic People circa 1200 C.E.
(Please note that this map is an approximation only as it is from Wikipedia).

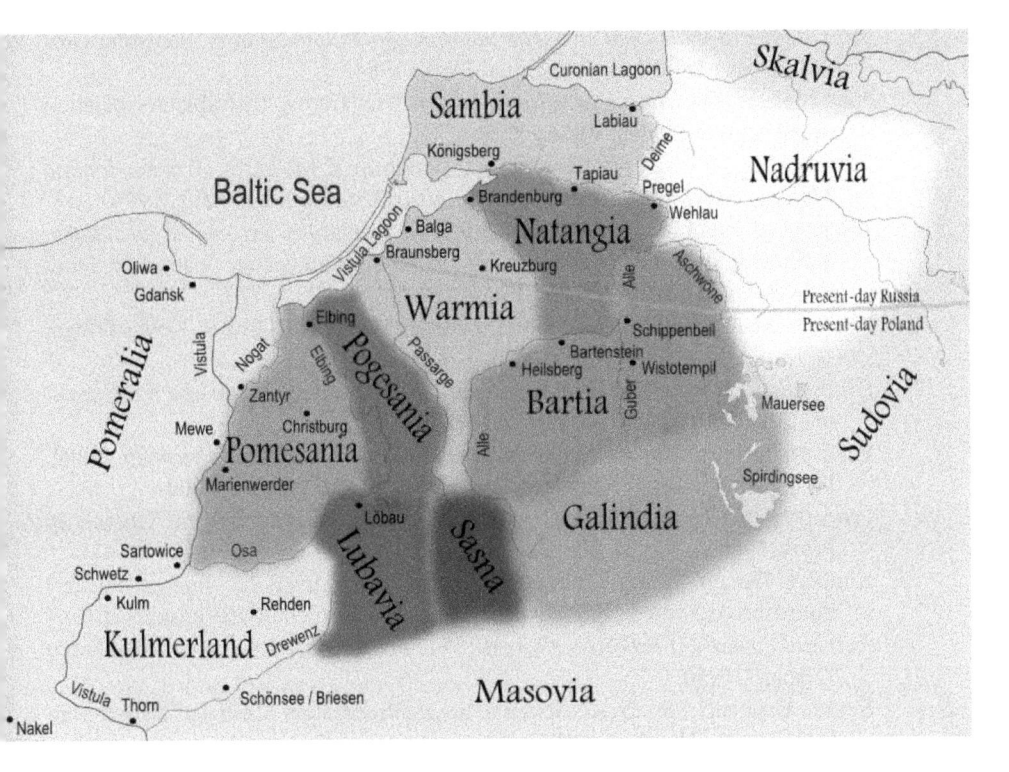

Map 2. Prussian Tribes circa 1250 C.E.
(Please note that this map is an approximation only as it is from Wikipedia).

Sources

Bruno, Saint: *Vita Sancti Adalberti, (Vita Sancti Adalberti Pragensis, episcopi et martyris Vita altera auctore Bruno Querfurtensis),* in *Monumenta Poloniae Historica,* Series Nova 4,2. Warszawa, 1969, 45-69.

Bychowiec Chronicle in *Polnoe Sobranie Russkix Letopisej,* XXXII. http://litopys.org.ua/psrl3235/lytov08.htm

Canaparius, *Vita sancti Adalberti episcopi Pragensis* in A. Mierzyński, *Źródła do mitologii litewskiej.* Warszawa, Druk K. Kowalskiego, 1892.

Chronicle of Greater Poland (Kronika Wielkopolska) in Historia Polski.eu http://historiapolski.eu/kronika-lechitow-i-polakow-t962.html (Retrieved: 2016-08-20)

Henry of Livonia, *Livonian Chronicle,* in *Genrix Latvijskij, Xronika Livonii,* perevod S. A Anninskogo. Moscow-Leningrad, Izdatel'stvo Akademii Nauk SSSR, 1938. http://www.junik.lv/~link/livonia/chronicles/henricus/index.htm (Retrieved: 09/08/2016)

Jan Długosz, *Annales seu cronicae incliti Regni Poloniae*, in H. Samsonowicz, Polska Jana Długosza. Warszawa, PWN, 1984.

John Malalas, *The Chronicle of John Malalas*. Melbourne, Australian Association of Byzantine Studies, 1986.

John Malalas, *Chronicon*, Slavonic translation *in* V. M. Istrin, *Xronika Ioanna Malaly v Slavjanskom perevode*. Moscow, Džon Uajli and Sanz, 1994.

Michael of Sambia, *Articuli per Prutenos tenendi et erronei contra fidem abiciiendi*, in A. Mierzyński, *Źródła do mitologii litewskiej*. Warszawa, Druk K. Kowalskiego, 1892, 131-133.

Mierzyński, A., *Źródła do mitologii litewskiej*. Warszawa, Druk K. Kowalskiego, 1892.

Old English Orosius, The, in N. Lund, ed., *Two Voyagers Othere and Wulfstan at the Court of King Alfred*. York, 1984, 16-17.

Peter of Dusburg, *Chronicle of Prussian Lands, Kronika Ziem Pruskich*, transl. Wyszomirski. Toruń, Uniwersytet im. Mikołaja Kopernika, 2004.

Procopius of Ceasarea, *History of the Wars*. Cambridge, Harward University Press, 1968.

Rimbert, *The Life of Anskar*. New York, Fordham University - Internet History Sourcebooks Project. https://sourcebooks.fordham.edu/basis/anskar.asp

Russian Primary Chronicle (Povest' Vremennyx Let). Moscow, Izdatel'stvo "Nauka", 1950.

Simon Grunau, *Die Preussischen Geschichtschreiben*. Leipzig, Verlag von Duncker und Humblot, 1876.

Tacitus, *Germania*, in H. Mattingly & S.A. Handford, *The Agricola and the Germania*. Harmondsworth, Penguin Books Ltd., 1985.

Thietmar of Merseburg, *Chronicon*, edited & transl. by M.Z. Jedlicki, ed. Poznañ, Instytut Zachodni, 1953.

Treaty of Christburg (Traktat dzierzgoński), Stowarzyszenie "Dom Warmiński", http://www.domwarminski.pl/index.php?option=com_content&view=article&id=7:traktat-dzierzgonski&catid=59&Itemid=183 (Retrieved: 20/07/2016)

Wigand of Marburg, *Chronica nova Prutenica*, in *Kronika Wiganda z Marburga*, transl. E. Raczyński. Poznań, Księgarnia Nowa, 1842.

Bibliography

Beresnevičius, G.: "Lithuanian Religion and Mythology" in *Anthology of Lithuanian Ethnoculture. Lithuanian Folk Culture Centre.* Translated by L. Tamošiūnienė http://www.thelithuanians.com/bookanthology/mythology/relmyth.html

Białuński, G., 1993: "Bogini Kurko - główny kult Galindii", Komunikaty Mazursko-Warmińskie (Olsztyn), 1, 3-10.

Białuński, G., 1999: Studia z dziejów plemion pruskich i jaćwieskich. Olsztyn, Ośrodek Badań Naukowych im. Wojciecha Kętrzyńskiego.
Biezais, H., 1975: *Germanische und Baltische Religion.* Stuttgart, Verlag W. Kohlhammer.
Boryś, W., 2006: Słownik etymologiczny języka polskiego. Kraków, Wydawnictwo Literackie.
Bojtár, E., 1997: *Forward to the Past: A Cultural History of the Baltic People.* Budapest, Central European University press.
Bowker, J., 1973: *The Sense of God.* Oxford, Oxford University Press.
Brückner, A., 1904: *Starożytna Litwa. Ludy i bogi. Szkice historyczne i mitologiczne.* Warszawa, Księgarnia Naukowa.
Długokęcki, W., 2007: "Uwagi o genezie i rozwoju wczesnośredniowiecznych Prus do początków XIII wieku", *Pruthenia,* II, 9-54.
Dowden, K., 2000: *European Paganism.* London, Routledge.
Dumézil, G., 1966: *Archaic Roman Religion.* Baltimore, John Hopkins University Press.
Gieysztor, A., 1982: Mitologia Słowiańska. Warszawa, Wydawnictwo Artystyczno Filmowe.
Gimbutas, M., 1963: *The Balts.* London, Thames & Hudson.
Gimbutas, M., 1971: *The Slavs.* London, Thames and Hudson.
Gimbutas, M., 1974: "The Lithuanian God Velnias", *in* G. J. Larson, *Myth In Indo-European Antiquity.* Berkeley, University of California Press, 87-94.
Ivanov, V. V., Toporov, V. N., 1980: "Baltijskaja Mifologija", *Mify narodov mira: Enciklopedija.* Moscow, Vol. 1, 153-158. http://www.pdps.lv/mois/_private/istorija/b/balt_mif.htm (Retrieved: 12/10/2016)
Labuda, G., 1972: *Historia Pomorza,* 1. Poznań, Wydawnictwo Poznańskie.
Łowmiański, H., 1986: Religia Słowian i jej upadek. Warszawa, P.W.N..
Możdżeń, J., 2011: "Synkretyzm religijny Prusów na podstawie kroniki Szymona Grunaua", *Pruthenia,* VI, 221-248.
Narbutt, T., 1835: *Dzieje narodu litewskiego,* 8. Vilnius, A. Marcinowski.
Okulicz-Kozaryn, Ł., 1993: Życie codzienne Prusów i Jaćwięgów. Warszawa, Państwowy Instytut Wydawniczy.
Okulicz-Kozaryn, Ł., 1997: *Dzieje Prusów.* Wrocław, Fundacja na Rzecz Nauki Polskiej.
Puhvel, J., 1974: "Indo- European Structure of the Baltic Pantheon", *in* G. J. Larson, *Myth In Indo-European Antiquity.* Berkeley, University of California Press, 75-86.
Rowell, S. C., 1997: *Lithuania Ascending: A pagan Empire within East-Central Europe, 9 3* . Cambridge, Cambridge University Press.
Schmalstieg, W. R., 2003: "Review. Baltų religijos ir mitologijos šaltiniai 2, XVI amžius, parėngė Norbertas Vėlius", *Archivum Lithuanicum,* 5, 299-

387. http://www.elibrary.lt/resursai/Leidiniai/Archivum_Lithuanicum/2003/al_03_06.pdf (Retrieved: 01/09/2016)

Shiroukhov, R. A., 2006: *Panteon baltijskix bogov*, MA Thesis, Immanuel Kant's Russian National University (Kaliningrad) https://vu-lt.academia.edu/RomanShiroukhov (Retrieved: 05/08/2016

Sulimirski, F., Chlebowski, W., Wawelski, W., 1882: Słownik geograficzny Królestwa Polskiego i innych krajów słowiańskich, *III*. Warszawa, Filip Sulimirski i Władysław Walewski. http://dir.icm.edu.pl/pl/Slownik_geograficzny/Tom_III/264 (Retrieved: 10/12/2011)

Swanson, G., 1964: *The Birth of the Gods*. Ann Arbor, The University of Michigan Press.

The Tower of Babel, *An Etymological Database Project* http://starling.rinet.ru/ (Retrieved: 10/06/2016)

Urban, W., 1989: *The Samogidian Crusade*. Chicago, Lithuanian Studies And Research Center.

Wach, J., 1973: "Religious Organisation", in T.F. O'Dea & J.K. O'Dea, *Readings on the Sociology of Religion*. Englewood Cliffs, Prentice-Hall, Inc.

Winn, S. M. M., 1995: *Heaven, Heroes and Happiness: The Indo-European Roots of Western Ideology*. Lanham, The University Press of America Inc.

Wojciechowski, L., 1983: "Wyprawy łupieskie w Słowiańszczyźnie Zachodniej w X-XII wieku", *Roczniki Humanistyczne*, XXXI, 62.

Zaroff, R., 1999: "Organized Pagan Cult in Kievan Rus'. The Invention of Foreign Elite or Evolution of Local Tradition?", *Studia Mythologia Slavica*, 2, 47-76. http://sms.zrc-sazu.si/En/SMS2/Zaroff2b.html

Zeps, V. J., 1962: "Review of i Die Gottesgestalt der lettischen Volksrelkgion", *American Anthropologist*, 64, 4, 884-885.

Table of contents

Foreword .... p. 5

Jiří Dynda, Slavic Anthropogony Myths. Body and Corporeality in the Slavic Narratives about the Creation of Man .... p. 7

Alexander V. Ivanenko, Towards the PSl. *striboga origin .... p. 25

Oleg V. Kutarev, Description of Rod and Rožanicy in Slavic mythology. B. A. Rybakov and his predecessor's interpretations ... p. 33

Kamil Kajkowski, Idols of the Western Slavs in the Early Medieval period. The example of Pomerania (northern Poland) .... p. 47

Stamatis Zochios, Slavic deities of death. Looking for a needle in the haystack .... p. 69

Marina M. Valentsova, Slovak mythological vocabulary on the Common Slavic background. Ethno-linguistic aspect .... p. 99

Aleksandr Koptev, Mythological triadism as the paradigm of princely succession in early Rus' according to the *Primary Chronicle* .... p. 127

Patrice Lajoye, Sovereigns and sovereignty among pagan Slavs .... p. 165

Roman Zaroff, Some aspects of pre-Christian Baltic religion .... p. 183